Free DVD  Free DVD

Essential Test Tips Video from Trivium Test Prep

Dear Customer,

Thank you for purchasing from Trivium Test Prep! Whether you're looking to join the military, get into college, or advance your career, we're honored to be a part of your journey.

To show our appreciation (and to help you relieve a little of that test-prep stress), we're offering a **FREE *NMLS Essential Test Tips* Video** by Trivium Test Prep. Our video includes 35 test preparation strategies that will help keep you calm and collected before and during your big exam. All we ask is that you email us your feedback and describe your experience with our product. Amazing, awful, or just so-so: we want to hear what you have to say!

To receive your **FREE *NMLS Essential Test Tips* Video**, please email us at 5star@ triviumtestprep.com. Include "Free 5 Star" in the subject line and the following information in your email:

1. The title of the product you purchased.

2. Your rating from 1 – 5 (with 5 being the best).

3. Your feedback about the product, including how our materials helped you meet your goals and ways in which we can improve our products.

4. Your full name and shipping address so we can send your **FREE NMLS *Essential Test Tips* Video**.

If you have any questions or concerns please feel free to contact us directly at 5star@triviumtestprep.com.

Thank you, and good luck with your studies!

NMLS Study Guide

3 Full Length MLO Practice Tests and NMLS SAFE Mortgage Loan Originator Exam Content

Elissa Simon

Table of Contents

TRIVIUM
—TEST PREP—

Online Resources

Trivium includes online resources with the purchase of this study guide to help you fully prepare for the exam.

Practice Tests

In addition to the practice tests included in this book, we also offer an online exam. Since many exams today are computer based, practicing your test-taking skills on the computer is a great way to prepare.

From Stress to Success

Watch "From Stress to Success," a brief but insightful YouTube video that offers the tips, tricks, and secrets experts use to score higher on the exam.

Reviews

Leave a review, send us helpful feedback, or sign up for Cirrus promotions—including free books!

Access these materials at: www.triviumtestprep.com/nmls-online-resources

Introduction

Congratulations on choosing to take the NMLS SAFE Mortgage Loan Originator (MLO) licensing exam! By purchasing this book, you've taken the first step toward becoming a licensed mortgage loan originator.

This guide will provide you with a detailed overview of the MLO exam, so you will know exactly what to expect on test day. We'll take you through all of the concepts covered on the exam and give you the opportunity to evaluate your knowledge with practice questions. Even if it's been a while since you last took a major test, don't worry; we'll make sure you're more than ready!

What is the SAFE Act?

The **Secure and Fair Enforcement for Mortgage Licensing Act (SAFE) Act** was enacted in 2008 as part of the Housing and Economic Recovery Act. To protect consumers and discourage fraud, the SAFE Act requires licensing for mortgage loan originators. Anyone who accepts residential mortgage loan applications or discusses their terms must be licensed under this law.

What Is the NMLS SAFE MLO Exam?

The **Nationwide Mortgage Licensing System and Registry (NMLS)** administers the MLO licensing exam and maintains records of licensure throughout the nation.

MLO exams are part of licensure nationwide, but some states may require additional tests. Check with the MLO licensing board in your state or province for complete information.

Licensing helps ensure that both new and experienced mortgage loan originators practice safely and ethically. This book will prepare you for the national MLO exam.

What Is on the NMLS SAFE MLO Exam?

The MLO exam consists of **120 questions**. Only 115 of these questions are scored; the remaining five questions are unscored, or *pretest* questions. Pretest questions are included to gauge their suitability for inclusion in future tests. You'll have no way of knowing which questions are unscored, so treat every question like it counts.

The questions on the MLO exam are multiple-choice with four answer options. The MLO has **no guess penalty**. In other words, if you answer a question incorrectly, no points are deducted from your score—you simply do not get credit for that question. You should therefore always guess, even if you do not know the answer. You will have **three hours and ten minutes** to complete the exam.

What Is on the MLO?		
Subject	Approximate Number of Questions per Subject	Percentage of Exam
Federal Mortgage-related Laws	29	24%
General Mortgage Knowledge	24	20%
Mortgage Loan Origination Activities	32	27%
Ethics	22	18%
Uniform State Content	13	11%
Total	120 multiple-choice questions (115 scored)	3 hours and 10 minutes (190 minutes)

How Is the MLO Scored?

The MLO is a pass/fail test. To pass the MLO, you must receive a minimum score of **75 percent**. Of the 120 questions on the test, 115 are scored. Your score is determined by how many of the 115 scored questions you answer correctly.

You will receive an unofficial copy of your score report immediately after the exam. Your official results will be posted in the NMLS. Your score report will include the percentage score and a breakdown indicating your performance on each section of the exam.

The number of correct answers needed to pass the exam will vary slightly depending on the questions included in your version of the test. That is, if you take a version of the test with harder questions, the passing score will be lower. For security reasons, different versions of the test are administered every testing window.

If you do not pass the test, you may take the test again after thirty days. You are entitled to three attempts. If you still do not pass on the third try, you must wait 180 days before retesting.

How Is the MLO Administered?

The MLO is administered at Prometric testing centers around the nation. Plan to arrive at least **thirty minutes before the exam** to complete biometric screening. Bring at least one form of **government-issued photo ID** and be prepared to be photographed and have your palms scanned. You may also be scanned with a metal detector wand before entering the test room. Your primary ID must be government-issued, include a recent photograph and signature, and match the name under which you registered to take the test. If you do not have proper ID, you will not be allowed to take the test.

You will not be allowed to bring any personal items into the testing room, including calculators and phones. You may not bring pens, pencils, or scratch paper. Other prohibited items include hats, scarves, and coats. You may, however, wear religious garments. Prometric provides lockers for valuables. You can keep your ID and locker key with you.

About Trivium Test Prep

Trivium Test Prep uses industry professionals with decades' worth of knowledge in their fields—proven with degrees and honors in law, medicine, business, education, the military, and more—to produce high-quality test prep books for students.

Our study guides are specifically designed to increase any student's score. Our books are also shorter and more concise than typical study guides, so you can increase your score while significantly decreasing your study time.

1 Federal Mortgage-Related Laws

Real Estate Settlement Procedures Act

Definitions and Purpose

A **mortgage broker** can shop rates, mortgage lenders, and loan programs to find the right product for borrowers based on their credit scores, debts, current assets, and income. Mortgage brokers are usually very competitive and can offer more lending solutions, which gives borrowers more choices. Mortgage brokers work for the borrower by negotiating the best loan and rate, and they get paid by commission once the loan closes.

Other lending intuitions, banks, and credit unions can offer mortgage loans to borrowers, but they are tied directly to their internal loan programs set by management and investors. This limits the type of loan programs available to borrowers.

The **Real Estate Settlement Procedures Act (RESPA)** was passed by the United States Congress in 1974 and became effective on June 20, 1975. RESPA has two main goals:

- to reduce loan settlement (closing) costs for consumers on their pending mortgage loans

- to protect consumers from deceitful lending practices

RESPA is also known as Regulation X under the Consumer Financial Protection Bureau (CFPB) Consumer Laws and Regulations. **Regulation X** requires lenders, brokers, and servicers of mortgage home loans to disclose the costs and process of the real estate settlement requirements needed to obtain a mortgage. The disclosures to the borrower provide guidance on prohibited lending practices such as kickbacks, escrow, and mortgage servicing requirements. RESPA protects several types of loans, including

- new home purchases,

- refinances of existing and assumable mortgages,

- home equity lines of credit (HELOC), and

- reverse mortgages on residential properties.

RESPA does not protect purchases of vacant land, commercial properties, or agricultural structures. Part of the closing costs set aside are escrow requirements. RESPA limits the amount of escrow collected on taxes and insurances at the time of closing.

1. full property address

2. estimate of the property value
3. amount of mortgage applied for>

There are four critical sections of RESPA for loan officers to know. They are summarized in Table 1.1. and discussed below in more detail.

Table 1.1. Critical Sections of RESPA	
Section	**Purpose**
Section 6 – Loan servicing protection	protects customers from loan servicing problems after loans are sold on the secondary market
Section 8 – Rules on kickbacks, fee-splitting and unearned fees	prohibits giving or accepting a kickback, fee, or anything of value in exchange for referrals
Section 9 – Seller-required title insurance	prohibits the seller from insisting the buyer purchase this type of insurance through a particular title company
Section 10– Escrow limits	protects the borrower from lenders who collect too much money and hold large escrow accounts

Helpful Hint

There are six RESPA triggers that complete a loan application:

1. full name
2. income
3. Social Security

When a new mortgage loan is officially closed with the borrowers, the lender goes through an internal audit of the file and final documentation. If all is in order, it is then packaged and sent to the loan investor. The investor then decides if this loan should be sold and serviced to a secondary market servicer company. When this occurs, RESPA requirements kick in. While some lenders do not sell their loans and instead keep them within their balance sheets, RESPA laws still apply and the borrowers on the mortgage loan are protected.

Per RESPA Section 6, if borrowers have questions or complaints on the servicing of their loan, the servicer MUST respond to the borrowers in writing within twenty business days; this includes any escrow account concerns. The mortgage loan servicer must then resolve (again, in writing) the complaint and make any changes to the account within sixty days. The servicer has the right to show reasoning and refuse any corrections. At that point, if no resolution can be completed, the borrower has the right to take legal action against the servicer within three years of the initial complaint.

RESPA does not allow any compensation, fee splitting, kickbacks, or exchange of items of value in transactions—from the application through the closing—that involve a mortgage loan. RESPA's **Section 8** prohibits any type of monetary exchange that benefits another party. Its rules include guidelines on giving gifts; splitting settlement, title, and lender closing fees; and giving referrals for preferred partners, such as title companies and realtors.

Kickbacks—briberies—are attempts to influence the outcome of monetary transactions for the benefit of others. For example, if a loan officer tells borrowers that they can cut their closing costs if they use his realtor, it is considered a kickback.

When a home is under contract, the sellers of the property choose which title company will represent them. The buyers of the sellers' home must pay for any title insurance that the lender requires. On a

Closing Disclosure, this is referenced as "owner and/or lender's title policy." **Section 9** of RESPA prohibits sellers from insisting that buyers purchase this insurance using a particular title company. This keeps the realtor and sellers of the property from aligning with title companies and charging higher fees and/or allowing kickbacks to the realtor.

Sellers can be liable for up to three times the amount of the title insurance charges if they violate RESPA. When awarding damages to a plaintiff, the court refers to this concept as **treble damages**.

Most mortgage loans come with **escrows**, the collection of real estate property taxes and homeowner's insurance. These are part of the mortgage loan monthly payment. Escrow accounts benefit borrowers by allowing large yearly bills, like property taxes, to be broken down into manageable monthly payments.

Under RESPA, a lender can only collect a limited amount of money for escrow. Based on the time of year, more or less taxes may need to be held in escrow. For example, property taxes are paid out twice a year. If a loan closes in October, all taxes have been paid for the year, so the collection of monthly money for taxes will be lower. However, if a loan closes in January, more months of taxes will be collected because the lender will be required to pay those taxes sooner. **Section 10** protects the borrower from having lenders collect too much money and holding large escrow accounts.

Quick Review Questions

1. What are the TWO goals RESPA?

2. What is the term that describes the concept that sellers can be liable for up to three times the amount of the title insurance charges if they violate Section 9 of RESPA?

Required Disclosures and Information

Under RESPA, mortgage loan lenders are required to send forms—called loan disclosures—to homebuyers and sellers at the time of a loan application. **Loan disclosures** provide information to the consumer on lender guidelines for collecting escrow account monies, allowable title settlement costs, and the transfer of mortgage notes for payment collection; they also set rules on fees that can and (and cannot) be charged by industry professionals.

Loan disclosures must be sent and acknowledged by the borrowers either digitally (e.g., through DocuSign) or with a hard-copy signature. The lender is also required to send loan disclosures within specified time frames during the process of the loan.

The following required loan disclosures vary based on the type of mortgage loan the borrower applies for and, per RESPA, must be sent within three business days:

> **Helpful Hint**
>
> If a mortgage loan application is denied, the loan disclosure date rule does not apply; however, a written denial letter and the reason for denial must be mailed to the borrower within thirty business days.

1. Affiliated Business Arrangement Disclosure (see TILA-RESPA below)
2. Mortgage Servicing Disclosure Statement
3. Home Loan Toolkit
4. Servicing Transfer Statement
5. Good Faith Estimate, Uniform Settlement Statement, Loan Estimate, and Closing Disclosure

The **good faith estimate (GFE)** and the **Uniform Settlement Statement (HUD-1)** are used for reverse mortgages and loans that do not fall under RESPA requirements. These include investment loans, bank statement loans for manufactured homes, and nontraditional income loans:

- For reverse mortgages, a GFE showing settlement closing costs is required to be sent within three business days.
- The **loan estimate** and **Closing Disclosure** replaced the GFE and HUD-1 for most other loans in 2015 and are discussed under Regulation Z later in this chapter.

Under RESPA, the **Mortgage Servicing Disclosure Statement** is sent to the borrower within three business days of the loan application. This disclosure states whether the lender will service the loan in-house or sell it to another lender or investor.

The **Servicing Transfer Statement** is sent if the lender sells the loan to another lender on the secondary market. The Servicing Transfer Statement includes

> **Helpful Hint**
>
> For HELOC loans, a brochure called "What You Should Know About Home Equity Lines of Credit" must be sent within the same time frame as other required disclosures.

- the name of the new lender servicing the loan,
- the lender's contact information and payment instructions,
- the date on which the first loan payment is due, and
- information concerning the steps to resolve complaints.

If the lender does sell the loan once it has closed and been funded, the lender must send a Servicing Transfer Statement to the borrower **fifteen days** before transfer. The new servicer must also send the borrower a notice within fifteen days following the transfer. Borrowers have a sixty-day grace period during which payments accidentally sent to the former servicer should be forwarded to the new servicer without late fees being assessed.

A home is the largest asset most people purchase, and the process and verbiage can be overwhelming. Under RESPA, the CFPB created the **home loan toolkit** to give borrowers a reference while shopping for the right mortgage loan for their new or current home. It provides simple mortgage terms and guidelines borrowers need to follow to ensure the loan will not cause a financial burden. It helps consumers determine their

> **Did You Know?**
>
> In the spring of 2022, Fannie and Freddie Mac started lending on manufactured homes to help address the lack of affordable housing. There are specific guidelines for single- and multi-wide homes, so it is important to understand the differences between the types of manufactured homes.

housing budget, figure out if they can afford a bigger home, or see if desired renovations make financial sense.

The home loan toolkit is a good guide for all borrowers to use when determining if a mortgage loan makes financial sense. It is especially useful with helping first-time homebuyers make sound financial decisions.

1. Federal Mortgage-Related Laws

Quick Review Questions

3. When must the borrower receive the Mortgage Loan Servicing Disclosure Statement?

4. If the lender sells the loan on the secondary market, how much time does it have to send the Servicing Transfer Statement?

Equal Credit Opportunity Act

Core Concepts

Through Regulation B, the Federal Reserve was originally in charge of implementing the **Equal Credit Opportunity Act (ECOA)**. **Regulation B** outlines discriminatory practices and prohibits lenders from participating in certain activities during the loan process. In 2010, the Dodd-Frank Act transferred responsibility for the ECOA to the CFPB, who now has the authority to supervise and enforce compliance of the regulations set forth in ECOA.

ECOA protects consumers who request credit through financial institutions. According to ECOA's Regulation B, credit cannot be denied or approved based on the following:

- age
- marital status
- race or color
- religious preference
- nation of origin
- sex

> **Did You Know?**
>
> Regulation B is the law under 12 CFR Part 1002.

If a consumer is denied credit based on any of these reasons, it is considered disparate treatment—discrimination. To ensure credit results are not based on these factors, ECOA keeps track of the credit decisions before, during, and after the consumer has been granted or denied credit.

Under ECOA, Regulation B controls and promotes equal credit consideration to creditworthy consumers based on income sources and past and current reliability of repayment on current credit lines. If a consumer is denied credit, Regulation B also requires the creditor to notify the consumers of the action taken. If borrowers are turned down for a mortgage loan application, the lender must provide the reason for the denial in writing within thirty days. The consumer must receive information about how to find out why their loan was denied.

If a lender does not comply within this time frame, the party that completed the application may pursue legal action, including punitive damages up to $10,000 or, if it is a class action settlement, $500,000 (capped at 1% of the lender's net worth).

There are exceptions to this regulation:

- Some states are community property states, so asking about marital status is permissible.
- Lenders may ask about age in certain situations (e.g., if the borrower is unable to legally sign a contract).
- Lenders may ask about ages of any dependents and how many children for which a borrower is financially responsible.

- Possible alimony or child support payments must be taken into consideration in a liability ratio of income versus debt.

Quick Review Questions

5. Who supervises and enforces compliance with Equal Credit Opportunity Act (ECOA) regulations?

6. Regulation B of the Equal Credit Opportunity Act (ECOA) makes it unlawful to discriminate against credit applicants based on what factors?

Adverse Action

Sometimes, mortgage loans are denied because of credit reasons or missing information. Under ECOA, when a mortgage loan application is denied, the lender or loan officer must disclose to the borrower the specific reason(s) for which the loan was denied. This written notice is called an **adverse action notice**

Notices of adverse action must be provided in writing, within thirty days of the completed loan application. A notice of adverse action details the reasons for which an application was denied. Common reasons a borrower will receive an adverse action notice include

- poor credit history,
- foreclosure,
- bankruptcy timing,
- no credit history or lines of credit,
- late mortgage payments,
- collections and/or judgments, and
- an incomplete application (e.g., length of employment and address history).

> **Helpful Hint:**
>
> If an application is denied due to missing information, the borrower has sixty days to correct the application.

Regulation B defines adverse action as "a refusal to grant credit for the amount or terms requested in an application." Adverse action is therefore not a denial of all credit; in fact, a borrower can ask for a new credit or term amount and may receive credit based on the new information requested.

Table 1.2. Overcoming Adverse Action

Reason for Adverse Action	Potential Solution
A borrower has no credit lines (open credit).	The borrower can provide other documents that demonstrate consistent payment history: • utility payments • cell phone bills • rent history
A borrower's credit score is too low to approve a mortgage application.	The loan officer (LO) provides the borrower with information about credit repair companies: • The application can be reconsidered while the borrower works to improve the credit score. • The borrower's credit score must improve within sixty days.

Table 1.2. Overcoming Adverse Action	
Reason for Adverse Action	**Potential Solution**
A mortgage application with **multiple applicants/guarantors** has been denied due to poor credit.	The loan can be restructured to remove and add additional borrowers: • A credit-challenged borrower is removed, and a nonowner-occupant borrower is added. • The loan can move forward by using the nonowner occupant's credit history and income.

When a mortgage loan is submitted to the lender, loan disclosures are created and sent to the borrowers. Per CFPB, one of the forms borrowers must sign is an appraisal delivery waiver. The **appraisal delivery waiver** is strictly a timing disclosure that causes great confusion to the borrowers:

- If they check the box for waiving their right three days before closing, closing will not be delayed.
- If they check the box requesting to review their appraisal three days before closing, a rescission time clock, which can delay closing, starts.
- Appraisals are always given to the borrower within a few days of completion to avoid any closing delays.

When accepting a mortgage loan application, the LO must review **Form 1003 (Universal Residential Loan Application)** for accuracy and completion. Since any missing information could result in adverse action, getting a full picture of the borrower's financial history is critical. It is the LO's job to

- verify income;
- review credit reports;
- ask the borrower detailed questions;
- confirm with the borrower all of the information provided on the application;
- document income, debt, assets, and the two-year history of everything required by loan program guidelines; and
- be able to determine if one or more borrowers is needed for the loan amount the borrower is seeking.

It is essential that the LO does not violate Regulation B when reviewing the loan application. The LO must be especially careful when reviewing the sections of the loan application concerning marital status and race:

- LOs cannot ask borrowers whether they are single, divorced, or widowed; instead, they may ask if a borrower is married, unmarried, or separated.
- If the borrower refuses to answer the ethnicity questions found on page 4 of the application, the LO can collect this data based on visual observation or surnames.
- If the application was done online, "N/A" is an acceptable answer to these personal questions, but the box indicating that the application was not taken face-to-face needs to be checked.

A few areas of concern when taking a mortgage loan application commonly center around income, debt, and employment history:

- A borrower must provide a full two years of employment and address history.
- To prove creditworthiness, employment history must be consistent with current employment.
- Any gaps in employment must be fully explained and reviewed with loan program guidelines.

> **Helpful Hint:**
>
> Since the COVID pandemic caused large disruptions of steady employment in many industries, getting the full picture of borrower employment has created an extra layer of underwriting

The easiest type of borrower to qualify for a mortgage loan is a steady W2 employee with years of income doing the same type of work. A challenging borrower is a part-time worker or gig worker. Loan program guidelines are harder for borrowers with these types of income because they are not usually consistent.

The ability to repay credit is another critical area, and the credit report history must support the borrower's future ability to repay a large mortgage liability. If there are late payments, judgments, and/or disputes on a credit report, this will raise red flags during the mortgage loan approval process.

Quick Review Questions

7. Which document discloses to a borrower the specific reasons for which a loan was denied?

8. Can a loan officer ask borrowers whether they are single, divorced, or widowed?

Truth in Lending Act and Regulation Z

Terms, Definitions, and Core Concepts

The **Truth in Lending Act (TILA)** of 1968 was passed to protect consumers when working with creditors and money lenders (e.g., mortgage lenders and credit card companies). This act was executed through the Federal Reserve Board and CFR Part 1026. TILA applies to many types of credit including

- credit cards,
- installment loans,
- some student loans, and
- mortgage loans.

Having TILA protection is a benefit to consumers: it helps them with credit education while they shop for large purchases.

Regulation Z of TILA protects consumers when they apply for and obtain mortgage credit. Home purchases, home equality lines of credit (HELOC), and reverse mortgages are all subject to Regulation Z. Other lines of credit (e.g., credit cards, installment loans ,and some student loans) are also subject to Regulation Z.

Mortgage lenders are required under Regulation Z to send loan disclosure forms to borrowers who have completed applications. **Disclosure forms** break down the costs and terms of the loan. By disclosing these costs to the borrowers throughout the loan process, there are no surprises, hidden settlement charges, or loan officer compensation questions.

Regulation Z also prohibits referral, or **steering fees**, which used to be hidden in a loan officer's compensation. For example, loan officers cannot force buyers to use realtors they have a relationship with

or specific lenders they prefer. Loan officers must always recommend services based on the borrower's best interest and cannot pass along any fees to borrowers that might have exchanged hands during the loan process. It is a direct violation of Regulation Z to do so and subject to criminal penalties if class action damages are awarded in the event of noncompliance.

Once a borrower applies for a loan, the loan officer has three business days to send loan disclosures from the lender to the borrowers. A loan officer will submit the loan file to the mortgage lender and send links for e-signatures on the loan disclosures.

A **business day** is counted as "offices open to the public." Business days are generally Mondays through Fridays, although some lenders are open on Saturdays. For example, if a loan application was completed on a Thursday, the lender must have loan disclosures emailed to the borrower by Tuesday, or Monday if that lender has an office open on Saturday:

- The business-day rule also applies to federal holidays.
- The lender is also required to mail hard copies of the loan disclosures to the borrowers by the third business day of receiving the loan application.

TILA guidelines are very clear when it comes to credit and advertising. The CFPB and Regulation Z enforce compliance in advertising for open- and closed-end credit (e.g., mortgages, car loans, and credit cards).

Regulation Z regulates trigger terms for all mortgage-related marketing documents and activities. A **trigger term** is a word or phrase that legally requires one or more credit agreement disclosures when used in marketing and advertising in conjunction with any credit solicitation. Through the regulation of trigger terms, the consumer is protected from being misled by inaccurate credit practices, bait-and-switch advertising, and other unfair lending activities. Any type of marketing message—print, digital, or TV/radio/telephone—must adhere to Regulation Z guidelines.

Certain trigger terms cannot be used in marketing campaigns without additional disclosures being made. These disclosures must be clear and easy to understand with the intent to keep lenders honest. In other words, a company cannot just advertise "small down payment" or "up to 36 payments."

Table 1.3. Following Regulation Z When Using Trigger Terms in Advertising	
Trigger Term	**Example of Required Disclosure**
amount of down payment	"must include 5% – 20% down"
number of payments	"12 months of payments"
period of repayment	"6-year loans available"
amount of any payment	"12 monthly payments at $50"
amount of any finance charge	"financing costs less than $250"

The **annual percentage rate (APR)** is different than the mortgage interest rate. A simple explanation of APR is that it is the total cost of a loan to the borrower over time. When comparing mortgage rates, the borrower should be comparing the APR rather than the simple interest rate. The APR gives a complete picture of the total costs of taking out a mortgage loan and includes other charges that are part of the mortgage loan, such as:

- mortgage insurance
- discount points

- loan origination fees

Each year, the CFPB is required to calculate and adjust dollar amounts based on the current APR reflected in the consumer price index. Regulation Z requires that this information be published and show the annual adjusted dollar limits and not-to-exceed points for dollar amounts on credit cards, high-cost mortgages, and qualified mortgage (QM) loans.

Per CFPB's lending rules, the **points and fees limits** described in Table 1.4. apply to borrowers obtaining a QM loan. These fee limits protect the borrower from overpaying in points and lender fees.

Table 1.4. Point and Fee Limits Under Regulation Z	
Loan Amount	Limits
$100,000 or more	3% or less of the total loan amount
$60,000 to $100,000	$3,000 or less
$20,000 to $60,000	5% or less of the total loan amount
$12,500 to $20,000	$1,000 or less
$12,500 or less	8% or less of the total loan amount

Adjustable-rate mortgages (ARMs) can be great loan programs for the right borrowers, but the CFPB makes sure borrowers applying for these loans are aware of risks within ARM terms. Regulation Z requires that the lending institution send the Consumer Handbook on Adjustable-Rate Mortgages (**CHARM booklet**) to any borrower applying for ARMs.

> **Helpful Hint:**
>
> These fee limits do not apply to nonqualified mortgages, which tend to be investment loans and nontraditional borrower income loans.

As implied by the name, the interest rates of ARMs adjust throughout the mortgage loan period. Typically, the payment and interest are lower at the beginning of the loan and move up every one to two years, capping out at the end of the set adjustment period. The CHARM booklet provides a side-by-side comparison, in easy-to-understand language, of how ARM programs work versus fixed-rate loan programs. (See Chapter 3 for more on ARMs.)

Under TILA and Regulation Z, a **dwelling** is considered the borrower's principal home and must be attached to real property. In other words, for a mortgage transaction, the property secured to the loan note must be the main residence of the borrower. Dwellings include

- a residential structure of one to four units,
- an individual condominium or cooperative unit, and
- a mobile or manufactured home.

A **residential mortgage loan** is tied to the dwelling through a deed of trust which is recorded with the county of the state where the property is located. When the mortgage loan is paid off, the deed of trust is re-recorded and released. An official release and paid-in-full deed of trust is then sent to the borrower.

When consumers open a line of credit, they are protected by TILA through a **right to recession**—a cooling off period:

- From the date of the credit application, a customer has three days to back out of the purchase.
- This gives the consumer a way out of an impulse purchase (e.g., a car) or taking on a large debt (e.g., a mortgage).
- Any money that is exchanged in the transaction is returned without loss to the consumer.

As the loan progresses through underwriting and most underwriting conditions for final loan approval have been met, the first **estimated closing disclosure** is sent to the borrower. This is a very important step in the right to rescission timing. By law, borrowers have three business days to determine if they want to continue with the mortgage loan or cancel (rescind) the application.

This right of rescission also protects the borrower's earnest money if the loan is a purchase loan. The **loan objection date** on the real estate contract is the last date for final loan approval.

> **Helpful Hint:**
>
> A good rule of thumb is that the first estimated Closing Disclosure must be signed before the loan objection date.

On the day the Closing Disclosure goes to the borrower, the borrower must acknowledge or sign the disclosure before midnight of that day for it to count as day one of the rescission period. E-signing is permissible.

For example, the Closing Disclosure (CD) goes out on Monday and is signed. The first allowed day of closing would be Thursday.

In a buyer's real estate market, seller contributions/concessions are a common line item on the real estate contract. **Seller contributions** help with the closing costs on the mortgage loan and allow sellers to avoid doing repairs the buyers may want completed before purchasing the home.

Quick Review Questions

9. What is a right to rescission?

10. Under the Truth in Lending Act (TILA) and Regulation Z, what is a dwelling?

11. A word or phrase that legally requires one or more credit agreement disclosures when used in marketing and advertising credit is called what?

Home Ownership and Equity Protection Act (HOEPA), High-Cost Mortgages, HOEPA Section 32

The **Home Ownership and Equity Protection Act (HOEPA)** was an amendment to TILA in 1994. HOEPA, which is enforced by the CFPB under TILA Regulation Z, addresses the abusive lending practices that used to occur when borrowers would refinance their homes and their high-rate HELOCs.

In 2013, CFPB issued the **2013 HOEPA Rule**, which requires homeowner counseling. Within three business days of receiving the loan application, lenders must provide a loan disclosure with a written list of homeownership counseling organizations that are closest to the borrower's zip code.

HOEPA Section 32 covers high-cost mortgage loans (Section 32 loans). A **high-cost mortgage** has an APR that exceeds the average prime offer rate (APOR) currently available in the mortgage market at the time of application. These loans are secured by the borrower's principal residence:

- A mortgage is considered high cost if the APR exceeds 6.5% over APOR.

- In high-cost mortgages, the total lender and broker points and fees also exceed 5% of the total loan amount.
- For a QM, these fees must not exceed 3% of the total loan amount.

HOEPA does not cover reverse mortgages, construction loans, US Department of Agriculture (USDA) loans, or Housing Finance Authority (HFA) loans.

Quick Review Question

12. What does the 2013 HOEPA Rule require?

Higher-Priced Mortgage Loans

In 2009, lawmakers amended TILA/HOEPA to include **higher-priced mortgage loans (HPMLs)**. These are also known as Section 35 loans. An HPML is distinguished from other mortgage loans because the APR of an HPML exceeds the APOR. HPML loans include

> **Helpful Hint:**
>
> High-cost mortgages are also first liens; however, if the APR is more than 6.5% points over APOR, points and fees exceed 5% of the total loan amount and come with a prepayment penalty.

- a first mortgage lien with an APR rate that is 1.5% higher than the APOR,
- a second mortgage lien with an APR rate that is 3.5% higher than the APOR, and
- a jumbo mortgage lien with an APR rate that is 2.5 % higher than the APOR.

For residential mortgage loans, borrowers are often concerned about closing costs. For first-time buyers, it can be especially difficult to come up with the down payment for a home purchase as well as closing costs that are standard in the mortgage loan.

> **Helpful Hint:**
>
> If a borrower puts 10% or more down on an FHA loan, the MIP is eliminated after eleven years of payments. The only other way to remove MIP is to refinance out of an FHA loan.

One common HPML is the Federal Housing Administration (FHA) loan. This type of loan is very popular for first-time homeowners because the down payment is low and credit scores can be lower to qualify. The debt-to-income (DTI) ratios are also higher, making this program more affordable.

The downside of an FHA loan is that mortgage insurance is required. This lump sum **up-front mortgage insurance premium (UFMIP)** is included in closing costs and equals 1.75% of the total loan amount. Then the mortgage insurance premium (MIP) is factored into the life of the loan through the APR. To avoid paying more over the life of the loan, borrowers should try to steer away from HPMLs.

Quick Review Question

13. What distinguishes an (HPML) from other mortgage loans?

MLO Compensation

Mortgage loan officer (MLO) compensation is regulated under TILA (12 CFR 1026.36(d)). Most MLOs are paid completely through commission. Like any sales job, each employer can vary salary and bonuses for

closing a high number of loans or dollar amounts monthly. The commission is paid either by percentage or 25 basis points (BPS), which equals one-quarter of one percent.

Non-commission paid salary-based jobs do exist for MLOs and are a great way to learn the business and build a client base. New MLOs usually need help getting started in the industry, so it is common for financial institutions to subsidize their income with a small monthly salary. The Federal Reserve Board prohibits **dual compensation**. That means that MLOs may only be paid by the borrower *or* lender—not both.

Mortgage loan brokers, who are licensed by each state, work directly with lenders for their compensation and are 100% commissioned. This commission is also known as a **loan origination fee**.

The lenders will pay MLOs 1% of the final loan amount funded; however, any loan amount over $500,000 is a negotiated percentage between the mortgage brokerage and loan officer. Out of that $500,000 mortgage loan, the brokerage will automatically receive $5,000 and the remaining amount is given to the MLO based on the fee structure set up between the brokerage and MLO.

Brokerage loan officers are paid through a percentage yield spread from the lender that is negotiated up front and part of the loan interest rate. The brokerage takes a percentage of the compensation and the rest goes to the loan officer. A loan officer who is salary-based under a national bank is compensated through bonus; salary is also negotiated up front.

Quick Review Question

14. What term describes the commission received by a mortgage loan officer (MLO)?

TILA-RESPA Integrated Disclosure Rule and "Know Before You Owe"

Disclosures

Under TILA and RESPA, the CFPB enforces guidelines lenders must follow under the **TILA-RESPA Integrated Disclosure rule (TRID)**. TRID was created as part of the overhaul of mortgage regulation following the 2008 subprime lending collapse of the housing market. The CFPB started the "Know Before You Owe" initiative to support borrowers.

TRID and loan disclosures are meant to simplify the current lending forms required by TRID. The Truth in Lending Disclosure, the good faith estimate, and the Settlement HUD-1 Statement were combined and released under TRID. This means fewer pages and less lender language confusion.

Under TRID, a mortgage loan application is triggered by six consumer points. A full loan application includes the following information from the borrower:

1. full name of applicant
2. value of property to be purchased
3. full address of applicant
4. Social Security number
5. income
6. amount of mortgage needed

The loan officer must send the application to a mortgage lender who must disclose the loan within three business days of the application. Once this information has been provided, the loan estimate is sent to the borrower electronically (if the borrower has completed an e-consent); hard copies are sent by mail.

At that point, a set of loan disclosures is sent to the borrower for signatures. The loan estimate is included in this package. The **loan estimate (LE)** is sent at the beginning of the loan and any time a change on the loan happens. To stay in compliance with TRID, the borrower must acknowledge each LE.

> **Helpful Hint:**
>
> Per TRID, all loan disclosures must be sent by email or mail within three business days once all mortgage loan application information is complete.

A package of loan forms, called **disclosures**, must be mailed, emailed and ink-signed or e-signed by the borrowers within a specific time frame. These documents combine the TILA and RESPA requirements for mortgage lending.

A loan estimate breaks down the borrower's estimated costs. These include:

- the interest rate,
- the monthly payment,
- the closing fees,
- the taxes and insurance,
- all title fees,
- the required amount of cash to close, and
- the required down payment.

If the loan's interest rate has been locked in with the lender, the loan estimate will show this. This three-page document is the first cost estimate for the loan and should be in line with expectations the loan officer has set with the borrowers. The LE costs are usually overestimated by the loan officer to avoid any 10% tolerance fees (see Chapter 5). There are multiple sections on the LE, each designed to be clear and easy to understand:

- Page one is straightforward, with personal details of the loan and lender, including
  - the mortgage loan amount,
  - the interest rate,
  - the monthly payment (including escrows),
  - the expiration date of a lock (if the loan is locked),
  - the type of loan and property, and
  - the borrowers' full names.
- Page two of the LE breaks down the estimated closing costs, including
  - the loan officer's origination charges,
  - services a borrower could and could not shop for on costs, and
  - escrow funds that will be collected at the time of closing.
- Page three breaks down the APR costs and gives the borrower the chance to compare the lender's costs against offers from other lenders:
  - Additional information on the loan (e.g., appraisal notes, homeowner's insurance, late payments, and servicing requirements) are also found on page 3.

If everything looks good, the borrower will accept the loan terms either by e-signing or ink-signing the entire loan package. This starts the **intent to proceed (ITP)** with the loan.

The **Closing Disclosure (CD)** is another very important disclosure under TRID. The CD is very similar to the LE and contains five to eight pages:

- For home purchases, the CD shows costs covered by the seller.
- For refinances, the CD shows fees that are part of the new loan and fees that have been paid by the borrower or lender.
- The CD also shows any payoffs to creditors.

To close on time

- the lender must deliver the CD three business days before closing, and
- the borrowers must sign (electronically or in ink) the CD three business days before closing.

Per TRID, the right to not move forward with the loan (i.e., the right-to-rescind time clock), only starts once the borrower signs the CD. The three-day right to rescission must be given to the borrowers. If the Closing Disclosure is not signed three days before closing, the closing date must be pushed by one day and every day until it is signed. This is a hard rule that cannot be changed.

Like the LE, the Closing Disclosure is an estimate of closing costs but should align very closely with the final numbers the borrower has agreed to with the loan officer.

Until the title company has "balanced" all numbers with the lender, the CD is subject to change; however, by the time the borrower is at the closing table, all numbers should be balanced so there are no closing surprises.

Mortgage bankers are not required to disclose their compensation to borrowers; however, mortgage brokers and their loan officers are required to do so. **Section A** on page 2 of the CD shows the cost of the loan officer's compensation. If the compensation is being paid by the lender, it becomes part of the loan rate pricing that has been negotiated with the LO and the lender. It will show up in Section A on the right side under "Seller" and be labeled "L" next to the amount. If it is paid by the borrower, or if there is no compensation to the broker/ LO, no amount will show in section A.

> **Helpful Hint:**
>
> The borrower should compare the first LE and first CD for differences and review them with the loan officer to make sure all loan credits and requested changes are reflected.

The **Affiliated Business Arrangement Disclosure** is a RESPA form that must be sent to the borrowers as part of their initial loan disclosure package if there is a business relationship between the referring party and the settlement provider. The lender must disclose the relationship of the provider and whether there is a direct financial interest in the referral of business. It also shows the range of costs this provider charges. A typical settlement provider is an appraisal management company or credit report servicer.

The special information booklet ("Your Home Loan Toolkit: A Step-By-Step Guide"), issued by the CFPB, was created as a tool for prospective homebuyers to use as they navigate the home-buying process. It is required by RESPA and only applies to mortgage loans for home purchases.

The special information booklet breaks down the closing costs found on the LE or HUD 1. This booklet is sent within the three-business-day TRID rule. It covers how to choose the best type of mortgage program, provides a breakdown of the closing services and costs, and discusses how to understand the CD. It also offers tips on successful homeownership.

Quick Review Questions

15. Under the TILA-RESPA Integrated Disclosure Rule (TRID), a mortgage loan application is triggered by six consumer points. What are these points?

16. Under the TILA-RESPA Integrated Disclosure Rule (TRID), loan disclosures should be sent within what time frame?

Other Information

TRID allows for certain changes due to **change of circumstance (COC)**. TRID has a 10% change rule that allows for costs to be adjusted on fees that the borrower cannot shop for:

- If the cost changes more than 10%, a COC to the original LE costs must be redisclosed to the borrower.
- For example, if the loan officer disclosed $200 for title fees and the actual fees are 10% higher, a new LE must be sent and signed/acknowledged by the borrower.

One common COC concerns the appraisal. Most LEs show an industry cost appraisal fee based on the type of property; however, if the property is unique (e.g., a mountain or rural property), the cost might be higher. A COC for the additional cost must be done. Regardless of COC, the borrower has the right to receive a copy of the appraisal report. Another common change is adding a rush charge to meet the contract deadline. If the borrower agrees to pay for the fee difference, then a COC must be done to include the new charge. The COC must be completed within three days of the new fee charge, or it becomes a tolerance charge, and the loan officer is responsible for the cost.

> **Did You Know?**
>
> **Loan consummation** is when the borrower signs the mortgage note.

Loan costs that are not allowed to change are also known as **zero tolerance fees**. Zero tolerance fees include

- fees paid to third parties (e.g., credit report fees);
- loan processing fees; and
- loan origination fees.

If borrowers are **escrowing**, the lender on their mortgage loan is collecting monthly money for property taxes and homeowner's insurance. Per CFPB, the servicer on the mortgage must send borrowers an annual escrow statement within thirty days of the annual loan time frame. For instance, if a borrower closes in July, the lender must send the annual escrow statement to the borrower in June. This escrow statement will show the amount collected for taxes and insurance premiums. Escrow must meet the requirements for the payouts to the county and insurance agency.

If the escrow is short, the servicer will make adjustments to it. Borrowers may make up the difference for the shortage, or the amount collected will increase in the following month's mortgage payment. If there is an overage, an escrow check will be sent to the borrowers.

1. Federal Mortgage-Related Laws

Quick Review Questions

17. Within how many days must a change of circumstance (COC) be completed?

18. Loan costs that are not allowed to change are called what?

TRIVIUM
—TEST PREP—

Answer Key

1. The two goals of the Real Estate Settlement Procedures Act (RESPA) are to reduce closing costs and protect consumers from deceitful lending practices.

2. The term *treble damages* describes the triple liability of sellers who violate Section 9 of the Real Estate Settlement Procedures Act (RESPA).

3. The borrower must receive the Mortgage Loan Servicing Disclosure Statement within three days of the loan application.

4. If the lender sells the loan on the secondary market, it has fifteen days to send the Servicing Transfer Statement to the borrower.

5. The Consumer Financial Protection Bureau (CFPB) supervises and enforces compliance with regulations set forth in the Equal Credit Opportunity Act (ECOA).

6. Regulation B of Equal Credit Opportunity Act (ECOA) makes it unlawful to discriminate against a credit applicant on the basis of age, marital status, race or color, religion, sex, or nation of origin.

7. An adverse action notice discloses to the borrower the specific reasons for which a loan was denied.

8. No, loan officers cannot ask if borrowers are single, divorced, or widowed; instead, they may ask if borrowers are married, unmarried, or separated.

9. A right to rescission is a three-day cooling off period during which a customer may back out of the purchase.

10. Under the Truth in Lending Act (TILA) and Regulation Z, a dwelling is considered the borrower's principal home. It may be any of the following:

- a residential structure of one to four units
- an individual condominium or cooperative unit
- a mobile or manufactured home

11. A trigger term is a word or phrase that legally requires one or more credit agreement disclosure when used in marketing and advertising in conjunction with any credit solicitation.

12. The 2013 HOEPA Rule requires homeowner counseling.

13. The annual percentage rate (APR) of a higher-priced mortgage loan (HPML) exceeds the average prime offer rate (APOR), which distinguishes it from other mortgage loans.

14. The commission received by a mortgage loan officer (MLO) is known as a loan origination fee.

15. The six points consumer points that trigger a mortgage loan application are: the full name of applicant, the value of the property to be purchased, the full address of the applicant, the applicant's Social Security number, the applicant's income, and the amount of mortgage needed.

16. Per the TILA-RESPA Integrated Disclosure Rule (TRID), all loan disclosures must be sent by email or mail within three business days once all mortgage loan application information is complete.

1. Federal Mortgage-Related Laws

17. A change of circumstance (COC) must be completed within three days of the new fee charge.

18. Loan costs that are not allowed to change are also known as zero tolerance fees.

2 Other Mortgage Laws And Authorities

Other Federal Laws and Guidelines

The Home Mortgage Disclosure Act

The **Home Mortgage Disclosure Act (HMDA)** was written to require mortgage lenders to collect data about

- the loan applications it receives to buy a dwelling,
- the loans on dwellings it originates, and
- the loans on dwellings it purchases.

This data is reported regularly to the federal government so that the government can ensure the lender is following fair lending practices. Some of this data is also disclosed to the public.

According to the HMDA, a **dwelling** is a residential structure. It may or may not be attached to a broader property. Table 2.1. provides some examples of what constitutes a dwelling:

> **Helpful Hint:**
>
> The HMDA is also known as **Regulation C**. It was codified into federal law as Regulation C of Part 1003 of Title 12 of the Code of Federal Regulations (CFR).

Table 2.1. Defining a Dwelling Under Regulation C	
What Is a Dwelling?	**What Is Not a Dwelling?**
<ul><li>single-family homes</li><li>condominiums</li><li>manufactured homes</li><li>multifamily residences</li><li>vacation or second homes</li><li>homes owned as investments</li><li>assisted living facilities</li></ul>	<ul><li>recreational vehicles</li><li>houseboats</li><li>temporary housing (e.g., hotels and college dorms)</li><li>rehab facilities</li><li>any building used mostly for commercial purposes</li></ul>

A lender must generate or collect forty-eight different pieces of information for each loan application it receives. The most important of these are discussed below.

Borrowers must provide certain financial information as part of their application, including

- gross annual income,
- total assets,
- employment history,
- tax returns,
- bank account information, and
- sources of the down payment.

> **Helpful Hint:**
>
> The entire list of information required by lenders can be found at https://consumerfinance.gov.

In addition to collecting this financial information, MLOs must also collect certain **personal information** from the borrower. Mortgage loan originators are restricted in the types of questions they can ask; see Table 2.2.

Table 2.2. What Can MLOs Ask a Borrower?	
Questions MLOs CAN Ask a Borrower	**Questions MLOs CANNOT Ask a Borrower**
<ul><li>What is your date of birth?</li><li>Are you married, unmarried, or separated?</li><li>How many children do you have?</li><li>Do you have other dependents?</li><li>Are you divorced? If so, do you receive alimony or child support?</li><li>How many people are applying for a loan?</li><li>Are you currently involved in a lawsuit?</li><li>What is your ethnicity and race?</li><li>What is your sex?</li></ul>	<ul><li>What is your age?</li><li>Are you single or widowed?</li><li>Are you pregnant or planning a family?</li><li>Do you have serious health problems?</li></ul>

Borrowers have the right to refuse to provide the following information:

- ethnicity
- race
- sex

In these cases, the borrower should be told that federal law requires this information to ensure that the lender is following fair lending practices.

If the borrower is asked to provide this information but refuses, the MLO should indicate on the data collection form that the borrower has refused. The borrower must be informed that the MLO is required to include the borrower's ethnicity, race, and sex on the form based on visual observation and the borrower's surname.

Finally, borrowers should be provided information explaining that the lender's HMDA data is available online with the Consumer Financial Protection Bureau. The data includes information about the ages, races, sex, incomes, and ethnicities of applicants and borrowers.

Quick Review Questions

1. The Home Mortgage Disclosure Act (HMDA) is also known as what?

2. Which type of personal information may borrowers refuse to provide?

The Fair Credit Reporting Act and Fair and Accurate Credit Transactions Act, 15 USC § 1681 et seq.

The **Fair Credit Reporting Act (FCRA)**, enacted in 1970, requires major credit reporting agencies to be more accurate in how they keep consumer credit reports.

An amendment to the FCRA, the **Fair and Accurate Credit Transactions Act (FACTA)** passed in 2003. It requires that major credit reporting agencies give consumers greater access to their own credit reports and help prevent identity theft.

A **consumer report** is created by a consumer reporting agency (e.g., Experian, TransUnion, Equifax). Businesses that may extend new credit (e.g., mortgage lenders) use the information contained in a consumer report to decide whether to extend new credit to a consumer. The report may access public records and existing credit accounts in order to determine which creditors the consumer already owes money to. Information gathered from consumer reports includes

- creditors the consumer already owes money to and how much;
- how the consumer is doing in paying back those creditors;
- how much credit is already available to the consumer, and in how many accounts;
- how much of that credit the consumer is currently using;
- whether the consumer has closed any credit accounts;
- how much medical debt the consumer has;
- whether the consumer filed for bankruptcy in the last ten years;
- whether the consumer has dealt with a collection agency in the last seven years;
- whether the consumer owes money from losing a civil lawsuit in the last seven years;
- whether the consumer has been arrested in the last 7 years;
- whether the consumer has ever been convicted of a crime;
- if the consumer owes back taxes or liens from the last 7 years;
- information on the consumer's personal character and reputation; and
- information on the day-to-day life of the consumer.

Information in the credit report is used to generate a **credit score** that helps estimate whether the consumer can pay back a new loan:

- The higher the credit score, the more likely the consumer can handle new credit.
- The lower the credit score, the riskier it is to give the loan—the consumer may not be able to repay it.

Any **fraud alerts**—statements by a consumer (or representative) to current creditors or law enforcement that the consumer has been, or soon may be, a victim of fraud or identity theft—must be included in the report. These statements may include notices to credit card companies that the consumer's credit card has been lost or stolen.

Lenders are required to develop **policies and procedures regarding identity theft**, which include ways of noticing common patterns or practices that may indicate that identity theft has taken place. More information on identity theft is in the FTC Red Flags Rule section below.

A credit report is accessed by a mortgage lender only when an applicant allows, in writing, the mortgage lender to do so as part of a mortgage application. The mortgage lender may use an automated underwriting system to decide whether to underwrite a home loan but must provide the consumer with a FACTA disclosure. A **FACTA disclosure** includes

- a copy of any credit reports the lender used in deciding on a loan,
- any factors that lowered the credit score, and
- the actual credit score itself.

When lenders notify consumers of their decision on a loan application, consumers receive

- their credit score,
- the option to get a free copy of their credit report from consumer reporting agencies, and

> **Did You Know?**
>
> A mortgage lender may use **risk-based pricing**—giving lower interest rates to people with high credit scores and higher interest rates to people with lower credit scores. The lender may even use information in a credit report to decide not to extend a loan at all.

Quick Review Questions

3. Which act requires credit agencies to help prevent identity theft and give consumers greater access to their own credit reports?

4. What must a mortgage lender provide to a consumer when deciding whether to underwrite a home loan?

FTC Red Flags Rule

Federal law requires each financial institution or creditor that offers customers a mortgage loan (or other covered account that allows multiple payments or transactions) to create an identity theft protection program. An **identity theft protection program** is a written plan creditors will follow to minimize the chances of customers' identities being stolen.

The plan must also maximize the probability that if a customer's identity is stolen, the theft can be detected, and the problem can be fixed with as little effect on the customer as possible.

> **Did You Know?**
>
> The written plan for an identity theft protection program must be approved and then overseen by a senior employee at the institution or the institution's Board of Directors.

The program must follow the **Federal Trade Commission (FTC) Red Flags Rule** (16 CFR Part 681) by identifying what the institution considers to be its **red flags**—suspicious things the institution notices that could indicate that identity theft has occurred or may be occurring. The identity theft protection program must be actively used to:

- prevent and reduce the risk of identity theft
- make it hard to steal an identity
- detect possible identity theft
- detail what the institution will do if it notices identity theft
- allow for regular training and retraining of staff (including MLOs) so they can notice red flags

The FTC and other agencies enforce this rule to keep customers' identities as safe as possible; this includes filing a suspicious activity report when required by law (see below).

Typically, a program's identified red flags consider ways that identity theft could happen when opening a new account or accessing a current account. Other red flags may be based on:

- past instances of identity theft at the institution
- methods of identity theft known to the institution
- documentation that does not look genuine
- how customers should identify themselves online or over the phone
- customer identifying information that looks suspicious
- the unusual use of a current account
- alerts or warnings from consumer reporting agencies
- notice from a customer that an identity has been stolen
- notice by law enforcement that a customer's identity has been stolen

---

Helpful Hint:

Given the changing nature of threats and technology, identity theft protection programs must be kept up to date regularly.

MLOs often work with new customers whose identity must be verified and safeguarded during the mortgage application process, and then safeguarded against identity theft after the mortgage is in place. Therefore, MLOs must be familiar with their institution's identity theft protection program and red flags.

When MLOs notice a red flag, they must follow their institution's program to deal with the problem as quickly as possible. This may include contacting the customer or notifying law enforcement. Common red flags are discussed in Table 2.3.

Table 2.3. Typical Red Flags	
When Setting Up a New Mortgage	**After a Mortgage Has Been Set Up**
<ul><li>An applicant's identifying information looks suspicious.</li><li>Documentation does not look genuine or seems inconsistent with other information.</li><li>A check of information provided by an applicant shows the information is fraudulent.</li><li>An applicant has the inability to answer the challenge questions to access a personal account.</li></ul>	<ul><li>There is an immediate or unexpected change of address.</li><li>There are sudden changes in a person's financial habits, including multiple new accounts.</li><li>A customer does not make the first payment, or makes the first payment but none after that.</li><li>A new credit account is being used in a way that usually indicates fraud.</li></ul>

Table 2.3. Typical Red Flags

When Setting Up a New Mortgage	After a Mortgage Has Been Set Up
<ul><li>All required information has not been filled in on an applicant's mortgage application.</li><li>There is unusual use of a current account.</li><li>There is a fraud alert, or a consumer report, that indicates that an applicant's credit has been frozen.</li></ul>	<ul><li>An account has been inactive for a long time and is suddenly being used again.</li><li>A customer provides notice of unauthorized transactions.</li><li>There is a data security breach at your (or another) institution.</li><li>A customer provides confirmation of a stolen identity.</li><li>Law enforcement provides notice that a customer's identity has been stolen.</li></ul>

Quick Review Questions

5. A written plan followed by creditors to minimize the chances of customers' identities being stolen is called what?

6. Suspicious things the institution notices that may indicate identity theft are called what?

The Bank Secrecy Act and Anti-money Laundering

The **Bank Secrecy Act/Anti-Money Laundering (BSA/AML)**, passed in 1970, requires financial institutions, including mortgage lenders, to keep records about their relationships with customers. The BSA/AML requires institutions to

- verify the identity of customers,
- perform due diligence on their transactions with customers, and
- protect customers from identity theft.

Compliance with BSA/AML regulations must be independently tested by auditors on a regular basis. Each institution is required to designate a BSA/AML compliance officer, and institution employees must be regularly trained on BSA/AML procedures.

The BSA/AML requires records to be kept well enough so that each customer's transactions with the institution can be reconstructed in the future if necessary. The Act also requires that a currency transaction report be filed with the Treasury Department for each customer cash transaction of $10,000 or more—whether in US or foreign currency—unless the customer is well-known to the institution and the institution has thus formally exempted the customer from this requirement.

> **Did You Know?**
>
> Currency transaction report exemptions must be reviewed on a regular basis, usually once a year or once every other year.

An institution should file a **suspicious activities report (SAR)** with the Treasury Department within thirty days of detecting one or more unusual transactions from a customer. **Unusual transactions** include

- those involving $5,000 or more that look like money laundering or terrorist financing, and
- any transaction that may go over the $10,000 limit or other rules under the BSA/AML.

SAR filings are always made known to an institution's BSA/AML officer as well as at least one person on the board of directors. Filing an SAR protects the institution from being sued for anything related to what is discussed in the SAR, even if no criminal act was found as a result.

An SAR should also be filed for any transaction that

- may involve other illegal activities,
- may be carried out in an attempt to avoid the disclosure rules of BSA/AML,
- does not seem to have any business purpose,
- is not something a specific customer is typically known to do, and/or
- is something that makes no sense to the institution.

The SAR should include

- information about the institution;
- the person(s) involved, if known;
- a detailed description of everything that looks suspicious;
- the amount of money involved;
- any loss to the institution; and
- what the institution has done in response.

> **Did You Know?**
>
> SARs are not filed for robberies, counterfeit money, or stolen securities.

Customers about whom an SAR is filed cannot be told of the filing. Each SAR is considered federal government property and should be kept by the lender for five years after it is filed.

Quick Review Questions

7. If an institution detects one or more unusual transactions from a customer, what must it file with the Treasury Department?

8. If an institution is filing an SAR about a customer, should the institution let the customer know?

The Gramm-Leach-Bliley Act and Privacy

The **Gramm-Leach-Bliley Act (GLBA)** was passed in 1999 to require financial institutions (including mortgage lenders) to create and carry out policies for safeguarding consumers' non-public information. MLOs must understand certain terms as defined by GLBA:

- A **consumer** is defined as a person who gets, or is trying to get, a financial product or service (e.g., credit) from a lender.
  - Notably, consumers generally provide personal information during the process.
- **Non-public information** is personally identifiable financial information.
  - Non-public information also includes any information generated by using personally identifiable financial information.

26   2. Other Mortgage Laws and Authorities

For example, it is permissible to use publicly available information to create a list of names and street addresses for marketing purposes. But the list cannot be created *from* personally identifiable financial information, such as account numbers.

A mortgage lender's process of safeguarding consumers' non-public information includes creating an information security program, supervised by a qualified person who reports to senior staff at least once a year. The program must

- keep the information confidential,
- keep unauthorized people from accessing the information, and
- keep up to date with new ways to improperly obtain such information.

Lenders must also ensure that the companies they use for outside services (e.g., appraisers, and settlement companies) have their own information security programs. By law, information security programs must include written risk assessments that identify "reasonably foreseeable internal and external risks to the security, confidentiality, and integrity of customer information" and assess "the sufficiency of any safeguards in place to control these risks."

The program must also include annual testing to ensure that consumer information is still being kept secure and encryption when sending data and multi-factor authentication so that customers are the only non-lenders able to access their individual information. The program must even include a written incident response plan that can be carried out if data becomes insecure.

Once a year, a lender must provide a written copy of its privacy policy to each of its customers. The policy mailing should also include information on how to opt out of the lender's marketing outreach and how to opt out of having the lender share the customer's nonpublic personal information with nonaffiliated third parties. The mailing may be sent to the customer's last known address in written form. The privacy policy may also be delivered electronically if a customer agrees to accept electronic delivery and confirms with the lender that the policy notice was received. After that, the lender may post its customers' annual notices of the privacy policy on its website in a conspicuous way.

Some lenders use the telephone as a method of collecting debts from those who owe the lender money. They may also hire telemarketers to use the phone as an advertising tool. The **National Do Not Call Registry** was created so consumers can choose not to receive telemarketing calls by adding their phone numbers to a national list to opt out of telemarketing calls. Besides contacting those who owe them money, lenders may use telemarketing with the following three groups:

1. consumers who have established business relationships with the lender
   - This is only applicable for eighteen months after the consumer's last purchase or last payment.
   - If the consumer requests that the lender not call again, the lender must stop calling.
2. consumers who inquire for information, or who submit an application
   - This is applicable for three months after the date of the application.
   - Again, if the consumer requests that the lender not call again, the lender must stop calling.
3. consumers who give the lender written permission to contact them

To ensure compliance with the law, lenders must provide training to telemarketers, which includes the following:

- Telemarketers must identify themselves by name, lender, and phone number.
- Calls may be made only between 8 a.m. and 9 p.m., local time.
- A lender must have a written policy for maintaining a do-not-call list.
- The policy must be available to be seen at any time.
- If a consumer requests that telemarketers no longer call, the lender must keep that phone number on its internal do-not-call list for five years.

Quick Review Questions

9. What distinguishes a consumer under GLBA?

10. How frequently must lenders provide written copies of their privacy policies to consumers?

Advertising

Regulation N (12 CFR Part 1014) defines mortgage credit products and regulates how they are advertised. Under federal law, **mortgage credit products** are forms of credit secured by a property or a dwelling that are available to consumers for personal use.

Mortgage loan originators who advertise mortgage credit products must follow strict rules according to Regulation N. All advertising of mortgage credit products must be totally accurate. Not every one of the following terms of contract must be included in advertising, but every term that does appear in advertising must be correct to prevent violations. Each term below is likely to appear in any contract signed by consumers, so MLOs should plan to go over all of the terms of the contract with consumers before they sign on the dotted line. Terms that must be accurate if appearing in a mortgage credit product advertisement include:

- the type of product being advertised
- who is doing the advertising
- the cost of the product
- the chances that a consumer will be eligible for the product
- the amount of monthly interest owed
- the interest percentage rate
- extra fees or costs
- costs and information about other products sold at the same time and their effects on the consumer's taxes or insurance payments
- the consumer's ability to refinance
- prepayment penalties
- possible changes in interest rates or terms
- comparisons between temporary rates and actual rates
- minimum payments
- what would trigger a consumer's default
- whether the product can be used to pay other debts
- the product's affiliations with any government program or other organization
- whether consumers can remain living in their homes if using the product

- how long consumers can remain living in their homes if using the product
- whether counseling is available before the consumer makes a final decision to use the product

In a commercial communication, it is a violation of Regulation N for anyone to materially misrepresent any term of contract of any mortgage credit product being sold. Commercial communication includes

- materials written on paper
- radio ads
- TV infomercials
- telemarketing scripts
- websites
- posters
- videos
- movies
- PowerPoint slides
- oral statements

> **Did You Know?**
>
> Misrepresentations are forbidden even if they are only done by implication or indirect means. MLOs should therefore take care to never misrepresent any mortgage credit product.

It is also a violation to try to get consumers to waive their protections against unethical mortgage credit product advertising. Those protections are detailed in Regulation N and include protection against misrepresentations of any of the above bullet points.

Mortgage loan originators who advertise mortgage credit products are required to keep copies of all materials used to advertise those mortgage credit products for two years after the materials are no longer used for advertising. This includes the names of the products and the terms under which they were offered for sale. It is a violation to not keep such materials.

Quick Review Questions

11. What law regulates how mortgage products are advertised?

12. For how long must an MLO keep copies of materials used to advertise mortgage credit products?

Electronic Signatures in Global and National Commerce Act

Where documents must be provided in writing, the **Electronic Signatures in Global and National Commerce (E-Sign) Act** allows them to be legally signed electronically.

Before agreeing to sign electronically, consumers must be given a statement that explains that records can always be provided on paper, regardless of whether the consumer agrees to sign electronically. In addition, before consenting to sign electronically, consumers must be told the following:

> **Helpful Hint:**
>
> To use electronic signatures in a transaction, *both* the mortgage lender and consumer must agree to sign electronically.

- how to get paper copies, and how much the copies may cost
- how to withdraw consent if they change their mind about signing electronically
  - Consumers who agree to sign electronically but then change their minds may be liable for fees or other consequences.
- how to update their contact information so the lender can contact them electronically

2. Other Mortgage Laws and Authorities

- which items can be signed electronically
- which items can still be signed on paper if desired
- the technical products (e.g., computer and software) required to electronically sign and keep copies of all documents

After consumers agree to sign electronically, MLOs should double-check that the consumers have online access to the documents that are to be signed. If a mortgage lender later changes any computer requirements needed to access electronic documents, the lender must

- inform the consumer of the new computer requirements;
- offer the consumer a chance to go back to pen and paper at no cost; and
- have the consumer sign an agreement, updated with the new computer requirements, to continue signing electronically.

Mortgage lenders keep some electronic records in digital cloud storage for a certain period of time. These records remain visible to everyone concerned (e.g., consumers, loan officers) as long as the record is kept as required by law. For legal purposes, keeping the electronic record is considered the same as keeping a traditional paper record:

> **Did You Know?**
>
> Oral communications and the recording of such communications are not considered electronic records.

- Each electronic record kept must be a digital copy that is unique, identifiable, unalterable, and reproducible.
- A mortgage lender must also track the employee who oversees the maintenance of each electronic document on file and ensure that any changes made to a record are authorized by that person.
- The unique electronic signature of each person who signs should be captured by the lender to allow signature matching at any time.
- Bank checks can be kept in electronic form by a lender if both sides of the check are kept electronically.
- Notarized documents and statements under oath can also be signed electronically and kept afterward, the same as a paper record.

If someone needs to see an electronic record or its history but cannot access it, this may be enough to nullify the legal effects of the record, even if the record was properly signed and handled at first. It is therefore imperative to ensure that electronic records can always be seen by everyone involved in a transaction for as long as the law requires it.

During any signing process, a consumer must be able to provide **proof of identity** to protect both the consumer and the lender from fraud. Common ways of verifying consumer identity include

- a separate password for each document,
- requiring the consumer's email address,
- recording the consumer's IP address when a document is accessed,
- recording the time of day of such access,
- automatically phoning the consumer and requiring a response,

- only granting access to documents for a certain number of minutes before the consumer is automatically logged out, and
- two-factor authentication.

Finally, electronic signings cannot be used for mortgage default, foreclosure, or eviction notices. Signatures for these documents as well as all documents related to a default, foreclosure, or eviction must still be done on paper.

Quick Review Questions

13. Can a mortgage lender force a consumer to sign documents electronically?

14. Can recordings of oral communications be considered electronic records?

USA PATRIOT Act

The **Uniting and Strengthening America by Providing Appropriate Tools Required to Intercept and Obstruct Terrorism Act (USA PATRIOT Act) of 2001** was passed after the terrorist attacks of September 11, 2001. The USA PATRIOT Act makes money laundering and terrorist financing more difficult and requires financial institutions to create written customer identification programs within their Bank Secrecy Act programs. Institutions must do the following:

- collect identifying information from consumers before they open an account
    - name
    - birth date
    - physical address
    - an identification number of some kind (e.g., Social Security number)
- tell each customer why this information is needed
- explain how the institution verifies a customer's true identity
- maintain records on each customer and secure photocopies of records against identity theft
- verify that customers are not on lists of terrorists
- explain what the institution will do if a customer's identity cannot be verified

A borrower's identity may be verified by documentary methods (e.g., using an unexpired government ID), non-documentary methods (e.g., checking references or utility bills), or through some combination of the two. Extra due diligence is needed to verify the identity of foreign customers.

An institution must also authenticate a customer's electronic account applications by verifying the information a customer gives and checking that it makes sense and does not involve past fraud.

The USA PATRIOT Act requires financial institutions to respond to federal government requests for information on customers whom the government suspects of being involved in money laundering or terrorist financing:

- Institutions receiving such a request may tell other institutions of the request but may NOT tell the customer about it.
- All institutions must certify once a year that they are willing to share such information with other institutions as needed.

Quick Review Questions

15. Is a bank required to ascertain that customers are not on lists of terrorists?

16. What responsibilities do financial institutions have if the federal government requests information about their customers?

Homeowners Protection Act

A **high-ratio loan** is when a customer's down payment is less than 20% of the total purchase price. In order to receive a high-ratio loan, customers are generally required to purchase private mortgage insurance. **Private mortgage insurance (PMI)** is designed to cover a mortgage lender's costs in case the mortgage goes to foreclosure and the house must be resold. Though PMI costs can be paid by others, it is most common for the borrower to pay them. PMI can be paid all at once at loan closing but is typically paid monthly, along with the payment on the mortgage.

Once borrower-paid PMI is no longer needed, a lender is supposed to cancel it, so the borrower does not continue to pay for it. The **Homeowners Protection Act**, also known as the PMI Cancellation Act, facilitates the process of canceling borrower-paid PMI and ensures uniformity in the process throughout the United States. Documents relating to PMI must be provided to the applicant at the time of closing. These include

- an explanation of the differences between lender-paid PMI and borrower-paid PMI, and
- a written amortization schedule and a notice explaining the PMI cancellation rules.

Under the Homeowners Protection Act, borrower-paid PMI must generally be canceled on a mortgage in two cases:

- automatically when the original mortgage is 22% paid off and the borrower's mortgage payments are up to date, OR
- as soon as the mortgage owner meets specific requirements (see below)

Borrower-paid PMI must also be canceled when the original mortgage is 20% paid off and the mortgage owner meets five specific requirements:

1. The borrower requests in writing that the PMI be canceled.
2. The borrower has a good payment history on the mortgage.
3. The mortgage is paid up to date.
4. The property has not lost any value since the loan was originated (such as by an appraisal).
5. The owner's equity in the home does not have a subordinate lien.

> **Did You Know?**
>
> If mortgage payments are up to date, PMI must be automatically canceled on the termination date specified in the original mortgage documents or on the first day of the first month after the mortgage payment is up to date.

Refinancing a mortgage loan ends the PMI on that loan but may affect the PMI needed for the refinanced loan. PMI never lasts past the halfway point of the length of any mortgage. Any PMI premiums collected past the termination date must be returned to the mortgage owner, and the owner must be notified in writing that PMI has been terminated and no longer needs to be paid.

Quick Review Questions

17. When do borrowers typically pay PMI?

18. Per the Homeowners Protection Act, when must PMI be canceled?

Dodd-Frank Act

The **Dodd-Frank Wall Street Reform and Consumer Protection Act (Dodd-Frank Act)** was passed in 2010 to change how the United States regulates its financial system. Understanding Dodd-Frank is essential for MLOs:

- It governs mortgage loan origination fees.
- It prevents unreasonable mortgage terms.
- It prohibits discrimination by race, ethnicity, gender, or age when mortgage terms are provided.
- It requires all mortgage lenders to be licensed.

Section 1411 of the Dodd-Frank Act ensures that mortgage lenders only provide loans that fit a consumer's **ability to repay (ATR)**. An officer therefore must make a good-faith determination that a consumer will actually be able to pay back the loan, as well as the property taxes and mortgage insurance that are often paid along with the monthly loan payment.

Determination of ATR should be made only after considering a consumer's credit history, income, other financial obligations, employment, and other money the consumer may be able to access.

Though a mortgage lender must verify income by examining a customer's pay stubs and federal income tax returns, income verification for a loan refinance can be skipped under the following circumstances:

- The consumer is up to date on the current loan.
- The refinance will not increase the principal due on the current loan.
- The refinance fees are less than 3% of the new loan amount.
- The refinanced interest rate is less than the old rate (unless moving from an adjustable rate to a fixed rate).
- The refinance will pay off the loan without any balloon payments.

Rules by the CFPB require a process of **TILA-RESPA Integrated Disclosure (TRID)** (also called "Know Before You Owe"). TRID allows consumers to understand how much they will owe on a mortgage loan before they sign anything.

At the start of the TRID process, mortgage lenders have three days after they receive qualifying information from a consumer to provide the consumer with a **loan estimate** of how much the lender may lend. That qualifying information comprises the consumer's name, income, and Social Security number, along with the property's address and estimated value, and the size of the loan desired.

> **Helpful Hint:**
>
> See Chapter 1 for details on TRID.

With the exception of the credit report fee, loan estimates must be provided without any up-front fees or income verification and must be provided at least seven business days before the closing date. If a

consumer provides income verification data at this stage, a lender may use it to give the consumer pre-approval for the loan.

At the end of the TRID process, lenders must also provide the consumer with a **Closing Disclosure** at least three business days before the closing date. If the percentage rate of the loan is changed, or a prepayment penalty is added, the consumer has three more business days after getting a changed Closing Disclosure to make a final decision on whether to accept the loan.

Table 2.4. Loan Estimate Versus Closing Disclosure	
What Is on a Loan Estimate?	**What Is on a Closing Disclosure?**
<ul><li>approximate information on monthly payments</li><li>fees that must be paid to obtain the loan</li><li>closing costs</li><li>how much cash the consumer will need to close the loan</li><li>whether the loan can be transferred to another servicer</li></ul>	<ul><li>how much the mortgage will cost (including how much the consumer will need for closing costs)</li><li>whether homeowner's insurance is required</li><li>the consumer's monthly payment on the loan</li></ul>

TRID disclosures are not required for the following:

- home-equity loans
- reverse mortgages
- mortgages secured by a dwelling that is not real property (e.g., mobile home or houseboat)

Quick Review Questions

19. Which part of the Dodd-Frank Act requires mortgage lenders to determine a consumer's ability to repay ATR?

20. Under the TRID process, how long do mortgage lenders have to provide the consumer with a loan estimate after they receive qualifying information from a consumer?

Regulatory Authorities

Consumer Financial Protection Bureau

The **Consumer Financial Protection Bureau (CFPB)** is an independent agency within the US Federal Reserve. It was created by the Dodd-Frank Act to promote fairness and transparency for mortgages and other financial products and services. The CFPB is responsible for

- implementing and enforcing federal consumer finance laws,
- ensuring that financial services providers are following the law,
- making sure markets work transparently for consumers, and
- establishing a toll-free consumer hotline and website for complaints and questions about consumer financial products and services.

Did You Know?

Terms in a Closing Disclosure must be as close to the terms specified in the loan estimate as possible, with no lender charges changeable and only a 10% increase in fees allowed for some third-party services.

The CFPB has oversight authority over banks, thrifts, and credit unions with assets over $10 billion, and their affiliates. It also supervises non-bank mortgage originators and servicers, payday lenders, and private student lenders of all sizes.

The CFPB provides information to consumers about their rights in the mortgage process. Consumers can access the **Know Your Rights** page on the CFPB website to find answers to frequently asked questions or concerns.

Section 1420 of the Dodd-Frank Act requires mortgage lenders to provide a coupon book or a written mortgage statement to consumers each billing cycle. The **written mortgage statement** must include

- contact information for the servicer;
- contact information for a housing counselor;
- information on how to report an error on a mortgage statement;
- the current payment amount;
- the amount of principal still due;
- the current interest rate and, if it will soon change, the new interest rate;
- how much of each payment is interest, principal, and escrow;
- the date the next payment is due without creating a late fee;
- the minimum payment needed to avoid a late fee;
- payment options (e.g., check, online) and their effect on principal;
- recent payment history;
- notice of delinquency (if behind on payments); and
- any penalties for prepayment.

Consumers can file a complaint online with CFPB at https://www.consumerfinance.gov/complaint, which allows complaints to be submitted online or through the phone number provided.

Quick Review Questions

21. How was the CFPB created?

22. What does Section 1420 require mortgage lenders to provide to consumers each billing cycle?

Department of Housing and Urban Development

The **US Department of Housing and Urban Development (HUD)** is a department of the federal government, supervised by a secretary who is nominated by the president and confirmed by the Senate. HUD was created partly to help consumers with every aspect of home ownership, including:

- finding a home to buy
- obtaining a mortgage to buy a home

- enforcing the Fair Housing Act to prevent discrimination against potential homebuyers
- avoiding foreclosure

HUD insures home loans through its **Federal Housing Administration (FHA)** which includes the mortgage-backed securities program of the **Government National Mortgage Association (Ginnie Mae)**. FHA programs help homebuyers

> **Did You Know?**
>
> Some FHA programs even allow buyers to make monthly payments based on what they can afford at the moment and have those payments increase in the future as their income increases.

- prequalify for a loan
- obtain a fixed-rate mortgage with a constant interest rate
- obtain an adjustable-rate mortgage whose interest rate may change
- obtain a reverse mortgage
- refinance an existing loan
- make a home more energy efficient

HUD's **Office of Housing Counseling** certifies agencies that provide advice and training to borrowers. These agencies counsel borrowers on:

- deciding to buy a home
- choosing and buying the home
- getting the home inspected before moving in
- financial decisions related to a home
- how to sell a home

A lender must provide a **Homeowner Counseling Disclosure** that includes a written list of at least ten such certified agencies near the applicant's current home to each borrower applying for a federal-related mortgage.

A borrower must meet with a counseling agency when the borrower is applying to buy public housing or when the borrower wishes to obtain:

- a high-cost mortgage
- a refinance
- a home equity loan or line of credit
- a reverse mortgage, and/or
- a loan with an excessive APR

The **Fair Housing Act** protects mortgage applicants from discrimination on the basis of race, color, national origin, religion, sex, or disability. It also prevents discrimination against parents with minor children and people who are pregnant. Under the Act, mortgage lenders may not use any of these criteria to

- refuse a mortgage loan to an applicant
- refuse to provide loan information
- provide different loan terms for one person over another
- appraise property unfairly
- refuse to purchase a loan

2. Other Mortgage Laws and Authorities

Lenders cannot threaten or intimidate anyone who exercises the rights to fair housing. They also cannot advertise in a way that seems to discriminate against any of the groups mentioned above.

Quick Review Questions

23. Does HUD issue home loans?

24. What law protects mortgage applicants from discrimination?

Answer Key

1. The Home Mortgage Disclosure Act (HMDA) is also known as Regulation C.

2. Borrowers may refuse to provide information about their ethnicity, race, or sex.

3. The Fair and Accurate Credit Transactions Act (FACTA) requires credit agencies to help prevent identity theft and improve consumer access to credit reports.

4. Mortgage lenders must provide consumers with the Fair and Accurate Credit Transactions Act (FACTA) disclosure.

5. A written plan followed by creditors to minimize the chances of customers' identities being stolen is called an identity theft protection program.

6. Suspicious things the institution notices that may indicate identity theft are called red flags.

7. If an institution detects one or more unusual transactions from a customer, it must file a suspicious activities report (SAR) with the Treasury Department.

8. No, customers about whom an SAR is filed cannot be told of the filing.

9. According to the Gramm-Leach-Bliley Act (GLBA) consumers generally provide personal information.

10. Lenders must provide written copies of their privacy policies to consumers each year.

11. Regulation N regulates how mortgage products are advertised.

12. A mortgage loan originator (MLO) must keep copies of all materials used to advertise mortgage credit products for two years after ceasing their use.

13. No. To use electronic signatures in a transaction, *both* the mortgage lender and consumer must agree to sign electronically.

14. No. Oral communications and recordings of them are not considered electronic records.

15. Yes. The USA PATRIOT Act requires financial institutions to verify that customers are not on any lists of terrorists.

16. The USA PATRIOT Act requires financial institutions to respond to federal government requests for information on customers whom the government suspects of being involved in money laundering or terrorist financing.

17. Borrowers typically pay private mortgage insurance (PMI) when they have high-ratio loans, meaning the down payment is less than 20% of the total purchase price.

18. Per the Homeowners Protection Act, private mortgage insurance (PMI) is canceled when the original mortgage is 20% paid off or as soon as the mortgage owner meets other specific requirements.

19. Section 1411 of the Dodd-Frank Wall Street Reform and Consumer Protection Act (Dodd-Frank Act) requires mortgage lenders to determine a consumer's ability to repay (ATR).

20. Under the TILA-RESPA Integrated Disclosure (TRID) process, lenders have three days after they receive qualifying information from a consumer to provide the consumer with a loan estimate.

21. The Consumer Financial Protection Bureau (CFPB) was created by the Dodd-Frank Wall Street Reform and Consumer Protection Act (Dodd-Frank Act).

22. According to Section 1420 of the Dodd-Frank Act requires mortgage lenders to provide a coupon book or a written mortgage statement each billing cycle.

23. Yes, the US Department of Housing and Urban Development (HUD) insures home loans through the Federal Housing administration (FHA).

24. The Fair Housing Act protects mortgage applicants from discrimination on the basis of race, color, national origin, religion, sex, or disability.

3 Qualified And Non-Qualified Mortgage Programs

Qualified Mortgages

According to the Consumer Financial Protection Bureau (CFPB), a **qualified mortgage (QM)** must meet certain guidelines. The following guidelines are the most common:

- equal monthly payments over the life of the mortgage
- loan term of thirty years or less
- limited points and fees
- limited APR
- no balloon mortgages or negative amortization
- lender-verified current income and existing debt of the borrower
- lender-verified debt-to-income (DTI) ratio

A lender must conduct a good-faith **ability to repay (ATR)** check to give reasonable certainty that a QM can be paid back. A lender must also ensure that the borrower's debt-to-income ratio is 43% or less.

As of November 1, 2022, the CFPB sets limits on the points and fees that a lender can charge for a QM, as shown in Table 3.1. The dollar amounts in the table are adjusted once a year, but because most mortgages are at least $100,000, the limit in most cases is 3% of the loan amount.

Table 3.1. Points and Fees a Lender May Charge for a QM	
Loan Amount	**Maximum Total of Points and Fees**
less than $12,500	8% of loan amount
$12,500 – $20,000	$1,000
$20,000 – $60,000	5% of loan amount
$60,000 – $100,000	$3,000
greater than $100,000	3% of loan amount

The CFPB also sets an upper limit for a QM's **annual percentage rate (APR)** of interest based on market conditions. The APR is equal to the mortgage interest rate, plus the effective interest rate that is created by spreading out the points or fees, and the prepaid interest at closing over the length of the mortgage. Mortgage interest is due on the first of each month.

The APR is therefore usually 0.05% to 0.5% higher than the given interest rate for the mortgage. In most cases, on the date the interest rate is set, the APR cannot exceed the **average prime offer rate (APOR)** by more than 2.25%, but this limit does change based on the size of the mortgage.

3. Qualified and Non-Qualified Mortgage Programs

Qualified mortgages can be prepaid (or repaid early), but during the first three years, lenders may charge extra for this privilege:

- up to 2% of the prepaid amount during the first two years
- up to 1% of the prepaid amount during the third year

If a lender imposes such charges, it must also make alternatives available that do not have a prepayment penalty.

After three years, no extra lender charges are allowed for prepayment. If the mortgage payments are up to date after three years, the mortgage is considered **seasoned**. At that point, borrowers can no longer sue lenders claiming that the lenders gave them loans they could not repay.

Quick Review Questions

1. For a qualified mortgage (QM), what must the borrower's debt-to-income ratio be?

2. What is the limit to which the annual percentage rate (APR) may exceed the average prime offer rate (APOR) in most cases?

Conventional/Conforming Mortgages

The **Federal National Mortgage Association (FNMA)**, commonly called **Fannie Mae**, was created in 1938 to make more money available for home mortgages. Fannie Mae provides **securitization** of mortgage loans made by lenders by borrowing money from the federal government:

- Fannie Mae uses that money to buy primary mortgage loans from lenders.
- Individual primary loans are grouped into a debt package of **mortgage-backed securities (MBSs)**.
- MBSs are sold to investors in a **secondary market** of bonds or other financial instruments that pay back debt over time.

Lenders use the money they get from selling mortgages to Fannie Mae to make more mortgage loans. Investors buy MBSs expecting that, as homeowners pay back their mortgage loans, investors will receive that paid-back money as both the original amount invested in MBSs and as extra income.

Investors pay a fee to Fannie Mae so that it will assume all financial risk for people who default (i.e., cannot pay back their mortgage loan). In those cases, Fannie Mae pays investors the mortgage and interest money the investors expected to receive from the borrower.

Soon after Fannie Mae became a partly private company, whose public part became known as Ginnie Mae, the federal government created the **Federal Home Loan Mortgage Corporation (Freddie Mac)**. Freddie Mac is an alternative to Fannie Mae and a way to make even more mortgage money available.

Freddie Mac also securitizes home mortgages and groups them together to create MBSs; likewise, investors pay Freddie Mac a fee so that it will assume all financial risk for people who default on their mortgage loans and will pay the investors the money they were expecting.

Thus, both Fannie Mae and Freddie Mac have rules for—and limits on—the types of mortgages they will buy and repackage. Mortgages they will buy are known as **conforming**, because the mortgages conform to

those rules and limits, or **conventional**, because those rules and limits are used for the vast majority of their mortgages.

Both Fannie Mae and Freddie Mac use automated underwriting systems to speed up the process of deciding whether they will purchase a loan:

- Fannie Mae uses Desktop Originator and Desktop Underwriter.
- Freddie Mac uses Loan Program Advisor.

Both Fannie Mae and Freddie Mac allow **interested party contributions (IPCs)**—contributions from parties other than the borrower—to help pay a borrower's closing costs. Even the seller will help with closing costs, but there are limits on what help can be offered. The total amount that a seller will help with closing costs cannot be more than the total amount of the closing costs themselves and must be used only for those costs; it cannot be used for repairs, the down payment, and so forth. Help from the seller is also limited to a percentage of the loan amount.

Both Fannie Mae and Freddie Mac also charge extra fees to buy loans with certain risk characteristics, such as refinancing loans where the borrower is taking cash out.

Quick Review Questions

3. What do lenders do with money gained through the securitization process?

4. What types of mortgages do Fannie Mae and Freddie Mac purchase?

Government Mortgages

There are two major types of home mortgages in the US: government mortgages and conventional mortgages. Both government and conventional mortgages are QMs:

- Government mortgages are offered through the government entities described below.
- Conventional mortgages are offered through private lenders and will be explained later in this chapter.

Federal Housing Administration Loans

The **Federal Housing Administration (FHA)** is a branch of the US Department of Housing and Urban Development (HUD). The FHA insures mortgages that are made by FHA-approved lenders:

- The FHA approves mortgage lenders who are willing to follow FHA guidelines.
- An **FHA mortgage** is a mortgage the FHA Is willing to insure because it meets FHA guidelines.
- FHA will not insure mortgages for those with above-average income.

The FHA **Single Family Housing Policy Handbook** (SF Handbook) contains information on FHA loans. To verify information, a loan officer uses the FHA's **Uniform Residential Loan Application (Form 1003)**, which is filled out by the borrower. Necessary information includes the borrower's

- employment situation
- assets
- income situation

- credit (including bankruptcies and foreclosures)
- debts

During this process, the officer also documents the borrower's identity and all sources of money that will be needed at closing, including any earnest money deposit and any gifts from friends or relatives that will be used for the down payment and the cost of a title insurance policy.

The FHA requires a one-time **up-front mortgage insurance premium (UFMPI)**, but this may be added to the amount being financed:

- The officer calculates the mortgage payment.
- The mortgage payment includes an annual mortgage insurance premium that is separate from the up-front payment.
- In most cases, the mortgage payment will be no more than 31% of a borrower's monthly income and no more than 43% when combined with the borrower's other debt.

The officer ensures that the borrower has no delinquent federal debt of any kind. Then the officer uses the FHA's **Technology Open To Approved Lenders (TOTAL) Mortgage Scorecard**, along with the verified information, to create the borrower's **minimum decision credit score**:

- The minimum decision credit score must be greater than 500 to obtain an FHA-insured mortgage of up to thirty years.
- If the score is greater than 580, then only a 3.5% down payment is needed.
- If the score is between 500 and 579, a 10% down payment is needed, and the interest rate will be higher.

A loan officer also ensures other aspects:

- that the property is habitable and has been appraised
- that the property's title is secure
- that the loan amount needed is within FHA loan limits at the time
- that the borrower will be living there and has homeowner's insurance

Finally, the officer creates the borrower's escrow account (discussed later in this chapter).

Quick Review Questions

5. Borrowers with what type of income are eligible for FHA loans?

6. What is the minimum decision credit score a borrower must have to obtain a 30-year Federal Housing Administration (FHA) loan?

Veterans Affairs and USDA Loans

The **US Department of Veterans Affairs (VA)** and its Veterans Benefits Administration, as well as the **US Department of Agriculture (USDA) Rural Housing Service**, both provide home mortgages for people in certain situations. The VA works to help the following borrowers purchase homes:

- active-duty military personnel
- military veterans

- National Guard and Reserve members
- eligible surviving spouses

The VA guarantees lenders that it will pay a portion of the loan to a lender if the borrower goes into foreclosure. This enables lenders to provide more favorable loan terms:

- This loan portion offered by the VA is known as an **entitlement**.
- The basic or full entitlement may be up to $36,000, or 25% of a loan amount of $144,000.
- VA applicants who need loans larger than $144,000 may qualify for a **bonus entitlement** up to the maximum amount a lender will lend the applicant, based on the applicant's financial situation.
- Applicants who already have another VA loan when applying for a new loan, or who defaulted on a previous VA loan, receive a **reduced entitlement**.
- Reduced entitlements require a down payment to get the loan.
- If the previous property with a VA loan is sold, the basic entitlement is restored for the new loan.

VA loans are also **assumable**, which means that if a property is sold, the new buyer can take over the loan at the same interest rate and other conditions as the seller. To receive these benefits, however, a veteran must meet a lender's requirements of credit and income and have a VA Certificate of Eligibility.

VA loans require applicants to have full-time employment with a certain amount of monthly **residual income**, or money left over each month to live on after paying the mortgage and other debts. The residual income required is measured in dollars (not in a percentage of income) and depends on where an applicant lives and on the number of people in the household.

Limited closing costs on a VA loan include

- a VA funding fee of between 1% and 3.6% of the loan value,
- a 1% loan origination fee that covers many of the lender's costs to set up the loan,
- an appraisal fee,
- itemized fees,
- optional discount points, title insurance, and appraisal.

Charges are listed in detail on the VA's website.

Table 3.2. VA Loans	
VA Loan Facts	**What Can VA Loans Be Used For?**
• no PMI • limited closing costs • no down payment required (though a lender may require a down payment) • may be used for more than one home over time	• homes • townhouses • farms • manufactured homes • some multi-family homes • some condominiums • to improve a home's energy efficiency • to refinance a home (in some cases)

3. Qualified and Non-Qualified Mortgage Programs

The USDA offers rural home loans through its Section 502 Direct Loan Program to help low- and very low-income applicants in rural areas buy a single-family home. Requirements for applicants are the following:

- being without a home that is considered safe, sanitary and decent;
- live on the property they are buying as their primary residence
- be US citizens or eligible non-citizens
- be legally able to take on a loan
- having no disbarments or suspensions in any federal programs
- be unable to obtain or maintain a loan from other sources

The USDA's Direct Loan Program offers 33-year mortgages for low-income borrowers and 38-year mortgages for borrowers with very low income. These loans typically do not require a down payment, and interest rates are fixed based on the current market rates at either approval or closing—whichever is lower. Usually, applicants must also have a credit score of at least 640. USDA mortgages do not require mortgage insurance but do have an annual "guarantee fee" paid from the borrower's monthly payments.

Quick Review Questions

7. What term describes the loan portion offered by the US Department of Veterans Affairs (VA)?

8. What minimum credit score do US Department of Agriculture (USDA) loan applicants require?

Conventional Mortgages and Nonconforming Mortgages

Conventional and Conforming Loans

A conventional loan one that is not offered through a government agency like FHA, the VA, or USDA. Instead, **conventional loans** are made by private lenders that offer money for home loans:

- Any conventional loan that conforms to (or follows) the rules set up by Fannie Mae and Freddie Mac is considered a **conforming loan**.
- Conforming loans can be sold by lenders to Fannie Mae or Freddie Mac after closing.

A typical conventional mortgage requires a 20% down payment, which can take years to save up for. In many cases, borrowers with good credit may qualify for lender programs that require only a 3% or 5% down payment for a conventional mortgage; in return, borrowers are required to purchase **private mortgage insurance (PMI)** until 20% of the loan has been paid off. PMI protects the lender from loss in the event of foreclosure.

Conventional mortgage lenders require borrowers to purchase hazard insurance as part of their homeowner's insurance policy. **Hazard insurance** covers much of the cost of severe damage that is caused by natural disasters (e.g., fire, hail, tornado):

- Loans for houses near a known flood plain require separate flood insurance, which is offered by the National Flood Insurance Program (NFIP).
- Loans for houses in areas prone to earthquakes often require separate earthquake insurance.

Borrowers can usually prepay their mortgage in less time than allowed without paying a financial penalty; however, as explained above, some lenders impose a penalty for paying off a mortgage in the first three years. More often, prepayment is required as part of an escrow account for the buyer; each monthly payment is calculated to include

- the loan interest from the previous month,
- some of the loan principal,
- part of the annual mortgage insurance cost,
- part of the annual homeowner's insurance cost, and
- part of the annual property tax.

With each monthly payment, the **escrow account** automatically receives and holds the money for

- the annual mortgage insurance cost,
- the annual homeowner's insurance cost, and
- the annual property tax.

The mortgage insurance, homeowner's insurance, and property tax are then paid by the lender from the escrow account; this typically happens annually and ensures that the three items are always paid without the need for the borrower to keep track of them.

Did You Know?

A loan for a non-owner-occupied rental property (one to four housing units where the borrower will not be living), typically requires a larger down payment (20% to 30%); charges a higher interest rate; and has a shorter term than a loan for a single-family home where a borrower will live.

To ensure that the money is always available for these, closing costs usually include a **prepayment** of several months' worth of payments for each (e.g., half of the annual property tax, two months of mortgage insurance, and the first year of homeowner's insurance). When the house is sold, these prepayments are returned to the borrower at closing as needed.

An escrow account may be canceled when the mortgage is paid off, the house is sold, or the account has existed for at least five years, provided at least 20% of the mortgage has been paid back.

Quick Review Questions

9. When must borrowers pay PMI?

10. What account is funded to pay property tax, mortgage insurance, and homeowner's insurance?

Nonconforming Loans

Nonconforming loans do not meet the rules described above for conforming loans. Fannie Mae and Freddie Mac will not buy a nonconforming loan from a lender.

A common type of nonconforming (or nontraditional) loan is a **jumbo loan**, which is a loan larger than the highest amount Fannie Mae or Freddie Mac will guarantee. As of autumn 2022, jumbo loans for a single-family home are those which are larger than $647,200—an amount that often becomes larger in high-cost areas.

Jumbo loan requirements may vary slightly and are based on an individual lender's rules. Applicants for jumbo loans often have a higher-than-average income and usually also need the following:

- a higher-than-average credit rating
- a lower-than-average debt-to-income ratio
- a down payment of at least 10%
- a second appraisal of the property to be purchased
- a higher-than-average amount of income/asset documentation

> **Helpful Hint:**
>
> Because the government is not involved in jumbo loans, lenders should be more careful than usual before issuing these types of loans to applicants—a default on such a loan could cost the lender a lot of money.

Types of nontraditional loans other than jumbo loans are discussed at the end of this chapter. CFPB requires that lenders issuing high-priced or high-cost loans create escrow accounts for buyers as explained above.

Quick Review Questions

11. A loan larger than the highest amount Fannie Mae and Freddie Mac will guarantee is called what?

12. Applicants for jumbo loans have what kind of income?

Subprime Lending

Mortgage loans can be divided into prime, subprime, and Alt-A:

- A **prime loan** is offered to customers with excellent credit histories.
- A **subprime loan** is offered to applicants with credit problems.
- An **Alt-A loan** is somewhere between prime and subprime, with some qualities and requirements of each that vary between lenders.

> **Helpful Hint:**
>
> Loan officers should become familiar with their lender's specific Alt-A programs as well as the concepts below that may appear in those programs.

The interest rate on a prime or subprime mortgage loan can be fixed or adjustable:

- A **fixed-rate mortgage** means the interest rate, as an annual percentage of the amount owed, remains the same for the entire length of the mortgage, even if the mortgage lasts for thirty years.
- An **adjustable-rate mortgage (ARM)** may have its interest rate changed at least one time during the length of the mortgage, based on prevailing index interest rates at the time.
  - For example, the rate may be 3% for the first five years, adjusted higher or lower at the five-year point, and then kept at the new rate for the remainder of the mortgage.
  - The amount that an interest rate may increase is often capped when the mortgage is given so that applicants know the maximum rate they may have to pay.

> **Helpful Hint:**
>
> ARM applicants may pay for a temporary rate **buydown**, which means the interest rate is made even lower at the beginning of the mortgage than otherwise expected.

Types of ARMs to know are outlined in Table 3.3:

Table 3.3. Types of ARMs

Type	Definition	Examples
Interest only	No principal on the mortgage is paid off for a period of time.	▪ A mortgage is for $320,000 but requires only interest payments for seven years. ▪ After seven years of paying regularly on the mortgage, the principal owed is still $320,000. ▪ At that point, the principal begins to be paid back, along with a higher interest rate.
Payment option	The applicant can choose whether to pay principal and interest together, interest only, or even only a part of the interest.	▪ If only part of the interest is paid at first, the total amount owed will increase over the years and must still all be repaid. ▪ The adjustable interest rate may increase and thus increase the monthly payment.
Hybrid	The interest rate is fixed for a period of years and then allowed to **float**—be changed periodically.	▪ A 5/25 ARM would provide a fixed-interest rate for the first five years. ▪ The floating rate would then be changed at regular intervals for the remaining twenty-five years.
Assumable	If a property is sold, the new buyer can take over the loan at the same interest rate and other conditions the seller had.	▪ A property with half of its mortgage remaining is sold, and the buyer takes up the loan under the same terms. ▪ Non-assumable loans are "due on sale": the seller's mortgage must be fully repaid at closing and the buyer must obtain his own mortgage separately.

Most prime mortgages have a fixed interest rate, while most subprime mortgages have an adjustable interest rate. Thus, ARMs often trigger a payment shock for applicants whose interest rates are suddenly raised substantially. In a **payment shock**, the higher interest rate creates a higher monthly payment that the applicant may not be able to afford.

In order to estimate the ability of an applicant to continue paying a loan, lenders typically estimate the amount of payment shock that is likely to occur if an interest rate changes to its maximum value.

As part of deciding whether to offer a prime or subprime loan, a loan officer should perform a **debt-to-income ratio assessment**, which calculates the percentage of an applicant's monthly income that goes to paying off debts of all types, including mortgages, property taxes, and homeowner's insurance:

- ▪ For example, an applicant has a monthly income of $5,000 and debt of $300 per month.
- ▪ With an expected mortgage/tax/insurance payment of $1,200 the applicant will pay $1,500 of the $5,000 monthly income toward debt.
- ▪ Thus, the applicant's debt-to-income ratio is 30%. (1,500 ÷ 5,000 = 30%)

> **Did You Know?**
>
> The CFPB requires QMs to have debt-to-income ratios of less than 43%; however, some lenders require debt-to-income ratios of less than 36%, with no more than 28% going toward mortgage/tax/insurance.

The government's **Statement on Subprime Mortgage Lending** describes the risks of subprime mortgages and related practices. Besides payment shock, the Statement mentions concerns that can increase the credit risk of extending an ARM to an applicant. These include

- limited (or no) verification of income;
- fees charged for lack of income verification;
- prepayment penalties (when the lender charges a fee for paying the mortgage back faster than expected);
- no limit (or a very high limit) on the maximum interest rate;
- extra mortgage-related products sold to an applicant, with costs that may require the applicant to refinance the mortgage with more fees and an even higher interest rate;
- applicants not understanding that besides paying the interest and principal on a mortgage, they will also be paying property tax, homeowner's insurance, and PMI; and
- the legal and financial costs that will become the burden of lenders if applicants are given loans they cannot repay.

As mentioned above, subprime borrowers have credit problems, such as

- past bankruptcy,
- credit delinquency,
- past eviction or foreclosure,
- too many creditors or too much debt already, and
- a short credit history.

Subprime borrowers typically face larger down payment requirements, higher interest rates, and higher loan fees. Their monthly payments are therefore likely to be larger than those for prime mortgages.

Before giving a loan to a subprime applicant, some lenders choose not to verify an applicant's income at all. Even then, lenders must still conduct a good-faith ability to repay (ATR) check to give reasonable certainty that a nonqualified mortgage can be paid back.

In these cases, a lender may provide loan amounts and conditions based on the applicant's "stated income" (what the applicant tells the lender his income is, verifiable by bank statements/deposits) or by a "non-income-verifying" loan that verifies the applicant's assets (e.g., current home, retirement fund, inheritance) instead of income.

Quick Review Questions

13. In what kind of mortgage is the interest rate fixed for a period of years and then allowed to float?

14. What is the maximum debt-to-income ratio permitted by the CFPB on a QM?

Non-Qualified Mortgages

Borrowers who cannot obtain a qualified mortgage may be able to obtain a **non-qualified mortgage (non-QM)** instead of a QM. Applicants may consider a non-QM because they lack the extensive financial documentation required by the CFPB to obtain a QM. Non-QMs may be appropriate for certain clients:

- investors
- self-employed
- small business owners
- those whose income is seasonal or irregular

Because a loan officer may verify income for a non-QM by using paperwork other than pay stubs and tax returns, these applicants may be able to produce other paperwork that demonstrates that their finances are flexible enough, their resources large enough, and their financial education extensive enough to handle monthly payments, even if the payments are larger than average because of the risk that the lender and applicant both undertake with a non-QM.

A loan officer must be extremely careful when suggesting a non-QM to certain clients who may lack sufficient financial resources to handle a sudden personal crisis or economic downturn. A loan officer should do more financial investigation and exercise more caution than usual before approving a non-QM for applicants such as

- those who are retired,
- those with a very high debt-to-income ratio,
- those with lower credit scores,
- those who have recently declared bankruptcy, and
- those who are in foreclosure on another property.

As mentioned above, some lenders choose not to verify a non-QM applicant's income at all. But even in that situation, lenders must still conduct a good faith ATR check to give reasonable certainty that a non-QM can be paid back. Monthly payments for non-QMs generally cost more than monthly payments for QMs due to

- a larger down payment requirement,
- a higher interest rate, and
- higher loan fees.

In addition, if a buyer's house loses value because of a decline in the housing market, the buyer is still obliged to pay according to the terms agreed upon at closing. Therefore, buyers with non-QM mortgages may not be able to sell their houses for as much as they paid for them. In such cases, the borrowers are either stuck in the house until the market improves or may be forced to sell for less than they paid and, as a result, need more cash at closing to complete the sale.

A non-QM is also riskier for the lender because it cannot be obtained from the government programs detailed earlier in this chapter and cannot be sold to Fannie Mae or Freddie Mac.

Common types of non-qualified (or nontraditional) mortgages are described in Table 3.4.

Table 3.4. Types of Non-Qualified Mortgages

Type	Description
Balloon mortgage	▪ The payment made at the end of the mortgage is at least twice as large (and may be ten to one-hundred times as large) as a regular monthly payment.
Interest-only payments	▪ Principal on the mortgage is never paid off. ▪ If the mortgage is $200,000 but requires only interest payments, even after five years of paying regularly on the mortgage, the principal owed is still $200,000.
Negative amortization	▪ The monthly payment is less than the amount needed to cover principal, interest, taxes, insurance (PITI); the unpaid portion is added to the loan. ▪ If the mortgage is for $200,000 but allows negative amortization, then even after five years of paying regularly on the mortgage, the amount owed may increase to $225,000 or more.
Long-term	▪ A loan term is longer than the typical thirty years (often forty or fifty years).

A balloon mortgage can be beneficial for certain applicants:

- applicants who want to buy now and expect to refinance the house before the balloon is due
- applicants who expect to have the balloon payment ready when due
- investors who plan to "fix and flip" (renovate/repair the house and sell it to someone else) before the balloon payment is due

Helpful Hint:

A major drawback to interest-only payments is that, by only paying the interest, buyers develop no equity in their houses while making the payments.

Quick Review Questions

15. Which types of borrowers are likely to pursue a non-QM?

16. What term describes a loan where the monthly payment is less than the amount needed to cover PITI and the unpaid part is added to the loan?

Answer Key

1. For a qualified mortgage (QM), a lender must ensure that the borrower's debt-to-income ratio is 43% or less.

2. The annual percentage rate (APR) cannot exceed the average prime offer rate (APOR) by more than 2.25%, but this limit can change based on the size of the mortgage.

3. To make more mortgage loans available, lenders use the money they get from selling mortgages to the Federal National Mortgage Association (Fannie Mae).

4. Federal National Mortgage Association (Fannie Mae) and Federal Home Loan Mortgage Corporation (Freddie Mac) purchase conventional or conforming mortgages.

5. Borrowers with low or average income are eligible for Federal Housing Administration (FHA) loans; the FHA will not insure mortgages for borrowers with above-average income.

6. A borrower must have a minimum decision credit score greater than 500 to obtain a Federal Housing Administration (FHA) insured mortgage of up to thirty years.

7. The loan portion offered by the US Department of Veterans Affairs (VA) is called an entitlement.

8. US Department of Agriculture (USDA) loan applicants must usually have a credit score of at least 640.

9. Borrowers who have less than a 20% down payment must pay private mortgage insurance (PMI).

10. The escrow account is funded to pay property tax, mortgage insurance, and homeowner's insurance.

11. A jumbo loan is one which is larger than the highest amount the Federal National Mortgage Association (Fannie Mae) and the Federal Home Loan Mortgage Corporation (Freddie Mac) will guarantee.

12. Applicants for jumbo loans usually have a higher-than-average income.

13. In a hybrid mortgage, the interest rate is fixed for a period of years and then allowed to float.

14. The Consumer Financial Protection Bureau (CFPB) requires qualifying mortgages (QMs) to have debt-to-income ratios of less than 43%.

15. A non-qualified mortgage (non-QM) may be suitable for investors, the self-employed, small business owners, and borrowers with seasonal or irregular income.

16. The term *negative amortization* describes when the monthly payment is less than what is needed to cover principal, interest, taxes, insurance (PITI) and the unpaid part is added to the loan.

4 Mortgage Loan Products

Fixed-Rate Mortgages

What is a Fixed-Rate Mortgage?

A **fixed-rate mortgage (FRM)** is a loan whose rate is fixed throughout the life of the loan. A common example is a 30-year fixed-rate mortgage, where the rate remains unchanged throughout the duration of the loan:

- There are many different types of fixed-rate loans, ranging from three to thirty years.
- Thirty-year or 15-year term loans are most common in residential home purchases and finances.
- Shorter terms exist for clients who wish to pay off their mortgage balances sooner; the shorter the mortgage term (designated by months or years), the higher the monthly payment.

In the United States, most homeowners seek out a 30-year mortgage. For many families, housing costs are the biggest financial monthly expense, and the 30-year fixed rate offers a lower payment. The 30-year term also gives clients the most buying power—another reason for its popularity. That means clients can afford the highest loan amount (which translates into the highest home purchase amount) when compared to shorter-term mortgages. Because mortgage companies review clients' debt-to-income ratios and limit the maximum loan amount, the 30-year term allows for the most overall leverage.

Some clients are less concerned with the monthly payment than the total amount of interest paid and/or the total time holding a loan. These clients may seek a shorter loan term (e.g., a 15-year fixed) in order to pay the loan off sooner and limit the total interest paid. When considering a homeowner's monthly payment, the three main factors are

- the loan amount,
- the interest rate, and
- the loan term.

Quick Review Questions

1. What type of loan has a rate that is fixed throughout the life of the loan?

2. What are the most common terms for FRMs?

Down Payments

When purchasing a home, a buyer can put more money toward a down payment in order to lower the monthly payment. This works the same way when refinancing a mortgage. The borrower can also apply funds to the transaction to lessen the mortgage payment:

- A typical down payment is 20% of the sale price of the home.
- Borrowers can pay less than 20% down, but they will usually have to pay private mortgage insurance (PMI).
- Certain programs (e.g., FHA) offer lower down payments to make homeownership accessible.

The **down payment** is essentially the borrower's equity in the property. In a home purchase, a lender finances a portion (typically the majority) of the property. The down payment is the money the borrower offers as a financial contribution toward the home.

The down payment means the borrower has a vested financial interest in the property, along with the lender. The larger the down payment, the less the overall risk to the lender since the lender will have less to lose should the borrower stop making payments and the loan goes into default.

Aside from a typical 20% down payment, there are scenarios in which clients may have higher down payments. These are usually cases where the property or borrower presents a higher overall risk (e.g., oceanfront homes susceptible to hurricanes). When the lender perceives a higher risk, a higher down payment is required.

Sometimes, down payments are lower or even nonexistent. These cases generally apply to affluent clients or when a government program is associated with the loan:

- Lenders may accept a lower down payment from a high-net-worth client because they perceive the client as less likely to default.
- In government programs (e.g., FHA, VA loans), the government guarantees a portion of the lender's debt.

Quick Review Questions

3. What is the amount of a typical down payment?

4. What if a borrower wants to purchase a high-risk property?

Recasts

Some lenders offer a recast. Rather than refinancing a loan, which involves a new loan application, and sometimes an appraisal, closing costs, and more, a **recast** simply maintains the current loan terms and amortizes the new lower balance over the current terms.

The largest advantages of a recast versus a refinance are the costs and time. Typically, a recast will be a nominal cost (as low as $200) and take only a few days for the lender to complete. This is compared to a refinance that may take thirty days or more and cost several thousands of dollars.

Recasts are common when clients have sold other properties or have had large income bonuses they wish to apply toward their mortgages to lower their monthly payments. Recasts allow clients to maintain their current terms and update their mortgage payments based on the new loan amounts.

Quick Review Question

5. When is a recast useful for borrowers?

Escrow

Most mortgage companies either have or require escrow to be a part of the total loan payment. In **escrow**, the mortgage company collects a percentage of the property's taxes and insurance, and then pays the county and insurance carrier as those become due. Escrow simplifies homeownership for some borrowers: they only need to make one payment each month, and the mortgage company pays the taxes and insurance when they become due. When escrowed, the monthly mortgage payment will include

- principal,
- interest,
- taxes, and
- insurance.

Not all clients wish to have their taxes and insurance managed by a mortgage company; some choose to pay separately. In these cases, the mortgage payment contains only the principal and interest. As the property tax and insurance become due, the clients pay those vendors directly from their individual funds.

Many mortgage companies require escrow as a loan requirement; otherwise, the lenders will charge a certain percentage within the rate. Mortgage companies prefer to reduce risk by managing tax and insurance payments to ensure they are paid on time; if the payments are not made on time, both the lender and the borrower could be responsible for legal or financial problems. For instance, if a home suffers property damage but the home insurance premium was not paid, the loss is multiplied.

Escrows generally include taxes, insurance, and sometimes homeowner's association (HOA) dues. It is most common to have the taxes and insurance (hazard and flood insurance if applicable) included, but there are instances in which one or the other—and possibly HOA dues—are required.

Quick Review Question

6. Why do most mortgage companies prefer escrow?

Adjustable-Rate Mortgages

Terms and Definitions

Adjustable-rate mortgages (ARMs) are an option for clients who are considering mortgages on real estate. Both FRMs and ARMs

- allow clients to purchase or refinance real estate,
- include a principal and interest component within their payments, and
- are generally due in monthly installments.

Unlike FRMs, ARMs have a fixed period (e.g., seven years) after which the interest rate and monthly payments will adjust based on the lender's rate metric. The payments are based on the agreed-upon amortization schedule, most commonly thirty years.

Most lenders derive the ARM rate rules from a public rate system. An **index rate** is a benchmark rate that is based on the overall market:

- Common benchmarks include the US Treasury rate or the London Interbank Offered Rate (LIBOR).
- The index rate changes as the market changes.
- Clients with better credit generally receive lower interest rates because they pose the least risk to the lender.

The lender then applies a margin against the index rate. The **margin** on an ARM is a percentage that the lender adds to the index, which equals the total interest rate:

- Margins vary by lender and change depending on the market cycle.
    - The margin impacts the lender's profitability.
    - The aggressiveness with which lenders seek loans varies and impacts how the margins are structured.
    - The margin does not change throughout the life of the loan.
    - As the index adjusts, the margin remains unchanged.

A borrower's **monthly payment** is calculated by taking the loan amount, rate, and amortization term into account, similar to an FRM. The **change date** is when the fixed period has ended on the loan. The lender adjusts the rate based on the index at the time of the change date. For example:

- The index is at 4% on the change date.
- The index was originally at 3% when the loan was established.
- The margin is at 1%.
- The borrower's new rate on the change date would be 5%, which is a 1% increase.

This changed interest rate increases the borrower's monthly payment. Lenders vary in their change dates, with some occurring only each year (after the fixed period), while others occur each month.

Typically, a shorter ARM period (e.g., three years) has a lower rate than a 10-year ARM because the lender can adjust the rate quickly if the index increases. Lenders view the loan funds as a capital cost. As interest rates change, the profitability of the loan is affected; therefore, lenders generally price longer terms higher than shorter terms.

Quick Review Questions

7. A benchmark rate that is based on the overall market is called what?

8. What is the name of the percentage that lenders add to the index that equates to the total interest rate?

Lender Responsibilities

Per the law and loan agreement, the lender must notify the client of an interest rate and payment change. Lenders notify borrowers several months in advance of a change, so they can prepare and reach out with any questions.

The lender must legally provide **disclosures** to the borrower on all related laws. These disclosures are required at the federal level and may vary depending on the loan itself and the state in which the loan is generated. Several of the disclosures involved are related to the following:

- conversions
- assumptions
- adjustments
- payment shock
- underwriting guidelines
- loan-level price adjustments

Lenders must inform borrowers how to find and understand the index. If a borrower's interest at the time of closing is below the overall market rate, the lender must inform the borrower about the available current margins and index.

The **Consumer Handbook on Adjustable-Rate Mortgages (CHARM booklet)** provides an overview of the ARM product and is part of the disclosures. Overall, it is important for the lender to explain—and the client to understand—that the mortgage has an adjustable-rate component and is not fixed throughout the term.

> **Helpful Hint:**
>
> Borrowers should monitor the index since it is public information and not controlled by the lender.

Quick Review Questions

9. What must lenders explain to borrowers of ARMs?

10. What booklet explains the ARM product?

ARM Scenarios

Like FRM payments, ARM payments contain principal, interest, and are due each month. The payment remains the same until the term ends, at which time it may be adjusted based on the current index.

Borrowers have several options when establishing an ARM. ARMs can range from a 3-year fixed period up to a 15-year fixed period and vary among lenders. When deciding on a mortgage, the client must consider the index and margin. For example, if the US Treasury rate is 3%, the lender's margin might be +1%, making the client's rate 4%.

A client may be offered a 7/1 ARM, which means the mortgage is fixed for seven years and can then adjust up or down with the US Treasury rate. ARMs typically have a minimum and maximum rate at which the client's rate can fully adjust. For example (keeping in mind that bank rules vary), after the fixed period, the 7/1 ARM loan might adjust (up or down) 2% of the index, but the lender has a minimum floor rate of 3%. This means that the total rate cannot adjust below 3%. Similarly, the lender might have a maximum of 10%, which means that the rate cannot adjust above 10%—even if the margin/index calculation totals 12%. These limits can be understood as protections for both the lender and borrower. Remember: margins

vary between lenders. The following is a spin-off example of the original 7/1 ARM example described above:

- A client has an initial rate of 4% (3% interest plus 1% margin).
- In year eight, the US Treasury rate adjusts up to 4%.
  - The client's rate then adjusts to 5%.
  - If the US Treasury rate adjusts to 7%, then the client's rate could only adjust up to 6% because of the maximum change of 2%.

When initially established, ARM mortgage interest rates tend to be lower than current market interest rates. This is because the lender offers a shorter fixed period than would be available through a different product (i.e., a 30-year fixed mortgage). The borrower can take advantage of a lower rate now, with the understanding that it could increase in the future (after the fixed period). Candidates for ARMs are borrowers who do not need a guaranteed low rate for a long period of time. These include

- borrowers who do not plan to remain in the home for a long time, or within the ARM fixed period;
- borrowers who plan to pay off the mortgage in a few years, which would cause them to be unconcerned with the future interest rate; and
- borrowers who believe rates will remain the same or adjust down in the future.

Clients must understand that ARMs are not fixed throughout the life of the product. If rates go up in the future, their rate will go higher. Any rate increase will also cause their payment to increase. It is important for borrowers to understand the long-term possibilities that exist for the ARM product. **Fully indexed rate mortgages** are found with variable mortgages offered by lenders and can be calculated by adding a specified index rate to a margin.

Quick Review Questions

11. When do ARM payments adjust?

12. Are borrowers who wish to remain in their homes for at least ten years good candidates for an ARM?

Other Mortgage Products

Balloon Mortgage Loan Products

In a **balloon mortgage**, the loan matures (i.e., balloons) before the amortization schedule achieves loan payoff. One example is a 5/15 balloon mortgage. In this case, the monthly payments would be based on a 15-year amortization schedule; however, the loan would balloon in five years.

Since balloon mortgages help lenders mitigate risk, lenders generally offer them for transactions that they consider to be risky. With a balloon mortgage, the lender has the option of having the loan paid off in less time, but the client still has a favorable payment amount. Some lenders will refinance or review a loan once it matures; others fully anticipate the loan to be paid off by the client or another lender. Given the perceived higher risk of this loan scenario, the balloon mortgage enables a purchase that may otherwise be unavailable to the client. In this way, balloon mortgages expand lending opportunities.

For example, if a borrower wishes to purchase a property that is built in a unique style, a lender may see this property as risky given its uniqueness to the neighborhood—in case of default, it will likely not sell easily. The lender may therefore offer a balloon mortgage to ensure a shorter commitment time on the property.

When considering a 5-year mortgage versus a 5/15 balloon mortgage, the monthly payments are much higher on a 5-year mortgage as opposed to a 5/15 balloon. The balloon mortgage offers the lender a lower time commitment while allowing the client to make affordable monthly payments.

Balloon mortgages range from one to fifteen years. The amortization terms vary as well. One scenario might be a 1-year balloon and a 10-year amortization schedule. Another possibility is a 15-year balloon on a 30-year amortization schedule. Scenarios vary widely and depend on the client, lender, and overall market.

Balloon mortgages are considered niche products and non-qualified mortgages (see Chapter 3); most lenders do not offer them. They are generally reserved for borrowers with higher credit scores and incomes.

Borrowers who are not planning on staying in a home for the long term may consider a balloon mortgage given that its term matures sooner than a traditional mortgage and it offers better payments. There may also be scenarios where lenders are *only* willing to offer balloon mortgages to borrowers. Such lenders may wish to limit their long-term credit exposure because property characteristics or other factors cause them to perceive a higher risk.

Quick Review Questions

13. When do lenders offer balloon mortgages?

14. What is the typical borrower profile for balloon mortgages?

Reverse Mortgages

In a **reverse mortgage**, the lender pays the homeowner, which is the "reverse" of a traditional mortgage. Reverse mortgages are designed for people who are sixty-two years old or older. They allow clients to receive a portion of their home's value without selling the home or making loan payments (as with a traditional mortgage). Homeowners access these funds through a variety of ways, including fixed- and variable-rate options:

- With fixed-rate option, the mortgage funds are received as a lump sum to the client.
- With the variable-rate option, the client can choose between installment payments (made to the client), a line of credit (to access as needed), or some combination of the two.

There are three types of reverse mortgages:

- federally insured
- proprietary
- single-purpose

Home equity conversion mortgages (HECMs) are federally insured reverse mortgages and are the most common. HECMs can be set up in three ways:

1. a lump sum of funds

2. a tenure option, in which the borrower receives a specific amount of funds each month

3. a credit line that the borrower accesses as needed.

Helpful Hint:

In a reverse-mortgage scenario, it is important for homeowners to continue making home insurance and property tax payments.

Lines of credit are proprietary—private lenders offer funds not backed by the government. A borrower may choose this option to qualify for more overall funds because there are no federal limits in place.

The **single-purpose reverse mortgage** is the least common. It is for a specific purpose and is available through local, state, and nonprofit agencies.

Interest on reverse mortgages is generally tied to the US Treasury rate or other public index, similar to a home equity line of credit. The overall interest will accrue until the borrower is no longer on the property.

Another type of reverse mortgage, the **conversion mortgage loan**, does not require any loan payments until the borrower dies or moves out of the property. The borrower must pay and maintain the taxes and insurance, but no debt payments are needed. Once the borrower moves or dies, the loan must be repaid in full.

The factors involved in determining the amount a borrower can receive from a reverse mortgage include

- the borrower's age (youngest on property title, or spouse);
- the home's value or FHA limit (currently $970,800)—the lesser of the two;
- current interest rates; and
- any balance of an existing mortgage.

Typically, the loan-to-value ratio works out to 50% to 65%. This means that a borrower who owns a home valued at $100,000 with no current loan balance could expect a loan of $50,000 to $65,000. The amount of title insurance required is the market value of the collateral property or the maximum amount of the mortgage, whichever is greater. The reverse mortgage balance becomes due when the borrower dies or leaves the property. In either scenario, the full loan balance plus accrued interest becomes due. As with most banking and financial products, there are **strict advertising requirements** when it comes to reverse mortgages:

1. The lender cannot market the loans with an affiliation to the US Department of Housing and Urban Development or the FHA.

2. All advertisements must be fair, accurate, and include required disclosures.

3. The lender must keep any marketing items for at least two years.

As with most other loans, lenders are required to provide **disclosures** to borrowers. One specific disclosure discusses the requirement of borrowers of reverse mortgages to obtain third-party counseling;

4. Mortgage Loan Products

this is to ensure that the borrowers have a high degree of understanding about the product. Another type of disclosure states that borrowers are not required to finalize a mortgage.

Quick Review Question

15. What are the age requirements for obtaining a reverse mortgage?

Home Equity Line of Credit

Home equity lines of credit (HELOCs) are open-ended mortgages that are secured by a client's home and available to use for a variety of purposes. Borrowers seek out HELOCs for property-specific uses, such as upgrades, maintenance, and renovations; however, they can be used for almost anything that the homeowner deems useful.

HELOCs are offered by lenders and provide flexibility to homeowners. They have a set term (e.g., ten years) in which they are available for use. During this period, the client can use credit, pay it down or off, and use it again. The lender will typically require the client to pay only any interest that becomes due on a used balance, and possibly some principal.

> **Helpful Hint:**
>
> Many lenders will simply refinance or review a HELOC once the open-end period is finished, which allow the client to have a new open-end period.

After the open-end term is finished, the lender requires any balance to be paid and then closes the line; sometimes the lender may "term out" any remaining balance. For instance, after the open-end term, the lender may look to convert any remaining balance on a 15-year closed-end term. The client then makes principal and interest payments each month to achieve a total payment over that time frame. The client cannot withdraw any additional funds during the closed-end period.

HELOC rates may be variable or fixed. Variable rates typically adjust based on a published external rate (e.g., LIBOR, Secured Overnight Financing Rate, or possibly a US Treasury rate). As with any mortgage, it is important for clients to understand the rate, term, and payment.

A **subordinated loan** is a secondary loan (as it relates to a real estate loan) or second mortgage. It is subordinated to any primary mortgage associated with a property, hence the name. Generally, a homeowner will use a primary mortgage (first lien) to purchase a home, and then later obtain a second mortgage (e.g., HELOC) for needs beyond the purchase. In some cases, a HELOC may also be used to purchase a home. The subordination is important when related to default on payment, as the first lender is the first to receive any available funds.

Quick Review Questions

16. Why do borrowers obtain home equity lines of credit (HELOCs)?

17. What is another term for a secondary loan (as it relates to a real estate loan) or a second mortgage?

Fundamentals of Construction Mortgages

A **construction loan** funds the construction of a property. Rather than a traditional mortgage, which is used to purchase or refinance an existing property, a construction loan is used to build a new property or construct an addition to an existing property. Generally, a borrower finds a local builder to perform the

actual construction and uses a lender to finance the project. Borrowers must understand the mechanics of a construction loan structure and should consider the following:

- Will the original lender be able to finance the entire project and facilitate permanent financing?
- If the construction loan is only to finance the build itself and does not automatically convert into a permanent loan after construction, will the current lender offer a permanent loan, or will the borrower need to seek an additional lender?

Some lenders offer only the construction draw financing (funds from which the builder may draw), while others have one loan that automatically converts into a permanent loan. Some require an additional closing to convert into a permanent loan.

Construction loan payments are on interest only, and interest is charged based on the amounts that have been distributed to the builder. This is because clients usually must carry another housing expense (e.g.,. mortgage or rent payment) as they wait for their home to be built. The interest-only payment is beneficial for several reasons:

- It allows clients to have a lower payment.
- Borrowers can manage their overall expenses while carrying a construction loan and another housing expense at the same time.

Lenders vary in the construction payment, and some do require principal and interest throughout the loan.

A **construction-to-permanent loan (CTP)** allows a one-time close on a construction loan. The lender reviews the building contract (between builder and client), architectural plans and specifications, and the land where it will be built. The lender then finances the needed construction amount through a one-time closing process.

The lender uses a future expected value—typically based on an appraisal—and then closes on that anticipated loan amount. From there, the bank distributes funds directly to the builder as needed throughout construction.

The client typically makes payments on the amount distributed (sometimes interest only), and the payment will naturally increase as the project progresses and more funds are disbursed to the builder. Once the project is completed, the lender automatically converts the loan into a principal and interest payment mortgage, without another formal closing.

Quick Review Questions

18. What type of loan funds the construction of a property?

19. What type of loan allows a one-time close on a construction loan?

Interest-Only Mortgages

Interest-only mortgages are offered by some lenders. These products allow clients to pay only interest—no principal—for a certain period of time. In doing this, clients benefit by having a lower overall monthly payment, given there is no required principal within the payment calculation. Like traditional mortgages, clients can pay more than the required interest amount if they want to pay down the principal balance.

> **Did You Know?**
>
> Interest-only mortgages are usually structured as ARMs, with a fixed period and then an adjustment period.

Interest-only mortgages can pose a higher risk to lenders because there may be little or no principal reduction over the course of the loan. As a result, they are generally only available to higher-net-worth individuals, or those with ample cash flow and resources.

Quick Review Questions

20. Who are typical recipients of interest-only mortgages?

21. Why are interest-only mortgages risky for lenders?

Purchase-Money Second Mortgages

Some clients use **purchase-money second mortgages** to buy a home. In a purchase-money second mortgage a first or primary lender provides most of the financing for a home, and a secondary lender provides a smaller amount of financing. Both of the loans are used simultaneously to close on a home purchase.

Borrowers may use these finances for entire home purchases; more commonly, borrowers put small amounts down themselves. A common purchase scenario would be an 80/10/10 purchase:

- The first lender provides 80% of the purchase price.
- The second lender provides 10% of the purchase price.
- The client provides the remaining 10% of the purchase price.

A purchase-money second mortgage allows the client to finance a higher percentage of the home purchase. For example, the first lender may only be comfortable financing a certain loan to value (e.g., 80%), and the client cannot or will not bring the other 20% needed. The purchase-money second mortgage allows another lender to contribute, making the purchase possible.

Why would the first lender not simply offer a higher loan-to-value? In this example, the lender perceives the equity position (80%) to be the maximum risk it is willing to take on the loan. Should the client stop making payments or another default scenario occurs, the overall exposure to the primary lender will be limited.

Quick Review Question

22. How do purchase-money second mortgages benefit lenders?

Answer Key

1. A fixed-rate mortgage (FRM) is a loan whose rate is fixed throughout the life of the loan.

2. The most common terms for fixed-rate mortgages (FRMs) are 30-year or 15-year loans.

3. A typical down payment is 20% of the sale price of the home.

4. If a borrower wants to purchase a high-risk property, a higher down payment may be required.

5. Borrowers who sell properties or reap large financial bonuses seek out recasts to apply the financial windfall to their loans and lower their monthly payments.

6. Most mortgage companies prefer escrow because it enables lenders to ensure that taxes and insurance are paid on time.

7. An index rate is a benchmark rate that is based on the overall market.

8. The margin is a percentage that lenders add to the index; the addition equals the total interest rate.

9. Lenders must notify borrowers of adjustable-rate mortgages (ARMs) of the interest rates and payment changes per the law and loan agreement. Borrowers should understand that their mortgages are not fixed.

10. The Consumer Handbook on Adjustable-Rate Mortgages (CHARM booklet) provides an overview of the adjustable-rate mortgage (ARM) product and is part of the disclosures.

11. Adjustable-rate mortgage (ARM) payments remain stable until the fixed term ends, after which the payment may adjust based on the current index.

12. No. Borrowers who do not plan to stay long in their homes are better candidates for adjustable-rate mortgages (ARMs); a borrower who plans to stay in the home for at least ten years would be a better candidate for a fixed-rate mortgage.

13. Lenders offer balloon mortgages when they consider transactions to be risky.

14. Balloon mortgages are generally restricted to borrowers with higher credit scores and incomes.

15. Reverse mortgages are available to people who are sixty-two years old or older.

16. Borrowers take on home equity lines of credit (HELOCs) for upgrades, maintenance, and renovations; they can also be used for whatever the borrower deems necessary.

17. A secondary loan or second mortgage is called a subordinated loan.

18. A construction loan funds the construction of a property.

19. A construction-to-permanent (CTP) loan allows a one-time close on a construction loan.

20. Interest-only mortgages are usually available only to high-net-worth individuals.

21. Interest-only mortgages are risky for lenders because there may be little or no principal reduction over the course of the loan.

22. Purchase-money second mortgages enable lenders to mitigate their risk exposure.

5 Loan Inquiry And Application Process Requirements

Loan Inquiry Process

Introducing Loan Inquiry

Mortgage applicants typically fill out Fannie Mae's **Form 1003** "Uniform Residential Loan Application" so that all data needed by a lender is standardized and in the same place:

- Form 1003 is usually filled out once at the beginning of the application process.
- It is filled out a second time near closing to ensure nothing important has changed.
- Without Form 1003/Form 65, Fannie Mae and Freddie Mac will not buy a loan from a lender.

> **Helpful Hint**
>
> Form 1003 is the same as Freddie Mac's Form 65.

The last section of Form 1003 provides information on the lender. The other eight sections of Form 1003 detail the following information about the borrower:

- personal information, including data on employment and income
- assets and liabilities
- real estate already owned
- property to be purchased
- intentions as to how the property will be used
- agreement of understanding as to how the provided information will be used
- past military service
- optional demographic information

In Section 1, borrowers list required personal information. If there is more than one borrower, each borrower must provide this same information:

- full name (first, middle, last);
- Social Security number; and
- all sources of income to be considered by the lender.

Section 4 contains the address of the property to be financed, along with its estimated property value and the expected loan amount needed. In Section 4d, borrowers list any gifts or grants they have or will have received, in order to get the loan. The following actors are forbidden from providing gifts:

- builders
- developers

5. Loan Inquiry and Application Process Requirements

- real estate agents
- anyone else involved in the loan transaction

Fannie Mae accepts the following as a borrower's **gift donors**:

- relatives (spouse, child, dependent, or anyone otherwise related by blood, marriage, adoption or legal guardianship)
- non-relatives (domestic partner or partner's relative, fiancé/fiancée, former relative or godparent)

As of March 2023, Form 1103 is also required. The **Supplemental Consumer Information Form (SCIF/Form 1103)** details an applicant's language preference and whether the applicant has had a homeownership education class and housing counseling.

> **Helpful Hint:**
>
> It is important that both lender and borrower double-check everything on Form 1003 before submitting all paperwork.

When a credit score is obtained by a lender from a credit reporting agency but disputed by the borrower, who believes the score is based on incorrect information, the borrower must contact the consumer reporting agency directly to discuss any discrepancies. If the lender generates the credit score, borrowers need to discuss any discrepancies with the lender. In such cases, the lender representative is usually a different person than the loan officer who is putting together the loan.

Quick Review Questions

1. What are the forms lenders must have borrowers fill out as required by Fannie Mae and Freddie Mac?

2. What form explains whether an applicant has had housing counseling?

Required Disclosures and Information

Under the TILA-RESPA Integrated Disclosure Rule (TRID), applicants have submitted a **loan inquiry** once they provide a lender with the six pieces of information mentioned above from Form 1003 Section 1 and Section 4 (full name, Social Security number, all sources of income, address of property to be financed, estimated property value, and expected loan amount needed). Within three business days after a loan inquiry submission, an applicant must receive the following from the lender:

- a **loan estimate** of how much settlement will cost and all specific transaction terms
- a written list of service providers and their contact information (if the lender allows shopping for settlement services) that the applicant may use,
- the **special information booklet** ("Your Home Loan Toolkit: A Step-By-Step Guide") that explains details of the home-buying process (this may also come from the applicant's mortgage broker); and
- a list of homeowner counseling organizations in the borrower's area (this may also come from the applicant's mortgage broker).

Quick Review Question

3. How many business days does the lender have to offer a loan estimate to the borrower once the borrower fills out Form 1003?

Borrower Applications

Borrower applications can be submitted in person, online, by mail, or over the phone. According to the Federal Deposit Insurance Corporation (FDIC), a loan officer must be licensed before directly "offering and negotiating the terms of a loan" for compensation or gain. This includes communicating information, such as specific loan terms, either verbally or in writing and also applies to the following situations:

- if the officer states that the offer is still conditional pending verification of information,
- if the officer states that other people must still make decisions before granting the loan,
- if the officer presents a revised loan offer, and
- if the officer knows that negotiating the lender's terms or binding the borrower are prohibited.

Unlicensed officers can volunteer and work for free. If they are getting paid, they may provide certain services including

- providing general information about loans and policies,
- the lender's specific rules for making a loan,
- deciding whether to underwrite a loan,
- telling a borrower that the lender has sent a written offer (without providing details),
- arranging a loan's closing, and
- going over loan details with a borrower.

> **Did You Know?**
>
> Loan origination software helps with making calculations and keeping information secure and all in one place.

Generally, unlicensed officers may not offer or negotiate loans. They may only do so by using a third-party licensed originator and not by directly contacting a borrower.

Once an application is submitted, a loan officer must manage the application's information, maintaining confidentiality (except as needed for the loan) and ensuring the information is entered accurately into the lender's loan origination software:

- Each lender has its own form for borrowers to fill out; the form authorizes the lender to obtain all information it needs from other people to verify the information on the borrower's Form 1003.
- A separate form is also needed for the lender to obtain borrower information from the Internal Revenue Service (IRS).
- Once these forms are filled out and signed by the borrower, the lender begins the process of verifying and documenting each piece of borrower information, including income, employment, and assets.
- Self-employed borrowers typically need to fill out a form that allows the IRS to send the business's recent tax returns to the lender.

> **Did You Know?**
>
> Anyone providing a financial gift to help the borrower buy a house must submit a signed letter stating that the money is a gift and is not expected to be repaid.

5. Loan Inquiry and Application Process Requirements

Table 5.1. Borrower Verification	
What Needs to Be Verified?	**How Is It verified?**
Income	▪ W-2 tax forms ▪ federal and state tax returns ▪ recent pay stubs from the borrower's employer

Employment	▪ contacting the borrower's employer and asking for the borrower's
	    ○ position,
	    ○ salary,
	    ○ work history, and
	    ○ chances of continued employment
	▪ In some cases, the borrower may need to fill out another form that lets the employer release that information to a lender.

Assets	▪ checking the cash in checking and savings accounts ▪ looking through recent bank statements for those accounts and sourcing the money ▪ checking that a borrower truly owns what they claim to own (e.g., real estate, stock, retirement accounts)

When determining the loan amount to offer a borrower, the lender must first estimate the down payment and closing costs needed for the loan. Then, the lender examines the borrower's bank account balances and any other liquid assets that could be quickly converted to cash. Finally, the borrower subtracts the actual down payment and closing costs to obtain the amount of liquid reserves that could be used to pay the mortgage if needed.

Lenders usually require borrowers to have at least two monthly payments worth of liquid reserves. In most cases, 100% of a bank account's cash is attributable to either down payment/closing or liquid reserves. The exception is for a large deposit, which is any single deposit that is more than half of the total monthly qualifying income. Large deposits on a bank statement must be traced to their source. Any large deposit amount whose source cannot be verified must be subtracted from the bank account's balance before calculating liquid reserves.

Quick Review Questions

4. Can unlicensed officers contact borrowers directly?

5. How can loan officers verify borrower income?

Suitability of Products and Programs

A loan officer must consider whether a given mortgage product and its terms are **suitable** for a given borrower and situation. The definition of suitability is a little fuzzy and varies among lenders. Generally, suitability goes beyond the economic rules about a borrower's liquid reserves and ability to repay (ATR).

A lender might be held liable in court if a jury thinks that the lender steered a borrower toward a mortgage whose terms seemed likely to cause the borrower to fail to make monthly payments, resulting in foreclosure.

To determine suitability, a lender should ask, "Can the borrower have success with this mortgage?" During the loan application process, a loan officer should try to find out more about a borrower's circumstances without prying into the borrower's personal life. Loan officers should try to estimate suitability by asking themselves the following questions based on the information they know or can gather from borrowers:

- Does this mortgage seem to fit the borrower's life experience of paying mortgages and maintaining homes?
- Does this mortgage seem to fit the borrower's current and foreseeable family situation and life circumstances?
- Does this mortgage seem to fit the borrower's current and foreseeable employment circumstances and income level?
- Does this mortgage seem to fit the borrower's current and foreseeable life goals?
- Does this mortgage seem to fit the borrower's ability to cope successfully with sudden family or employment problems?
- For investors: Does this mortgage seem to fit the borrower's risk tolerance in the event that the investment fails?

Quick Review Question

6. Is the lender liable if the borrower fails to repay?

Accuracy and Timing of Disclosures

Accuracy

The fees paid by a borrower to get a mortgage are explained to the borrower at the beginning of the loan process:

- In many cases, the exact fees are known early on.
- In other cases, the exact amount is not known until closer to the end of the process.
- Some fees may even change at the last second.

To avoid unpleasant surprises, lenders must provide a **good faith estimate** of these fees, which are divided into three categories:

1. **Zero tolerance fees** must remain unchanged from the original fee estimate first given to a borrower. These fees include

- government transfer taxes,
- property taxes,
- private mortgage insurance, and
- origination fees and services.

5. Loan Inquiry and Application Process Requirements

For example, if a borrower is told that these fees add up to $1,500, the lender cannot charge any more than $1,500. If the fees end up being higher, the lender will absorb the loss. Thus, lenders must be careful that these fee calculations are correct from the beginning.

2. **Ten percent tolerance fees (10% tolerance fees)** may go up by no more than 10% of the total fee amount first given to a borrower; otherwise, the lender must provide updated paperwork and costs within three days of learning about the increase. This allows the borrower to decide whether to continue. These types of fees include

- government recording fees,
- title insurance, and
- other services provided by anyone whom the borrower chose from a lender's provider list.

For example, if a borrower is first told that 10% tolerance fees add up to $1,000, these fees cannot cost any more than $1,100 (10% of $1,000 = $100; $1,000 + $100 = $1,100) at the end of the process unless the borrower is told differently within three days. Missing this three-day window would limit the lender to charging only $1,100, regardless of the final costs. Before calculating the 10% tolerance fee, fees ultimately not charged are removed from the total. For example:

- A $1,000 total estimate includes a $200 survey fee.
- If the survey is never needed, then the total drops to $800 ($1,000 – $200).
- As a 10% tolerance, the maximum fee total drops to $880 (10% of $800 = $80; $800 + $80 = $880).
- Within three days, the borrower must be informed of any amount charged over $880; otherwise, it must be refunded to the borrower at closing.

3. **Good faith tolerance** fees refer to services chosen by a borrower and not performed by someone on the lender's provider list. These may increase by any amount from the original estimate (if the estimate was made in good faith). Good faith tolerance fees also apply to

- amounts that will go into an escrow account, and
- fees originally subject to the 10% tolerance that were moved to the good faith tolerance category because the fees were performed by someone not on the lender's provider list.

For some **changes in circumstance**, a lender may change the closing costs without referring to the tolerances above. These changes in circumstances include

- changes requested by the borrower, such as choosing a type of loan that is different from the one specified on the initial application;
- changes of an interest rate that was not "locked in";
- the borrower needing or wanting at least ten extra business days before closing;
- a change in the down payment amount;
- a significant change in the appraisal value of the home;
- new information on a borrower's credit status, including changes from a new loan or missed loan payment;
- the lender being unable to document a borrower's income;
- more than sixty extra days needed to close a construction loan; and
- an extraordinary event that could not be foreseen.

Quick Review Questions

7. Property tax is what type of fee?

8. Title insurance is what kind of fee?

Timing of Disclosures and Counseling

Lenders have up to thirty days to evaluate a loan application. After the thirty days, lenders must notify the borrower as to whether

- the application is approved;
- a counteroffer of loan terms is offered; or
- adverse action has been taken on the application.

If the borrower did not complete the application and the lender took adverse action as a result, the borrower must be notified within thirty days of the adverse action. If the lender provides a counteroffer that the borrower does not accept, the lender has ninety days to notify the borrower of what the lender will do if the borrower does not accept the counteroffer. If the notification relates to adverse action on an application, the lender must notify the borrower by

- listing the reasons for the action, or
- telling the borrower that there is a sixty-day window to request those reasons and that the lender has thirty more days after such a request to provide those reasons.

If an application is incomplete, the lender must notify the borrower:

- If the missing information is not provided within a reasonable time, the application will be discarded by the lender.
- If the missing information is provided, the application must then be evaluated as noted above.

> **Helpful Hint:**
>
> Reasons for adverse action must be specific; they cannot be vague statements, such as "you did not meet our internal policies" or "your credit score was not high enough."

If a creditor provides early disclosures of needed information, the information must be sent within three business days of an application's completion and at least seven business days before the planned closing date.

If the annual percentage rate (APR) will be different at closing than what was planned at the beginning, that information must be given to the borrower at least three business days before the planned closing date. A borrower may shorten or skip these waiting periods by notifying the lender in writing. Once an application has been received, a lender has three business days to provide the borrower with a list of homeowner counseling services in the nearby area.

Quick Review Questions

9. How many days do lenders have to evaluate a loan application?

10. If the APR will be different at closing than was planned, when must the lender notify the borrower?

5. Loan Inquiry and Application Process Requirements

Loan Estimate

Within three business days after a loan inquiry submission, an applicant must receive from the lender an initial **loan estimate (LE)** document of how much settlement will cost as well as all of the specific transaction terms. There is only one major exception to this: if the lender denies the loan application within three business days, the lender does not need to send an LE.

The lender also has three business days after a loan inquiry submission to provide the borrower with a special information booklet ("Your Home Loan Toolkit: A Step-By-Step Guide") that explains details of the home-buying process. This may also come from the applicant's mortgage broker.

When the initial LE is provided, a lender may refer a borrower to another business affiliated with the lender that can provide settlement services. The lender may receive profits from that affiliated business if it gives the borrower an **Affiliated Business Arrangement Disclosure** along with the loan estimate. The disclosure must

> **Did You Know?**
>
> If the lender mails an initial LE or special information booklet on the third business day, the borrower is considered to have received it three business days later.

- inform the borrower of the business relationship,
- provide an estimated range of costs for using the affiliate,
- tell the borrower in capital letters that it is not required to use the affiliated business, and
- allow a place for the borrower to sign and acknowledge the receipt of the disclosure.

Besides the disclosure, a lender must "not receive any payment from the affiliated company other than a return on the ownership interest or franchise relationship."

Typically, the charges and terms in an initial LE must last for at least ten business days after the LE is issued. The lender may allow even more time in the following circumstances:

- If a borrower provides "intent to proceed" with the loan within that time, then the initial LE charges and terms are used to set up the loan.
- If a borrower waits to provide "intent to proceed" until after the lender's time period has expired, the lender may create a revised LE within three business days that may change any or all of the charges and terms.

A lender must provide a loan estimate to a borrower at least seven business days before the loan is consummated (closed):

- If the APR of the loan changes, or if closing costs increase by more than the 10% tolerance described above, then an updated LE must be reissued to a borrower within three business days, and the borrower must receive it at least four business days before the loan is closed.
- The final LE must be provided at least one business day before the Closing Disclosure is given to the borrower.

Quick Review Questions

11. How many days does the lender have to send the LE?

12. For how long do the terms in an initial LE last?

Delivery Methods

Time periods of three business days mentioned above begin when a lender meets a borrower face-to-face and gives the borrower needed documentation:

- If a lender sends documentation by standard mail or overnight delivery, the borrower is assumed to have received the documents three business days after being sent.
- The time period does not begin until after the borrower is assumed to have received the documentation.

For documents delivered **electronically**, the borrower must have consented to receive electronic delivery (as noted in Chapter 2):

- The first time a borrower receives documentation electronically, the date of receipt counts as the first day the borrower sees it online—not the day the lender sent it.
- After a borrower has accepted and used electronic delivery once, all future documents are considered received by the borrower three business days after they are sent by the lender, even if the borrower does not actually look at the documents during that time.

If the borrower looks at the documents online during this three-day period, then the three days begin when the borrower first views the documents.

Quick Review Question

13. A borrower who has already been receiving documents electronically is considered to have received the documents how many days after the lender sends them?

Closing Disclosure

A lender must provide a borrower with an initial **Closing Disclosure (CD)**, which contains all general information about the loan terms, projected monthly payments, and detailed information about the costs of closing the loan. The CD must be sent at least three business days before the closing.

A lender can also provide the borrower several contractual documents at the same time as the initial CD. These contractual documents include

> **Helpful Hint:**
>
> A business day is typically any weekday on which a bank office is open. Weekday holidays are not considered business days. In most cases, weekends are not considered business days.

- the promissory note, and
- the mortgage or security instrument.

Although these contractual documents can be provided at closing, providing them at least three business days before closing is a good habit for loan officers to develop.

Any changes to the APR or loan—as listed on the initial CD—must be updated on a new Closing Disclosure and received by the borrower at least three business days before closing. If the lender adds a prepayment penalty that was not on the initial CD, this information must also be noted and updated on a new Closing Disclosure and received by the borrower at least three business days before closing.

5. Loan Inquiry and Application Process Requirements

73

Any errors in fees, or costs that are discovered after a borrower gets a Closing Disclosure but before closing (including those due to clerical errors), may be corrected at closing and before anything is signed. In such cases, the borrower may ask for—and receive—a one-day delay to study those errors and their impacts on the loan.

At closing, the lender provides a final **Closing Disclosure** that is signed by the borrower and lender, agreeing to all loan terms:

- If something changes after the signing that makes the final Closing Disclosure inaccurate, a lender has thirty days after closing to make needed corrections.
- These changes are usually the result of non-clerical or non-numerical errors, as clerical and numerical errors should have been found during multiple checks by many people before signing.
- A lender has sixty days after closing to refund the borrower any extra money paid at closing.

If the borrower ever fails to make a payment after closing, the lender must notify the borrower within forty-five days after the missed payment that homeowner counseling is available to the borrower. In most cases, the lender will require the borrower to sign a **Homeownership Counseling Disclosure** indicating that the borrower has been told that counseling is available and where to get it.

Quick Review Questions

14. When must the lender provide the borrower with information concerning any changes to the CD?

15. If errors in a CD are discovered before closing, how much extra time may a borrower ask for in order to study the errors?

Answer Key

1. Mortgage applicants must fill out the Uniform Residential Loan Application, which is Form 1003 for the Federal National Mortgage Association (Fannie Mae) and Form 65 for the Federal Home Loan Mortgage Corporation (Freddie Mac).

2. Form 1103, the Supplemental Consumer Information Form, details an applicant's language preference and whether the applicant has had a homeownership education class and housing counseling.

3. The lender must send the loan estimate within three business days after the borrower completes Form 1003.

4. No. Generally, unlicensed officers may not directly offer or negotiate loans with borrowers.

5. Tax forms like W2s, federal and state tax returns, and pay stubs from the employer can all be used by loan officers to verify income.

6. Possibly. A lender might be held liable in court if a jury thinks that the lender steered a borrower toward an unsuitable mortgage.

7. Property tax is a zero-tolerance fee.

8. Title insurance is a 10% tolerance fee.

9. Lenders have thirty days to evaluate a loan application.

10. If the annual percentage rate (APR) will be different at closing than was planned, the lender must notify the borrower at least three business days before the planned closing date.

11. The lender must send the loan estimate (LE) within three business days.

12. The charges and terms in an initial loan estimate (LE) must last for at least ten business days after it is issued.

13. After a borrower has accepted and used electronic delivery once, all future documents are considered received by the borrower three business days after they were sent by the lender.

14. Any changes on the Closing Disclosure (CD) must be received by the borrower at least three days before closing.

15. The borrower is entitled to a one-day delay to study Closing Disclosure (CD) errors and their impacts on the loan.

6 Qualifications: Processing And Underwriting

Borrower Analysis

Assets

Assets are monies that can be verified through documentation. They are used for down payments, closing costs, and to follow certain loan program guidelines. Only money that can be legally documented may be used for mortgage loans. Common assets include

- checking accounts,
- savings accounts,
- investment accounts,
- retirement accounts,
- lines of credit on homes,
- life insurance,
- certificates of deposit (CDs),
- money market accounts,
- business accounts, and
- cryptocurrency.

Other assets that can be used are **gift funds**. These are monies given to the borrower for down payment, earnest money, and closing costs. Documentation is required when gift funds are used as assets for the mortgage loan. Undocumented cash—any money that cannot be verified through bank documentation—is not an acceptable form of down payment and will not be considered as verified money. On the Form 1003 loan application, assets are listed in Section 2. They are listed by

- account type,
- name of the associated financial institution,
- account number,
- and the current balance of the account.

> **Did You Know?**
>
> Once cash has been in a bank account for sixty days, it is considered "seasoned" and can be documented.

Reserve funds are monies meant to cover an income shortfall. They are required in certain loan programs because the underwriter wants to be sure that the borrower has enough funds to make loan payments in the event that the borrower faces financial difficulties. If the borrower will be living in the home for which the loan is taken out—known as owner-occupied—it is common for the lender to require three to six months in reserve funds. Reserve funds are usually an underwriting requirement when

applying for loans for a second home or vacation home and for all investment real estate transactions. The reserves do not need to be in cash. The following documentation can be used for reserves:

- 401(k)
- traditional and Roth individual retirement accounts (IRAs)
- investment accounts
- trust funds
- certificates of deposit
- vested life insurance
- annuities

Reserve funds are always required for investment property mortgage loans. Because investment property can be risky, the underwriter or loan program requires anywhere from three to six months of cash reserves to minimize risk if the investment property does not have a positive monthly cash flow. The real estate market can change quickly—rents rise and fall, and the costs of an investment can fluctuate. Cash reserves must cover the monthly fixed costs of the property and any loans tied to that property.

> **Helpful Hint:**
>
> For first-time home buyers, lenders look for consistency and a history of on-time rental payments.

The loan officer (LO) needs prior authorization from the borrower to verify assets and liabilities. The disclosure form, **Borrower Authorization of Third Party** or **Borrower's Signature Authorization**, must be signed in ink or electronically by each borrower before a credit report can be pulled and third-party vendors doing business with the borrower can be contacted. These forms give brokers and loan officers permission to act on behalf of the borrower.

Quick Review Questions

1. What term describes monies given to a borrower for down payment, earnest money, and closing costs?

2. What type of funds are required to qualify for investment property mortgage loans?

Liabilities

Liabilities are outstanding monetary obligations a person owes as a debt to others. Common liabilities include

- credit cards,
- auto loans,
- home lines of credit, and
- installment loans for personal property.

On the Form 1003 application, liabilities are monies owed by the borrower(s). They must be listed on the application in Section 2 under Assets/Liabilities. The borrower must list each liability separately and estimate all outstanding debt. The loan officer will confirm the liabilities against the borrower's credit report. Before submitting the loan to the lender, the LO should adjust the liabilities for accurate debt-to-income ratios.

When qualifying a borrower for a mortgage loan, several ratios apply. The **debt-to-income ratio (DTI)** is critical when determining the amount of loan a borrower can secure. DTI is calculated as a percentage of the borrower's gross monthly income against the borrower's monthly debt liabilities payments.

Any debt with more than ten months of payments remaining to satisfy the payment obligations must be disclosed as a liability. Revolving lines of credit must also be disclosed. Debt with fewer than ten months of payments remaining (e.g., an auto loan) does not have to be disclosed and is considered a short-term debt. The following type of liabilities—debt— need to be disclosed when applying for a mortgage loan:

- all house payments for mortgaged properties
- all revolving credit lines (e.g., credit cards)
- all installment loans that have more than ten months of outstanding payments left to satisfy the debt
- all lease payments, (e.g., auto leases)
- all lines of credit secured by real estate (e.g., HELOCs)
- alimony and child support payments awarded and recorded by a court of law
- all tax payments that are on a repayment schedule
- outstanding liens and collections on a repayment schedule

When completing the liability section of Form 1003, the LO is responsible for investigating debt owed by the borrower. Loan qualification can easily get misrepresented if debt obligations are not accurate.

Quick Review Questions

3. What term describes outstanding monetary obligations a person owes as a debt to others?

4. A borrower has three months remaining on a car loan. Is this debt considered a liability?

Income

A **self-employed borrower** has many options for mortgage loans. For a self-employed borrower, qualifying for a mortgage loan may involve providing a simple profit and loss (P&L) statement and a year of bank statements. Being self-employed might require extra documentation, but due diligence is critical when qualifying these types of income.

As of 2022, close to ten million borrowers were self-employed in the United States. The newest form of self-employment is gig work, which involves independent contractors doing freelance or temporary work. In recent years, there has been a 51 percent increase in borrowers with gig work income.

Because of this large demographic, mortgage lenders are developing new loan programs for this type of income; however, Fannie Mae, Freddie Mac, and the FHA are usually slower to update their guidelines for self-employed income documentation. Because of these guidelines, self-employed borrowers can be a challenge to loan officers.

Some of the challenges when qualifying self-employed borrowers revolve around consistent income and the length of time they have been self-employed. A two-year minimum of stable and growing income is required for most loan programs. The following documentation is needed for a typical self-employed borrower:

- 1099 forms for two years

- two years of personal and business full tax returns
- current IRS tax transcripts
- twelve to twenty-four months of bank statements for business and personal accounts
- business Schedule K1 forms
- Schedule C forms
- quarterly and year-to-date profit and loss statements
- business invoices/contracts or Secretary of State license showing business is current in state filings

Each self-employed borrower is different, and there is a very good chance there is a loan program for which such a borrower can qualify. The loan officer must take the time to gather all the correct documents and understand the borrower's business or industry since self-employment income may vary from year to year.

Did You Know?

Cash businesses typically will not qualify for a traditional mortgage loan. Hard money loans and debt-service coverage ratio (DSCR) loans may help these borrowers. DSCR loans are typically used for investment property where rent is used as cash flow. Hard money loans are usually for real estate flippers.

If income received from **capital gains** is a one-time transaction, it is not considered stable monthly income and will not be considered to qualify for the loan. To allow the income to be shown as consistent, the underwriter requires two years of federal taxes on the borrower's Schedule D tax form, which will be used to average the income for qualifying purposes.

Borrowers who are retired or disabled can still obtain mortgage loans. Per the Equal Credit Opportunity Act (ECOA), lenders cannot turn down borrowers due to age or disability. As with income-producing borrowers, lenders will want to see that borrowers who are retired or disabled are receiving consistent Social Security Administration (SSA) or disability payments. This can easily be proven by providing the yearly SSA letter the borrower receives or by providing two or more months of bank statements showing that the borrower received direct deposits from SSA.

For a conventional mortgage loan, lenders can "gross up" this nontaxable income to 25% more, which allows the borrower to qualify for a larger mortgage payment. Most lenders gross up SSA non-taxable income by multiplying the amount of net or non-taxable income by 1.25.

The LO must be diligent when getting a two-year job history on an application. A borrower should not be qualified without a full employment picture. When a borrower has any break in employment within the two years it must be explained and documented.

Underwriters require consistency when determining loan approval. Simple letters of explanation drafted and signed by the borrower usually meet this need.

Verification of employment, past and present, also helps guide the underwriter's review of income history. Dates of employment on the verifications must match Form 1003. When borrowers have less than two years of income history, the gap must be explained. For example, during the COVID-19 pandemic, many people lost jobs or pay due to the lockdowns. These are reasonable gaps; however, when a person moves from job to job or to a different industry within two years, the underwriter might interpret these events as red flags.

A borrower's monthly income varies based on the type of income received. Most LOs and lenders use spreadsheet software that calculates the different types of income. Form W2 income is straightforward and uses a formula for each of the following payment schedules:

- salary
- biweekly
- weekly
- semimonthly
- monthly

Lenders use gross monthly income to qualify borrowers. Full-time employment is considered working thirty-six hours or more per week. Some borrowers receive overtime, bonuses, or commission-based compensation. Loan programs vary regarding whether these sources can be considered as consistently reliable income. In general, these types of income must be documented through verification of employment. To be considered by the underwriter when calculating monthly gross income, the borrower must show two years of receiving these types of income. Seasonal employment typically describes jobs related to seasonal industries (e.g., a ski instructor at a ski resort). Income from such jobs can be considered if it can be verified with the employer.

Quick Review Questions

5. Can capital gains income be considered to qualify for a mortgage?

6. How can a borrower on Social Security demonstrate income to qualify for a mortgage?

Credit Report

Credit reports provide lenders with snapshots of borrowers' credit usage and history:

- A mortgage credit report is slightly different than a consumer credit report.
  - The formula used for the credit score for lenders holds a different weight for risk compared to the one used to determine a credit card or auto loan risk.
  - Mortgage loan scores will not be as high as what borrowers usually see when they check scores on their own.

The mortgage loan score determines the borrower's ability to obtain the amount to be borrowed, the interest rate, and the type of loan program for which the borrower can qualify:

- Higher credit scores open up better interest rates and loan programs to borrowers.
- Borrowers with scores under 580 may need to rent until they can increase their scores or have a cosigner on the mortgage.

A credit report will show the following information about the borrower:

- full name
- Social Security number

Did You Know?

Mortgage lenders use a tri-merge report that uses data from the three major credit bureaus—Experian, Equifax, and Transunion. The tri-merge report offers a better understanding of a borrower's overall credit risk.

- current and past addresses
- outstanding liabilities
- payment history (including late payments and how many months of late payments)
- old credit lines that are closed and have a zero balance

The underwriter prioritizes reviewing

- on-time payments,
- the length of credit lines, and
- the amounts owed on credit lines.

Any late payments must be explained. Any collections or disputes may need to be paid before or at closing. If there are late mortgage payments, some lenders will not approve the loan and the borrower will not qualify for most loan programs. There are always exceptions; letters of explanation can help a borrower explain to the underwriter what caused the late payment.

> **Helpful Hint:**
>
> Outstanding collections, liens, and disputes will be at the bottom of the credit report.

A **good credit score** is determined by on-time payments, length of credit history, amount of credit being used against the credit limits, and the number of credit lines currently open. Making a few small changes can help borrowers improve their credit scores within a month; these changes include making more than one payment a month, keeping low balances on lines of credit (or paying them in full monthly), and keeping several credit cards to show that the borrower can handle credit.

Loan officers can **rescore** a pulled credit report. The credit agencies have tools that give scenarios based on payments toward certain lines of credit or collections. A rescore can increase a borrower's score so that a better interest rate can be locked in. Many LOs have access to credit repair companies and will recommend a borrower work with them before trying to purchase a home.

Quick Review Questions

7. How is a mortgage credit report different from a consumer credit report?

8. Can a borrower with a history of late mortgage payments ever obtain a new mortgage?

Qualifying Ratios

Qualifying ratios, described below, are applied to a borrower's assets and liabilities and allow the borrower to qualify for a mortgage loan. To determine if a borrower has the **capacity**, or ability, to take on a mortgage loan, lenders investigate the borrower's

- total monthly income,
- employment history consistency,
- credit usage,
- savings, and
- monthly debt payments.

An underwriter reviews this information and applies two different ratios—debt-to-income ratio (DTI) and loan-to-value (LTV) ratio—to the documentation provided. All loan programs have guidelines for allowable

maximum ratios. If a borrower exceeds the allowable maximum ratios, the loan must be restructured to be approved.

Debt-to-income (DTI) ratio is a percentage of the total amount of pre-taxed (gross) income against the total housing expense (monthly payment). DTI is calculated by dividing the total monthly debt payments by the monthly gross income the borrower brings in.

The **front-end DTI ratio**, sometimes called the **housing ratio**, encompasses principal, interest, taxes, and insurance (PITI). Still, front-end DTI is a benchmark ratio, meaning that it may be exceeded if the borrower can offset a higher ratio with **compensating factors** (e.g., substantial extra cash reserves).

> **Helpful Hint:**
>
> For a qualifying front-end ratio, PITI cannot exceed 28% of gross monthly income.

The **back-end DTI ratio** includes a borrower's PITI plus all monthly debt obligations, including

- mortgage payment,
- credit cards,
- auto and student loans, and
- other installment loans or ongoing debt (e.g., child support).

Back-end DTI ratio is also known as total debt-to-income ratio, bottom ratio, or total expense ratio. For a qualifying back-end DTI ratio, PITI plus other debts cannot exceed 36% of gross monthly income without compensating factors. Back-end DTI does not include household debt like utilities or groceries and gas.

As a general guideline, DTI must fall between 35% and 43%. Again, the loan program determines how high the DTI can be to allow the borrower to qualify for the mortgage loan.

One of the critical ratios the underwriter looks at when qualifying the loan for the borrower is **the loan-to-value (LTV) ratio**:

- The higher the loan amount is, the risker the loan becomes.
- Higher risk loans usually come with higher interest rates.
- Anything less than 80% of the loan amount to property value is considered a good ratio.

A typical Fannie Mae/Freddie Mac ratio is an 80% LTV; these are known as conventional loan programs. No private mortgage insurance (PMI)—discussed later in this chapter—is required because the value of the property has enough cushion against the loan amount to be secured against the home.

The LTV ratio is calculated by dividing the loan amount being borrowed by the property's appraised value. For example, a borrower is purchasing a home with an appraised value of $200,000. If the borrower puts 20% down—$40,000—then the LTV ratio is 80%. A lender's **automated underwriting system (AUS)** programs determine DTI:

- Fannie Mae's AUS is called Desktop Underwriter (DU).
- Freddie Mac uses Loan Prospector (LP).
- Without an approved finding through these systems, the underwriter cannot approve the loan.
- AUS guidelines will not give eligibility approval findings over 46.9% front end and 56.9% back end.

Each loan program has strict guidelines for loan-to-value ratios. The LO must understand how much a borrower can put down on a property and determine the loan program for which the borrower will qualify.

Fannie Mae and Freddie Mac have several programs for borrowers who cannot afford a 20% down payment. Fannie Mae's HomeReady and Freddie Mac's Home Possible mortgage programs for low-income borrowers allow an LTV ratio of 97% (3% down payment) but require PMI until the ratio falls to 80%.

Once the value of the property has increased, and at least 20% of equity has been invested against the loan amount, many homeowners should refinance their existing loans. Getting out of first-time home buying programs or low-down-payment loans saves borrowers thousands in mortgage insurance premiums while lowering their monthly payments. A good LO will keep in contact with borrowers and advise them when it's a good time to refinance.

Another ratio the underwriter and loan programs consider when qualifying a borrower for a mortgage loan is the **housing expense ratio**. Like DTI and LTV, this ratio considers the total amount of housing costs versus the total amount of income being earned each month. Ideally, less than 30% of the borrower's income should be spent on housing costs. Each loan program has specific guidelines that must be followed when qualifying the borrower.

Calculating the **total-debt-to-total-assets-ratio** only applies to mortgages in certain situations. For instance, a company's total debt may be taken into consideration if the business income is being considered as income for securing a mortgage loan. If a business is trying to secure a business property, the total-debt-to-total-assets-ratio is used by taking total debt and dividing it against the company's assets.

Quick Review Questions

9. How is DTI calculated?

10. Expenses like the monthly mortgage payment, property taxes, and homeowner's insurance are part of what qualifying ratio?

11. How do loan officers determine the DTI ratio?

12. For a qualifying front-end ratio, PITI cannot exceed what percent of gross monthly income?

Ability to Repay

In qualified mortgages, the **ability to repay (ATR)** means the lender has determined, in good faith, that the borrower can repay the mortgage loan based on the terms for which the lender has approved them. The lender must have reviewed the loan application and the borrower's documentation of assets, liabilities, and income. The lender considers eight factors when determining ATR:

1. consistent monthly income
2. current verified employment status
3. monthly repayment obligations on non-housing debt liabilities
4. monthly repayment obligations on any subordination financing used for obtaining the mortgage loan
5. monthly payments relating to the mortgage loan (e.g., taxes/insurance, HOA)
6. cash or investment balances as required by the loan program
7. DTI ratios
8. credit history

If the LO cannot obtain approved ratios from the AUS, then the LO must work with the borrower to find a solution. If a borrower's ratios are tight, possible solutions include

- lowering the amount of the loan,
- finding more income from other sources to use towards the loan,
- using gift money to make a larger down payment, or
- adding a non-occupant co-borrower or cosigner.

Before offering a **pre-approval letter** that states that a borrower has been pre-approved to shop for homes, the LO should have reviewed the documentation provided by the borrower. Unlike a pre-approval letter, a pre-qualification letter can be offered to a borrower who does not provide documentation. A **pre-qualification letter** will not hold the same weight for a realtor as a pre-approval letter; however, until a loan estimate has been provided to the borrower, documentation to verify income/assets and liabilities cannot be requested per the TILA-RESPA Integrated Disclosure rule (TRID).

Regulation Z contains safe harbor provisions for qualified mortgages. **Safe harbor provisions** protect lenders against lawsuits from consumers who claim they received mortgages from a lender when in fact the borrower was not qualified to repay the mortgage loan.

The requirements a lender reviews for loan approval are based on the underwriting analysis of the borrower's income, assets, and debt. Lenders have automatic software that runs through red flags on a mortgage application. The loan will be kicked out for restructuring if the AUS finds anything that violates the safe harbor provisions. The following are considered red flags:

- a mortgage monthly payment that is over 43% of a borrower's income (for qualified mortgages)
- certain characteristics (e.g., negative amortization, balloon payments, or an interest-only mortgage)

Finally, the lender cannot charge more than 3% in points and origination fees for a loan greater than $110,260 (as of 2021)

Quick Review Questions

13. A lender has reviewed all necessary documentation and believes that the borrower can repay the mortgage loan based on certain terms. What term describes this circumstance?

14. What will happen if a borrower wants to pay 50% of her income in monthly mortgage payments?

Other Issues

When refinancing a mortgage, there must be a clear advantage to the borrower. This advantage is called the **tangible net benefit (TNB)**:

- Borrowers receive a TNB disclosure at their first loan e-signing or mailed package.
- TNB disclosure forms vary by state.
- TNB disclosures require borrowers and lenders to acknowledge the benefits that are tangible for the refinance.

Borrowers refinance their current mortgages for a variety of reasons, including

- to take advantage of a lower interest rate;
- to cash out the equity of the home for home improvements, debt consolidation, or to purchase another home;
- to eliminate PMI;
- in response to a change in loan program structure;
    - to move from an adjustable-rate mortgage to a fixed-rate mortgage (or vice versa), or
    - to change from an FHA program to a conventional program;
- to obtain lower monthly payments; and
- for a shorter amortization schedule (e.g., a 15-year loan rather than a 30-year loan).

Underwriters must consider different **occupancy types**. Declaring the occupancy of the property is critical since it protects lenders from mortgage fraud:

- If a borrower will be living in the property as a primary residence, the property will be considered **owner-occupied**.
    - The Form 1003 loan application requires the borrower to disclose this information.
- If the property is being purchased as an investment or second home, different loan programs and guidelines must be applied when approving the loan.

If a borrower needs help to purchase a home, such as adding a relative (who will not live on the property) as a co-borrower to increase the amount of income being considered, the person who provides the financial support is known as a **non-owner occupant** on the loan. This is a common way for a first-time home buyer to qualify for a loan.

Usually, the borrower must move into the property within thirty to sixty days of securing the mortgage loan. Each loan program has specific guidelines, but most loan programs require the owner to live in the property for at least twelve months before turning it into an investment.

A **verification of deposit** form may be sent to the banking institutions listed on the loan application to verify the deposit of earnest money. The borrower's third-party authorization form must be sent along with the verification of deposit form.

Most of the time, electronic bank statements are acceptable for verifying deposits. The underwriter requires the last two months (or more) of bank statements and a transaction history showing the current balance. In addition to verifying the earnest money check or wire clearing, the underwriter will look for any large deposits that are not payroll related. Such large deposits must be documented and explained. Based on the loan program, if gift funds are being used as down payment or closing costs, verification of those funds is required as well.

Quick Review Questions

15. When refinancing a mortgage, there must be a clear advantage to the borrower. What is this advantage called?

16. What does it mean if a property is owner-occupied?

Appraisals

Purpose and Process of Appraisals

Mortgage lenders lend money to borrowers on properties that retain their value in the real estate marketplace. To understand the property's value and protect the lender, an appraisal is required. An **appraisal** is an evaluation that determines the fair market value of the property the lender is financing.

Most loan programs and lenders require an appraisal as part of their underwriting process. An appraisal must be completed by a real estate **appraiser**. Appraisers must be licensed and or certified through the **Appraiser Qualifications Board (AQB)**:

- A minimum of seventy-five hours of education is required to start as an appraiser trainee.
- A **licensed appraiser** can appraise residential homes valued at less than $1 million.
- **Certified residential appraisers** have no limitations when accepting appraisal bids.

As licensed appraisers receive more experience and education, they can become certified, at which point they will be able to receive job bids on larger and more complex properties.

Each lender's approved third-party vendor list includes **appraisal management companies (AMCs)**. Once the lender and borrower confirm their **intent to proceed (ITP)** on the loan, an appraisal can be ordered through the lender's AMC.

A bid for the appraisal will not be accepted until payment has been secured. VA appraisals are the exception; the appraisal is paid at the time of closing. Once the appraisal is completed, the lender sends the report to the borrowers.

> **Did You Know?**
>
> A borrower cannot choose the appraiser or company doing the appraisal.

Per TRID, the lender must provide a copy of the paid appraisals three days before closing. Most lenders advise the borrowers to waive the right to receive the appraisal within three days of closing so that closing is not delayed if the appraisal is received three days or less before closing. To acknowledge this, borrowers sign the **appraisal waiver** as part of the loan disclosure package.

Sometimes, lenders do not require appraisals; they may be **waived** if there is enough equity in the property or if the borrower is making a large down payment.

The cost and type of appraisal depend on the loan program and the type of property being financed. Appraisals are typically straightforward for single-family homes, most condos, and townhomes. Appraisals become more complex for multi-unit homes, duplexes, and manufactured homes. Other issues, like substantial acreage, excess square footage, or a remote location, can affect the property's value and further complicate the appraisal. The cost of an appraisal varies based on the complexity of the property and the AMC's agreement with the mortgage lender:

> **Did You Know?**
>
> The Dodd-Frank Act replaced the Home Valuation Code of Conduct (HVCC) with the AIR certification.

- A full appraisal for a single-family property for a conventional mortgage loan typically costs $650 to $750.
- Rush fees could add an additional $100 to $200.

The type of appraisal needed by the lender is determined by the type of loan. Government loan programs like VA, USDA, and FHA have specific approaches to valuing a property. Appraisal types vary depending on the type of mortgage:

- Conventional and FHA appraisals are typically valid for up to four months.
- VA appraisals are valid for six months.

Most lenders will accept a transferred appraisal as long as the previous lender has released the appraisal to the borrower or new lender.

The **Uniform Residential Appraisal Report (URAR)** is the standard form for single-family home appraisals. Condominiums are appraised using Form 1073. The lender submits the appraisal to Fannie Mae and Freddie Mac through the **Uniform Collateral Data Portal (UCDP)**. Every single-family conventional completed appraisal comes with the following documents:

> **Did You Know?**
>
> The URAR is also called Form 1004.

- The **Appraiser Independence Requirements (AIR)** certification is a set of strict standards that licensed and certified appraisers must follow when doing appraisals for all conventional single-family property loans.
    - The AIR was developed by Fannie Mae, Freddie Mac, and the Federal Housing Finance Agency (FHFA).
- **Submission Summary Reports (SSRs)** are uploaded into the Fannie Mae and Freddie Mac UCDP system with information about the appraisal.
- An **invoice** shows that the borrower has paid the cost of the appraisal.
- An **XML appraisal file** is a type of file format that can be read by a Mortgage Industry Standards Maintenance Organization (MISMO) system.
- Lenders use the **appraisal report** (usually provided as a PDF document) to understand the appraisal comps and the value of the property.
    - A copy of the appraisal report goes directly to the borrower.
    - The borrower must sign a disclosure stating that a copy of the report has been received.

HIgher-priced mortgage loans (HPML) require additional written disclosures from lenders to borrowers within three business days of their application being received. The following disclosure is sent to the borrowers in their initial lender disclosure package:

- "We may order an appraisal to determine the property's value and charge you for this appraisal. We will give you a copy of any appraisal, even if your loan does not close. You can pay for an additional appraisal for your own use at your own cost."

A certified or licensed appraiser completes the appraisal, which involves physically visiting the interior of the property. Within three business days of the transaction closing date, the applicant is entitled to a free copy of each written appraisal conducted for the mortgage. If the property being considered for a mortgage loan is a flipped property, an additional appraisal is required. A property is considered flipped if it has sold within 180 days of the seller's closing date.

Once a mortgage loan has been submitted to the lender and consent has been obtained from the borrower, the loan disclosure package is sent to the borrower. The loan disclosure package includes the appraisal waiver, which must be acknowledged by the borrower. This package also typically includes the **Intent to Proceed (ITP statement)**, which gives the lender the green light to move forward with the loan officer. Once the ITP statement is signed, the credit card authorization for payment of the appraisal can be sent to the borrower (if needed), and the appraisal can be ordered.

Quick Review Questions

17. Who conducts an appraisal?

18. For how long is a conventional appraisal valid?

Appraisal Types

The type of appraisal used for mortgage lending depends on the loan program and borrower. Most home purchases are completed using a sales comparison appraisal for all loan programs.

The lender must confirm that the value of the home aligns with the current housing market and the borrower's sales contract. The **sales comparison appraisal** (also called the **market data approach**) protects the lender from over lending on the property's value. It also confirms the property value for the borrower.

To conduct a sales comparison appraisal, the appraiser compares the property to three recently sold homes similar in square footage, location, and number of rooms. The appraiser then assigns a value based on current housing market trends.

When establishing a line of credit for a construction loan, lenders use a cost approach appraisal. The **cost approach appraisal** uses the land as the value and considers the cost of improvements or depreciation of any current structures on the land. For example, if there are two plots of land of similar size and one has a house and one does not, the appraiser might compare these two properties and adjust the value of the empty lot by the cost of the construction of a house that is similar to the one on the other plot of land. New builders can add the lot price to the cost of the house to be built. The appraisal will confirm the final asking price of the new home and lot together.

Any mortgage loans being underwritten for investment income require an **income approach appraisal**, which uses a cap rate percentage to determine the potential income from the property. The investor's annual rate of return should equal the cap rate.

Quick Review Questions

19. What is the most common type of appraisal?

20. What kind of appraisal is used for a construction loan?

Title Report

The title work on the property is one of the first items that needs to be ordered once a loan has been started. Every purchase contract lists the title company that will be doing the closing and title documents for the seller and the buyer. For refinances, the existing title on the property is pulled and reviewed for any outstanding liens.

Title companies ensure that a property has a clean title (e.g., no liens) and facilitate the closing process. Title companies have specific duties, including

- recording all necessary closing documents with the county clerks (e.g., deeds of trusts);
- handling all wire transfers to the lenders; and
- dispersing checks or wires to lenders, loan officers, borrowers, and any creditors being paid off at closing.

A **preliminary title report** will show the property address, name of existing owners, and any outstanding liens or encumbrances that must be addressed before reissuing the new policy title into the lender's name. A **clear title** on the property is critical for the new borrower or new mortgage loan. The loan cannot close if outstanding liens are not satisfied or removed.

When a borrower goes under contract for a property purchase, the seller decides which title company to use for their loan closing and title paperwork for the property. If a borrower is refinancing a home or investment property, the borrower chooses the title company. The title company pulls recorded documents, such as the deed of trust, and outstanding balances on existing liens on the property.

Once a loan has been submitted to a lender, a title work request is sent to the title company on the property contract or on the request for refinancing from the broker. It is important to start the process at the beginning of the new loan and meet the title work contract deadline, or in the case of a refinance, start working on any issues on the title of the property. Any liens found during a title search on the address can take time to resolve. A clear title is a must when closing a new loan on the property.

Quick Review Questions

21. Who decides which title company to use?

22. A property has an outstanding lien. Can its loan close?

Insurance

Flood Insurance

Lenders require homeowner insurance on all mortgage loans. The standard insurance policy covers certain types of water damage caused in the home; however, standard homeowner's insurance will not pay out on claims for damage from natural flooding due to weather. For that reason, mortgage lenders require

separate flood insurance for homes at risk of flooding. Flood insurance is purchased in addition to regular homeowner's insurance.

Congress mandates that lenders require flood insurance for all properties located in a **Special Flood Hazard Area (SFHA)**. Realtors, lenders, and insurance agents must consider these areas of possible flood risk. The **Federal Emergency Management Agency (FEMA)** maintains a flood map that shows flood risk zones for properties around the nation. All consumers can determine the zone risk number by going to https://www.fema.gov/flood-maps.

Did You Know?

Some states will send a flood insurance loan disclosure in the original disclosure package if the property has been flagged as being in a flood zone.

The **National Flood Insurance Program (NFIP)** is managed by FEMA. NFIP covers homeowners, renters, and businesses when a flood occurs. Flood insurance covers buildings or mobile homes and any personal property secured by the mortgage loan. It does not cover land affected by the flood. The limits of coverage for flood policies are $250,000 for residential property structures and $100,000 for personal contents.

Private flood insurance also provides coverage for the home and belongings. The main difference is that private insurance is not backed by the government. The insurance agency is responsible for paying out claims. Private flood insurance also covers other flood expenses (e.g., temporary living expenses if a borrower is displaced from flooding). Higher coverage is also available for purchase and is typically paid out much more quickly than NFIP claims.

Quick Review Questions

23. When is flood insurance required?

24. Who determines which properties are at risk of flooding?

Private Mortgage Insurance

When a borrower pays less than a 20% down payment on a property on a conventional loan, **private mortgage insurance (PMI)** is required to protect the lender from foreclosure on the property. PMI is factored into the payment of the borrower's loan through escrow. PMI shows as part of the borrower's monthly loan payment. It can be removed from a mortgage loan once there is more than 20% equity in the property. Mortgage loans that require PMI offer a few advantages:

- Borrower can get into a home faster if they do not have enough money saved for a 20% down payment.
- In a buyer's market, borrowers can move more quickly with a lower down payment.
- If interest rates are low or falling, borrowers can secure better rates and, in the long run, the PMI can be removed with a refinance.
- Because PMI can be removed, it is a short-term expense that allows borrowers to enjoy the advantages of home ownership.

A lender will automatically remove PMI once the equity has reached 78% of the original purchase price. This is calculated using the LTV ratio. As long as the borrower has not missed or been late on any

6. Qualifications: Processing and Underwriting

payments, the PMI can be dropped. A borrower can accelerate the removal of PMI from a mortgage loan by doing the following:

- making extra payments or adding a small amount each month to pay the principal of the loan
- tracking the equity of the home and asking the lender to reevaluate the loan to remove the monthly PMI cost once the home's value has increased by 20% percent
- refinancing the current loan

Quick Review Questions

25. When is private mortgage insurance (PMI) required?

26. When is private mortgage insurance (PMI) automatically removed?

Other Issues

Homeowners' (hazard) insurance protects the lender and homeowner from any claims against the home. Hazard insurance covers the structural base of the home and is part of the homeowner's insurance policy. Borrowers are required to have homeowner's insurance on a property and must provide evidence of insurance before closing.

The amount of coverage is determined by the amount of the loan being secured against the property. It is usually escrowed into the monthly payment of the loan and paid out to the insurance agency once a year. If there is enough equity in the home, the home insurance can be paid annually by the borrower rather than put in escrow.

When a mortgage loan is still in place on a property and there is no current homeowner's policy or not enough coverage, the lender obtains **force-placed insurance** to cover their interest and minimize their risk. Force-placed insurance is needed under the following circumstances:

- the current homeowner's policy has expired
- the borrower has not responded to annual renewals
- the borrower has provided inadequate coverage
- the borrower cannot find insurance because the property is deemed risky or uninsurable

Force-placed insurance will cover only the amount outstanding on the loan or replacement coverage on the property due to fire and theft. The lender is usually the only beneficiary of forced-placed coverage; however, if a claim is made, the lender may share proceeds to help the borrower repair the damaged property.

Quick Review Questions

27. What type of insurance is required before closing?

28. What type of insurance does the lender obtain if the homeowner's policy expires and the borrower does not renew the policy?

Answer Key

1. The term *gift funds* describes monies given to a borrower for down payment, earnest money, and closing costs.

2. Reserve funds are always required for investment property mortgage loans.

3. The term *liabilities* describes outstanding monetary obligations a person owes as a debt to others.

4. No; a debt with less than ten months of payments remaining does not have to be disclosed.

5. Yes, if the capital gains income is consistent over two years, it can be considered to qualify for a mortgage.

6. To qualify for a mortgage, borrowers on Social Security can provide the yearly Social Security Administration (SSA) letter or at least two months of bank statements showing that their direct deposits from SSA were received.

7. A mortgage credit report uses a different formula and may show a lower score than a consumer credit report.

8. A borrower with a history of late mortgage payments may find it difficult to obtain a mortgage; however, there are always exceptions.

9. The debt-to-income (DTI) ratio is calculated by dividing the total monthly debt payments by the monthly gross income the borrower brings in each month.

10. The front-end debt-to-income (DTI) ratio includes the monthly mortgage payment, property taxes, homeowner's insurance, and HOA fees.

11. Loan officers use an automated underwriting system (AUS) to determine the debt-to-income (DTI).

12. For a qualifying front-end ratio, principal, interest, taxes, and insurance (PITI) cannot exceed 28% of gross monthly income.

13. The term *ability to repay (ATR)* means the lender has determined that the borrower can repay the mortgage loan.

14. If a borrower wants 50% of her income to go to monthly mortgage payments, the lender's automated underwriting system (AUS) will require that the loan be restructured. For qualified mortgages, borrowers should not have monthly mortgage payments that are more than 43% of their income.

15. The tangible net benefit (TNB) is the advantage gained by a borrower when refinancing a mortgage.

16. In an owner-occupied property, the borrower lives at the property.

17. The lender chooses an appraisal management company (AMC), and a licensed or certified appraiser conducts the appraisal.

18. Conventional appraisals are typically valid for four months.

19. A sales comparison appraisal is the most common type of appraisal.

20. A cost approach appraisal is used when a lender is funding a construction loan.

21. In a sale, the seller chooses the title company; in the case of a refinance, the owner chooses the title company.

22. No, a mortgage cannot close on a property with an outstanding lien.

23. Lenders must require flood insurance for all properties located in a Special Flood Hazard Area (SFHA).

24. The Federal Emergency Management Agency (FEMA) maintains a flood map that shows flood risk for properties around the nation.

25. Private mortgage insurance (PMI) is required when the borrower puts less than 20%down on a loan.

26. Private mortgage insurance (PMI) is automatically removed once the property's equity has reached 78% of the original purchase price.

27. Evidence of homeowner's insurance is required before closing.

28. If the homeowner's policy expires and the borrower does not renew it, the lender obtains force-placed insurance to minimize risk.

7 Closing Loan Process For Mortgages

Settlement/Closing Agent

What Is a Settlement Agent?

The closure process of a mortgage loan is complex, technical, and requires the involvement of various stakeholders, including the lender, borrower, attorneys, and settlement agents.

> **Helpful Hint:**
>
> Settlement agents are also known as closing agents or escrow agents.

A **settlement agent** is a professional who facilitates the transfer of ownership of a property from the seller to the buyer. Settlement agents are responsible for ensuring that the legal and financial obligations of the transaction are met and that all required documents are properly executed.

A settlement agent plays a crucial role in the loan closure process and is responsible for the following:

- coordinating the transfer of funds between the lender and borrower
- ensuring that all documents required for the loan are in order and signed
- preparing and providing all the paperwork required for the loan to be finalized:
  - the title and deed
  - the closing statement
  - the loan agreement
  - all other documents related to the closing
- reviewing the loan documents to ensure that the terms and conditions of the loan are properly stated:
  - the interest rate
  - the repayment schedule
  - additional fees or charges
- verifying that all required documents, including the deed and title, are properly executed
- ensuring that the closing statement is accurate and complete

The settlement agent is also responsible for coordinating the closing process, which includes the following:

- scheduling the date and time of the closing
- arranging for the delivery of the documents
- ensuring that all parties involved in the process are present
- ensuring that all the funds required for the loan are transferred and that all documents are properly signed

Finally, the settlement agent must ensure that the title and deed are properly recorded with the local government. This requires filing all necessary paperwork with the appropriate agencies, such as the county clerk and the county recorder. The settlement agent must also ensure that the deed is properly registered with the state and that the title is properly recorded with the county.

Quick Review Questions

1. Who facilitates the transfer of ownership of a property from the seller to the buyer?

2. How does the settlement agent ensure that the title and deed are properly recorded with the local government?

Understanding the Closing Disclosure

To ensure the loan closes smoothly and all parties are aware of their rights and responsibilities, borrowers need to thoroughly understand the documents and details involved in the process. One of the most important documents associated with a mortgage loan closing is the **Closing Disclosure (CD)**, which provides borrowers with a detailed summary of the costs associated with the loan as well as any other financial considerations. As of October 2015, the Closing Disclosure replaces the **HUD-1 Settlement Statement** for the majority of loans; in some cases (e.g., transactions that do not involve a seller), a shortened version of the CD Settlement Statement is used.

> **Did You Know?**
>
> The CD must be given to the borrower at least three days before the closing and must be signed by both the borrower and the seller.

The lender issues the CD after the loan has been approved. This document outlines all of the costs associated with the loan, including

- the loan amount;
- interest rate;
- closing costs (appraisal fees and title insurance premium);
- any other fees or charges associated with the loan;
- loan terms;
- information about payments (e.g., repayment schedule, monthly payments); and
- other important information.

Quick Review Question

3. When must the borrower receive the CD?

Reviewing the Closing Disclosure

The borrower and seller need to review the CD before the closing to ensure they understand the terms of the loan agreement. By reviewing the CD and understanding the loan details, the borrower and seller can ensure they are entering into a loan agreement that is beneficial to them.

Typically, the borrower and seller can review the CD before the closing; in most cases, the lender must provide the borrower and seller with a copy of the CD three days before the closing. The borrower and seller should carefully review the document to ensure they understand the terms of the loan agreement, including any fees that may be due at closing. Lenders can clarify any questions or concerns the borrower or seller may have about the CD.

It is also essential to bring a copy of the CD to the closing, along with any other documents required by the lender. At the closing, the borrower and seller will review and sign the CD and any other closing documents to finalize the loan transaction. Once the loan is closed, the borrower and seller will receive a copy of the signed CD. This document should be kept safe, as it may be needed for future reference.

Quick Review Question

4. When does the borrower sign the Closing Disclosure?

Explanation of Fees and Documents

Settlement Statement Fees

Closing costs are the additional fees and expenses incurred when purchasing a home. They are due at the transaction's closing and can include a wide range of fees, from loan origination fees to title insurance fees. Closing costs can add up to several thousand dollars, so it is important to understand what to expect before signing on the dotted line.

The CD outlines all of the charges associated with the purchase of a home. In order for the parties involved to make an informed decision, it is important that they understand what each fee is, as well as its purpose:

> **Did You Know?**
>
> For conventional mortgages, the origination fee is a fixed amount. In other cases, more often for jumbo or portfolio-type loans, the origination fee is a percentage amount ranging from 0.5% to 2%.

1. The **origination fee** is generally the first fee listed on the CD.
   o The lender charges the origination fee to cover processing costs (i.e., processing the loan and preparing the paperwork).
   o The fee amount can range from $0 to 2% of the loan, accounting for credit risks and competitiveness with other mortgage products.
   o To win the borrower's business, some lenders may not charge an origination fee, or they may offer a credit that offsets the fee.
2. The **title search fee** covers the title search cost.
   o The title search ensures that the seller is the rightful owner of the property.
3. The **title insurance premium** covers the cost of title insurance, which protects the buyer from any claims or liens that might arise from a title search.
   o Lenders often require title insurance ranging from a few hundred to more than one thousand dollars.
   o Generally, this amount is a percentage based on the loan amount.
   o Different states may have different ways to calculate the title insurance premium.
   o The title insurance premium amount is typically calculated as a percentage of the loan.
4. The **survey fee** covers the cost of a property survey.
   o It is important to ensure there are no boundary disputes or encroachments.
5. The **recording fee** covers the cost of recording the deed with the local government.
6. The **transfer tax** is paid to the local government based on the property's sale price.
7. The **appraisal fee** covers the cost of an appraisal of the property.

      o   This fee is important to ensure that the buyer pays a fair market value for the property.

8. The **credit report fee** covers the cost of obtaining the buyer's credit report.
    o The lender must be sure that the buyer can qualify for the loan.
9. The **discount points** are paid to the lender to lower the loan's interest rate.
    o Discount points are a type of prepaid interest that buyers may pay to obtain a lower interest rate on their loan.
    o Discount points can add up to thousands of dollars, so it is important to consider the costs versus the benefits in deciding whether to pay them.
10. The **prepaid interest** covers the cost of any interest that has accrued since the beginning of the month.
11. The **closing fee** covers the cost of the closing process.

Other closing costs are not generally on the CD, but they are important to know:

- **Prepayment penalties** are imposed if a buyer pays off the loan earlier than expected. These penalties can range from a few hundred to thousands of dollars. Prepayment penalties are very uncommon on residential/personal mortgages and generally found on commercial properties.
- **Prepaid items** typically include property taxes, homeowner's insurance, and other related fees. These fees are typically estimated and will be paid before the closing date.
- **Miscellaneous expenses** vary depending on the type of loan and the market:
    o inspection fees
    o HOA transfer costs
    o borrower's proration of expenses
    o other miscellaneous costs

> **Did You Know?**
>
> If a client is doing a refinance and has previously purchased a title insurance policy, the client may get a reissue rate.

Quick Review Questions

5. Which fee covers lender processing costs?

6. Which fee covers the cost of the closing process?

Understanding the Required Documents

The loan closing process of a mortgage is complex and requires a great deal of paperwork. Understanding the documents required when using a property as collateral is essential for a smooth property transaction and loan approval. From the initial application to the closing paperwork, there are several required documents that must be completed and submitted to the lender:

1. The **loan application**, which must be signed and dated in order to be valid, outlines the borrower's financial information:
    o employment status
    o income

- o loan amount requested
- o other assets and debts

2. The **credit report** reveals the borrower's credit history and score:
   - o It helps the lender determine the borrower's creditworthiness and whether the borrower can meet the minimum requirements for the loan.
3. **Proof of income** shows that the borrower can make loan payments:
   - o pay stubs
   - o tax returns
   - o other verifiable income documents
4. **Proof of assets** shows that the borrower has the funds to cover the loan:
   - o bank statements
   - o asset statements
   - o other financial documents
5. The **title search report** verifies that the borrower owns the property and checks for any liens against the property.
6. The **closing documents**:
   - o promissory note
   - o security instrument
   - o Closing Disclosure

A **promissory note** is an agreement between the borrower and the lender in which the borrower agrees to repay the loan following the terms and conditions of the promissory note. The promissory note is legally binding and states the amount of the loan, the interest rate, and the repayment schedule. It also outlines any other conditions or requirements (e.g., escrow payments or late fees).

Quick Review Questions

7. Which documents demonstrate that a borrower can make loan payments?

8. Which documents show that a borrower has the resources to pay a loan?

Security Instruments and Eligible Signatures

When a mortgage loan is approved, the closing process begins. The closing process involves signing several documents that are legally binding, including a security instrument. The **security instrument** is the agreement between the borrower and the lender. It can be a **deed of trust** or a **mortgage** and. serves as the legal instrument that grants the lender the right to take possession of the property if the borrower defaults on the loan.

The security instrument must be properly executed and recorded in the public record to be valid; to be legally binding, it must be signed by both the borrower and the lender. Typically, the borrower signs the security instrument in the presence of a notary public. The lender may also require a signature from a third party, such as a real estate attorney or title company representative. In some cases, the lender may also require a signature from a witness. Any signature not made voluntarily or without legal authority will be deemed invalid, and the security instrument will also be considered invalid.

When closing a mortgage loan, it is important to ensure that all signatures on the security instrument are valid and legally binding. This security instrument document is an essential part of the closing process and

serves as the legal agreement between the borrower and lender. By ensuring that all signatures are in order, the lender and borrower can be sure that their rights and obligations are clearly outlined and legally enforceable.

Quick Review Question

9. What legal instrument grants the lender the right to take possession of the property if the borrower defaults on the loan?

Power of Attorney

A **power of attorney (POA)** is a legal document that enables a person (the principal) to appoint another person (the agent or attorney-in-fact) to act on behalf of the principal to manage financial, legal, and personal affairs. A POA is especially important for managing affairs when the principal is incapacitated due to illness, disability, or other reasons. It may also be used when the principal cannot attend a closing due to scheduling conflicts.

A POA gives the agent the authority to conduct financial transactions (e.g., paying bills, collecting benefits, or making purchases) on the principal's behalf. Additionally, the POA can grant the agent authority to make medical decisions and sign legal documents (e.g., wills and trusts) on the principal's behalf. The agent must act in the principal's best interests and always follow the terms of the POA.

Quick Review Question

10. Who represents the principal in a POA?

The Note Disclosure Process

The note disclosure process of a mortgage loan protects both the lender and the borrower by providing clear and detailed information about the loan. The **note disclosure** is a document that outlines the terms of the loan, including

- interest rate,
- fees, and
- payment terms.

It also outlines the borrower's obligations, including

- paying taxes,
- paying insurance, and
- other conditions.

All of this information must be provided to the borrower in writing, and the borrower must sign the note disclosure to indicate that the loan terms are understood. The note disclosure is typically provided to the borrower at the time of closing along with other documents, such as the deed of trust.

Quick Review Question

11. When does the borrower receive the note disclosure?

The Assumption Clauses

An **assumption clause** is a part of the loan agreement that states under what circumstances the loan may be assumed by another party. Assumption clauses apply when the borrower transfers ownership of the property to another party, with the new owner taking over the terms of the loan, including the interest rates and repayment terms. Assumption clauses can vary from lender to lender; however, they generally include

- stipulations on who may assume the loan (e.g., a spouse or other family member); and
- any fees associated with the loan transfer.

In some cases, the new borrower may be required to pay an up-front fee to the lender to assume the loan. Additionally, lenders may require the new borrower to be creditworthy and eligible for the loan, and the lender may require a new appraisal of the property to ensure that it still meets their lending standards.

The assumption clause also typically outlines the process for transferring the loan, including any documents that must be signed and submitted. For example, the new borrower may be required to provide proof of income, a credit report, and other forms of documentation.

The assumption clause will also define what happens if the loan is not assumed, such as whether the original borrower or the new borrower will be responsible for the loan payments. In some cases, lenders may also include a "due on sale" clause in the assumption clause, which requires that the loan be repaid in full if the property is sold to another party. This clause protects the lender from potential losses if the property value decreases after the loan is assumed.

Some lenders will not allow for loan assumptions, while others may require the original borrower to remain on the loan for the entire term.

Quick Review Questions

12. What part of the loan agreement states the circumstances under which a loan may be assumed by another party?

13. What clause requires that a loan be repaid in full if the property is sold to another party?

The Escrow Analysis Statement

The **escrow analysis statement** is provided to the borrower by the lender at the time of closing. It includes a detailed breakdown of the loan and its associated costs. The borrower and the lender must sign the statement to close the loan. The escrow analysis statement includes

- the amount the borrower must pay each month to the lender,
- the amount that will go into the escrow account,
- the amount of any taxes and insurance that are being held in escrow, and
- the amount of any balances in the escrow account.

The escrow analysis statement is a critical document that must be reviewed before the mortgage loan can be closed. The borrower needs to understand the details of the loan, including the amount of the loan and the terms of the loan. It is also important for the borrower to understand the amount held in the escrow account each month and any taxes and insurance held in escrow.

Quick Review Question

14. Which document includes a detailed breakdown of the loan and its associated costs?

Title and Title Insurance

What Is Title Insurance?

One of the key components of the closing process is the purchase of title insurance. **Title insurance** protects the homebuyer from any claims or losses resulting from title defects. The title insurance company searches the public records to determine any liens, encumbrances, or other title defects that may affect the buyer's ownership rights. Title insurance has many benefits:

- It protects the buyer's interest in the property.
- It ensures that the title is free and clear of any liens or encumbrances.
- It is typically purchased by the buyer.
- It provides coverage for the duration of the ownership of the property.

It is important to note that title insurance does not do the following:

- guarantee against any defects in the title
- protect against title defects that occur after the policy is issued

The policy provides coverage for any defects that were not detected prior to the purchase of the property, such as a lien or encumbrance that was not recorded in the public records. It will also provide coverage for any title defects that may have been missed during the search, such as an unrecorded title transfer. In addition, the title insurance policy will provide coverage for certain title-related legal expenses, including attorney's fees and court costs.

Title insurance also provides coverage for any judgments or liens filed against the property after the policy has been issued (e.g., judgments or liens filed against the property's prior owner or against the title company itself). The policy also provides coverage for any claims of ownership of the property by another party.

Finally, title insurance covers any fees, costs, or other charges associated with foreclosure. This coverage is important as foreclosure proceedings can be costly and time-consuming. The title insurance policy will also cover any losses resulting from title defects after the policy is issued.

Quick Review Questions

15. What protects the homebuyer from any claims or losses resulting from title defects?

16. Does title insurance guarantee against title defects?

Easements, Encumbrances, and Deeds of Reconveyance

The closing of a mortgage loan is a complex process that involves a variety of documents, fees, and other legal considerations. Depending on the complexity of the loan and other factors, the process can be relatively simple or involve multiple scenarios.

Regardless of the complexity of the loan, understanding the priority of each element of the closing process can help ensure a successful outcome. This includes understanding the legal implications of easements, encumbrances, and reconveyance deeds.

> **Helpful Hint:**
>
> To ensure that all of the necessary documents are properly filed and that the property's title is clear, it is important to understand the implications of a deed of reconveyance when closing a loan.

Table 7.1. Comparing Easements, Encumbrances, and Deeds of Reconveyance

Element	Definition	Explanation/Examples
Easements	legal agreements that allow a third party to use a portion of the property owned by someone else	<ul><li>involve the right of the third party to use the property for a specific purpose (e.g., building a road)</li><li>part of the closing process</li><li>must be identified and recorded to be legally binding</li></ul>
Encumbrances	liens or claims placed on a property by a third party	<ul><li>examples include a mortgage, a tax lien, a judgment lien, or a mechanic's lien</li><li>must be identified and addressed during the closing process</li><li>must be paid off or resolved for the property to be</li></ul>

Table 7.1. Comparing Easements, Encumbrances, and Deeds of Reconveyance		
Element	Definition	Explanation/Examples
		transferred to the buyer
Deed of Reconveyance	a document filed after a mortgage loan's closing to transfer the property's title back to the original owner	• used when a loan is paid off or refinanced

Quick Review Questions

17. What term describes the legal agreements that allow a third party to use a portion of a property owned by someone else?

18. What term describes liens or claims placed on a property by a third party?

Funding

The **rescission period** is designed to give borrowers time to review the loan papers, ensure they are fully aware of the loan's terms and conditions, and decide whether to go through with the loan. During this time, borrowers can decide to back out of the loan if they wish to do so. The rescission period is only applicable when refinancing a home—not purchasing one. The rescission period is an important part of the loan process and protects the borrower from any potential issues that could arise with the loan. It is important to understand when the rescission period begins and ends so that borrowers can make an informed decision

The rescission period begins when the borrower signs the loan papers. The period ends on the third business day following the signing and extends for three additional business days. A rescission form, which indicates that the borrower has three business days to cancel the loan, is part of the closing documents and must be signed by the borrower.

The rescission period ends when the third business day passes after signing the loan papers. At this point, the loan is considered final, and the borrower is legally obligated to repay the loan as outlined in the loan papers. The lender will then begin collecting payments and other loan-related activities. It is important to understand when the rescission period ends so that the borrower is fully aware of the obligations and implications of the decision to accept the loan.

Funding is the process of providing the loan money to the borrower; it is typically completed after closing. At this point, the lender will transfer the funds to the borrower's escrow account and hold the money until it is ready to be used. Once the funds are transferred, the lender can no longer change the loan terms.

Quick Review Questions

19. When does the rescission period begin?

20. What term describes the process of providing the loan money to the borrower?

Answer Key

1. A settlement agent facilitates the transfer of ownership of a property from the seller to the buyer.

2. The settlement agent files all necessary paperwork with the appropriate agencies to ensure that the title and deed are properly recorded with the local government.

3. The Closing Disclosure (CD) must be given to the borrower at least three days before the closing date.

4. The borrower signs the Closing Disclosure at closing.

5. The origination fee covers lender processing costs.

6. The closing fee covers the cost of the closing process.

7. Proof of income documents demonstrate that a borrower can make loan payments.

8. Proof of assets show that a borrower has the resources to pay a loan.

9. The security instrument grants the lender the right to take possession of the property if the borrower defaults on the loan.

10. The agent or attorney-in-fact represents the principal in a power of attorney (POA).

11. The borrower typically receives the note disclosure at closing.

12. The assumption clause describes the circumstances under which a loan may be assumed by another party.

13. A "due on sale" clause requires that a loan be repaid in full if the property is sold to another party.

14. The escrow analysis statement includes a detailed breakdown of the loan and its associated costs.

15. Title insurance protects the homebuyer from any claims or losses resulting from title defects.

16. No, title insurance does not guarantee against title defects.

17. The term *easements* describes the legal agreements that allow a third party to use a portion of a property owned by someone else.

18. The term *encumbrances* describes liens or claims placed on a property by a third party.

19. The rescission period begins when the borrower signs the loan papers.

20. The term *funding* describes the process of providing the loan money to the borrower.

104   7. Closing Loan Process for Mortgages

8 Financial Calculations Used In Mortgage Lending

Period (Per Diem) Interest

The borrower's first monthly payment is due on the first day of the second month after closing:

- For loans closed during January, the first monthly payment is due March 1.
- For loans closed during May, the first monthly payment is due July 1, and so on.

The interest on a home loan, as part of each monthly payment, is paid for the previous month. For the examples above, a payment due on March 1 includes the interest on the loan for the month of February; a payment due July 1 includes the interest on the loan for June, and so on.

If, however, a loan closes in the middle of a month—January 20, for example—**per diem interest**, or **period interest**, covers each day between closing and the first day of the next month. Period interest is calculated in one of two ways:

- by using a 365-day year
- by assuming that every month is thirty days long (i.e., a 360-day year)

If the loan is closed near the beginning of a month, the per diem interest will cost almost as much as the interest on a regular monthly payment. The later in a month the closing is scheduled, the fewer days there are before the end of that month and, therefore, the less per diem interest that must be paid by the borrower.

Per diem interest must be calculated by a loan officer and included with the Initial and Final Closing Disclosures given to the borrower. Because the per diem interest amount changes each day depending on the closing date, the per diem interest amount will be different on the two disclosures if the closing date changes. This should be pointed out to the borrower as a slight change in the conditions of the loan, which is considered acceptable and legal. Per diem interest can be calculated as follows:

- Multiply the loan amount by the annual interest percentage rate (as a decimal).
- Divide that product by 360 or 365 (see above) to create a per-day rate.
- Finally, multiply the quotient by the number of days remaining in the month, including the day of closing. (This is the number of days for which per diem interest is owed.)

Table 8.1. contains examples of per diem interest calculations.

Table 8.1. Examples of Per Diem Interest Calculations	
Example	**Equation to Find Per Diem Interest**

▪ per diem interest for a $200,000 loan, 5% annual interest rate, loan closing on March 11
   ○ 365-day calendar
   ○ interest charged for the last 21 days of March (includes closing day)
	$200,000 × 0.05 ÷ 365 × 21 = **$575.34**

▪ per diem interest for a $300,000 loan, 3.5% annual interest rate, loan closing on July 17
   ○ 360-day calendar
   ○ interest charged for the last 15 days of July (closing day included)
	$300,000 × 0.035 ÷ 360 × 15 = **$437.50**

When the borrower eventually sells the property, the per-diem interest on the property's loan is calculated for the days between the first of the month and the day of closing. At closing, the original borrower pays the per diem interest cost for the days between (and including) the first of the month and the closing date, and the new borrower pays the per diem interest for the rest of that month. The new borrower then pays the next month's interest on the first monthly payment after closing.

Quick Review Questions

1. When the original borrower sells the property while still holding the loan, who pays per diem interest for the closing date and the remainder of the days in the month?

2. What is the per diem interest for the following loan?
   - $500,000 loan amount
   - 6.25% annual interest rate
   - closing date of September 28
   - 365-day calendar
   - interest charged for the last three days of September

Payments

Monthly Payments

Borrowers pay home loans back through monthly payments; they typically make one equal payment, due on the first of each month, over the life of the loan. A monthly payment on a home loan contains four parts: principal, interest, taxes, and insurance (PITI):

TRIVIUM
—TEST PREP—

Principal is the original loan amount. At closing, the lender provides an **amortization table** to the borrower that shows how the last of the loan amount will be paid back with the last monthly payment at the end of the loan. The amortization table shows the amount of principal contained in each payment, which increases by a few dollars each month. For instance, for a 30-year loan with 360 monthly payments, the principal will be paid back in full after the 360 payments have been made.

The paid-back portion of the principal, along with the down payment, is the borrower's **equity** in the home. Equity increases over time as the borrower makes payments. If a borrower puts down $20,000 on a property, and then makes monthly payments that pay off another $5,000 of the principal, the borrower will have $25,000 worth of equity in the home. This $25,000, which would normally not be available until the house is sold, may be accessed through a home equity line of credit (HELOC). (See Chapter 4 for more on HELOCs.)

If the house is sold before the principal is completely paid off, the borrower will receive the $25,000 equity at closing after paying the rest of the principal back (along with fees and per diem interest) to the lender using the money provided by the new borrower. Many borrowers use their equity to make a down payment on their next property purchase.

Interest is the fee for borrowing the principal, which is calculated as an annual percentage of the loan amount. As with principal, an amortization table shows the amount of interest contained in each payment, which decreases a few dollars each month:

- For example, for a $300,000 loan at 4% annual interest, the interest paid in the first year is 300,000 × 0.04 = $12,000, or $1,000 per monthly payment.

Taxes include state and local property taxes that are based on the assessed value of the property; they are usually paid once or twice annually. The more expensive a property is, the higher the taxes are:

- The amount of the previous year's taxes is divided by 12 to create the approximate monthly amount needed for taxes; it is added to each monthly payment.
- If taxes were $1,800 last year, the monthly payment for taxes would be 1,800 ÷ 12 = $150.

Insurance includes private mortgage insurance (PMI), for loans with less than a 20% down payment, and hazard insurance. The sum of these costs is divided by 12 to determine an approximate amount for insurance that is built into each monthly mortgage payment. Homeowner's insurance begins at closing. The cost of insurance is referred to as the **premium**. If the premium is $3,000 per year, insurance as part of PITI is calculated as follows:

$$\frac{\text{premium}}{12} = \$3,000 \div 12 = \textbf{\$250 per month}$$

Since the cost of homeowner's insurance varies nationwide, borrowers typically contact several insurance companies for quotes. Factors that affect the price of homeowner insurance include

- local weather,
- the number of insurance claims in the past,
- the size of the home, and
- the composition of the roof.

For most borrowers who need PMI, it is usually required until the seven-year mark since it takes about seven years to reach 20% equity in a home on a 30-year loan. The annual cost of PMI for most mortgages (not including the up-front premium) is 80 basis points or 0.8% of the loan amount:

- For a $300,000 loan, annual PMI would be 300,000 × 0.8/100 = $2,400.
- $2,400 ÷ 12 = $200
- Each monthly payment would include $200 for PMI.
- Once an owner has 20% equity in the home, PMI is removed, and the monthly payments reduce (in this case by $200 per month).

To ensure that a homeowner's taxes and insurance are consistently paid, a lender creates an escrow account for each loan. Each monthly payment made to the lender is divided into the four PITI categories. The **escrow account** holds the monthly tax and insurance payments until the time comes for the lender to pay the property tax, homeowner insurance, and PMI for the borrower. In this way, these items are always paid as long as the borrower makes timely mortgage payments.

Escrow also protects the lender. Unpaid taxes create a lien on the house that must be paid before the lender's lien would be paid, so ensuring taxes are up to date is in the lender's best interest. PMI protects the lender from losses if a borrower fails to pay off the loan. See Chapter 4 for more on escrow.

To ensure that money is always available to pay the taxes and insurance when they are due, closing costs include **prepaid items**, or several months' worth of payments of taxes and insurance paid in advance. Typical prepaid items required by lenders include

- at least two months of annual property tax,
- two months of PMI,
- the first year of homeowner's insurance, and
- per diem interest.

As each payment comes in, money is added to the escrow account; this way—even after all items are paid for the year—the escrow account still has money in it. When the home is sold, these prepayments are returned to the borrower at closing. The borrower often rolls them over to be used for the same purposes on the next property purchase.

The Closing Disclosure specifies the monthly payment. Calculating monthly payments means considering all of the factors. For example, if a borrower takes out a $300,000, 30-year loan at 5% interest with a 5% down payment, then the following information is true about the loan:

- monthly principal = $342.44
- monthly interest = $1,187.50

- annual taxes = $1,800
- annual homeowner's insurance = $1,500

The total monthly payment is calculated using the following steps:

- First, calculate the taxes and insurance.
    - To calculate monthly taxes, divide the annual tax amount by twelve:

$$\frac{\$1,800}{12} = \$150$$

    - To figure monthly homeowner's insurance, divide the insurance premium by twelve:

$$\frac{\$1,500}{12} = \$125$$

- Since the down payment is less than 20% of the property price, the borrower must pay PMI.
    - To calculate PMI, first subtract the down payment to get the loan amount:

$$\$300,000 \times 0.05 = \$15,000 \text{ (down payment)}$$

$$\$300,000 - \$15,000 = \$285,000$$

- To find the annual PMI, use the formula: $\frac{\text{loan amount} \times 0.8}{100}$
    - annual PMI $= \frac{\$285,000 \times 0.8}{100} = \frac{\$228,000}{100} = \$2,280$
- Divide by 12 to get the monthly PMI: monthly PMI $= \frac{\$2,280}{12} = \mathbf{\$190}$
- Add taxes and insurance to the monthly principal and interest as given in the example above:
    - monthly principal $= \$342.44$
    - monthly interest $= \$1,187.50$
    - monthly taxes $= \$150$
    - monthly homeowner's insurance $= \$125$
    - monthly PMI $= \$190$
    - $\$342.44 + \$1,187.50 + \$150 + \$125\ \$190 = \$1,994.94$
    - The total monthly payment is $\mathbf{\$1,994.94}$.

Monthly payments can be lowered by reducing the expense of the PITI categories. Borrowers can do the following to lower their monthly payments:

- obtain lower principal and taxes by buying a less valuable house
- decrease principal by increasing the down payment
- decrease interest and homeowner's insurance by shopping around for the best rates
- decrease interest by refinancing the house at a lower rate if possible
- eliminate PMI with a down payment of at least 20%

If a borrower's payment is delayed enough to incur a late fee but does not include the late fee, the lender may pay the late fee first and then apply the rest of the payment to the interest and principal owed. But if paying the late fee first leaves a partial payment that then becomes late because the late fee was taken, charging another late fee for that would create a pyramid effect—an illegal cascade of late fees.

If a house must be foreclosed on because the borrower fails to make payments, the lender files a lien. If the house is sold in foreclosure, lien holders are paid in an established **order of payments**, where taxes and government fees are paid first and lien holders are paid in the order of when a lien was filed (first to last) until the money from the sale is gone.

Quick Review Questions

3. What is the annual cost of PMI for most mortgages?

4. A borrower purchases a $500,000, 15-year loan at 6% interest. The borrower puts 20% down, and the following information is true about the loan:

- monthly principal = $1,375.43
- monthly interest = $2,000
- annual taxes = $2,100
- annual homeowner's insurance = $1,200

What is the total monthly payment?

Down Payment

A **down payment** is a percentage of the purchase price paid by the borrower at closing. All lenders require a down payment.

The amount of the down payment varies with the purchase price and the borrower's circumstances. The larger the down payment, the less money is borrowed for the loan, which means the monthly payment will also be less (since both the principal to be paid back and the interest on that principal will be less.)

As discussed in Chapter 3, FHA loans require a down payment of at least 3.5% of the purchase price (if the minimum decision credit score is greater than 580; lower scores require a 10% down payment and higher interest rates). Though conventional mortgages require a down payment of at least 20%, some lenders offer loans that require down payments of only 3%, 5% or 10%.

For loans with lower down payment requirements, the borrower must also purchase PMI until 20% of the original purchase price is paid to the lender. For example, if a property is purchased for $300,000, the following down payment calculation scenarios can be considered:

- The loan amount for a $300,000 property depends on the down payment:
    - a 3% down payment = $300,000 × 0.03 = $9,000.
    - the loan amount is $291,000 because $300,000 − $9,000 = $291,000.
- If the borrower chooses to put down more money for the same $300,000 property, the loan number changes:
    - a 5% down payment = $300,000 × 0.05 = $15,000
    - the loan amount is $285,000 because $300,000 − $15,000 = $285,000.
- In another example, the purchase price is $350,000:
    - a 3.5% down payment = $350,000 × 0.035 = $12,250
    - that makes the loan amount $337,750 ($350,000 − $12,250 = $337,750)

In all of these examples, PMI would be required since the down payment amount is less than 20% of the purchase price.

Quick Review Questions

5. Find the down payment and loan amounts for a property with a purchase price of $420,000 and a 10% down payment.

6. Find the down payment and loan amounts for a property with a purchase price of $550,000 and a 20% down payment.

Determining Qualifying Ratios

A property's **loan-to-value (LTV) ratio** is the percentage of a property's selling price that will be paid by the loan amount. LTV can be calculated in two ways, each expressed as a percentage:

$$\frac{\text{loan amount}}{\text{property's appraised price}}$$

Example

1. A property appraised at $400,000 that is purchased with a loan of $360,000 has an LTV of 90%:

$$\frac{360,000}{400,000} = 0.9 = 90\%$$

$$\frac{\text{property's appraised price} - \text{down payment}}{\text{property's appraised price}}$$

2. A property appraised at $300,000 with a down payment of $60,000 has an LTV of 80%:

$$\frac{300,000 - 60,000}{300,000} = \frac{240,000}{300,000} = 0.8 = 80\%.$$

Loans with an LTV of more than 80% require the borrower to purchase PMI because the down payment is less than 20% of the loan. See Chapter 6 for additional details on LTVs.

Lenders must verify a borrower's current income and existing debt. As discussed in Chapter 6, a borrower's **debt-to-income (DTI) ratio** is the monthly amount a borrower pays in debts, divided by monthly income. For example, if a borrower has income of $7,000 per month and no credit card or other debt, then the PITI would be $2,500 per month if the loan is approved. To determine the borrower's DTI, divide debt by income:

$$\frac{\text{debt}}{\text{income}} = \frac{\$2,500}{\$7,000} = 0.357 = \mathbf{35.7\%}$$

For qualified mortgages, the CFPB requires a DTI ratio of less than 43% of the borrower's monthly income. The debt calculation includes PITI. The mortgage in the example described above would be qualified because the DTI is less than 46%.

Some borrowers have high DTI, surpassing the 43% threshold. In some cases, the borrower may be able to take action to reduce the DTI. For example, if a borrower has an income of $5,000 per month, credit-card

debt of $200 per month, and a monthly car payment that is $300, the PITI would be $1,800 per month if approved for the loan. To determine DTI, the borrower's total monthly debt must first be determined:

$$\$200 + \$300 + \$1,800 = \mathbf{\$2,300}$$

The total monthly debt must then be divided by the monthly $5,000 income:

$$\frac{\text{debt}}{\text{income}} = \frac{\$2,300}{\$5,000} = 0.46 = \mathbf{46\%}$$

Since the borrower in this example surpasses the 43% threshold, the mortgage would not be qualified; however, because the ratio is not much higher than 43%, a loan officer could ask the borrower how soon the car will be paid off. If the borrower is about to make the last car payment, then the total debt amount would decrease:

$$\$2,300 - \$300 \text{ (car payment)} = \$2,000 \text{ debt}$$

Then, to determine the new DTI, this new debt amount would be divided by the monthly income:

$$\frac{\$2,000}{\$5,000} = 0.40 = \mathbf{40\%}$$

By paying off the car, the borrower would create a DTI that is acceptable for a qualified mortgage. In such situations, obtaining more information allows the loan officer to determine whether a qualified mortgage may be in reach before the day of closing on the property.

Quick Review Questions

7. A borrower has an income of $4,000 per month, credit card debt of $300 per month, and a monthly payment on a new car of $450. Principal, interest, taxes, and insurance (PITI) would be $1,500 per month if the loan is approved. What is the borrower's DTI ratio?

8. A borrower earns $6,000 per month and has credit card debt of $350 per month. Principal, interest, taxes, and insurance (PITI) would total $2,200 per month. What is the borrower's debt-to-income (DTI) ratio?

Discount Points and Interest Rate Buydowns

In the mortgage world, the word **_point_** means 1% of the amount of a loan. Sometimes the fees to get a loan are expressed as a fixed dollar amount plus some number of points (e.g., $2,000 + $\frac{1}{2}$ point).

The following formula can be used to determine the total amount of fees:

- fixed dollar amount + point × 1% × cost of property

For example, if the lender fees to get a loan are $1,500 + \frac{3}{4}$ point, the total fees for a $300,000 loan would be the following:

$$1,500 + \left[\left(\frac{3}{4}\right)(0.01)(300{,}000)\right]$$

$$1,500 + 2,250$$

$$\$3,750$$

To reduce the loan's overall interest rate, some lenders allow a borrower (or even the builder or seller) to **buy down**, or pay a fee at closing expressed in **discount points**. For example, a borrower needs a $200,000 loan at 6%. The lender offers to reduce the loan interest rate by 0.5% at a cost of 1 discount point. In that case, the borrower pays a fee of 1% of $200,000 ($200,000 × 0.01 = $2,000) at closing. The lender reduces the overall interest rate from 6% to 5.5%.

The lower interest rate after the buydown may be **permanent**, lasting for the life of the loan. In some cases, however, the buydown is only **temporary** and the interest rate goes back to its original percentage rate after a certain number of years. For example, a lender offers to reduce the loan interest rate for the first year of the loan by 1% at a cost of $\frac{3}{4}$ of a discount point. The borrower needs a $300,000 loan at 5%:

- The borrower pays a fee of $\frac{3}{4}$% of $300,000 at closing:

$$\frac{3}{4}\% = 0.0075$$

$$0.0075 \times \$300{,}000$$

$$= \$2{,}250$$

- The lender reduces the interest rate for the first year from 5% to 4%.
- After the first year, the rate goes up to the original 5% for the remainder of the loan period.

Buydowns may last for more than one year. For example, a lender offers to reduce the loan interest rate for the first year of a loan by 2% and for the second year by 1% at a cost of 1 ½ discount points. The borrower needs a $500,000 loan at 7%:

- The borrower pays a fee of $1\frac{1}{2}$% of $500,000 at closing:

$$1\frac{1}{2}\% = 1.5\% = 0.015$$

$$\$500{,}000 \times 0.015$$

$$= \$7{,}500$$

- The lender then reduces the interest rate for the first year from 7% to 5%.
- After the first year, the rate goes up to 6% (7 − 1 = 6) for the second year, and then up to the original 7% after that.

Quick Review Questions

9. If the lender fees to get a loan are $\$2{,}250 \; + \; 1\frac{1}{4}$ points, what are the total fees for a $400,000 loan?

10. If a lender offers to reduce the loan interest rate by 0.25% at a cost of $\frac{1}{2}$ discount point, and the borrower needs a $300,000 loan at 4%, how much would the borrower pay to obtain the lower cost?

Closing Costs and Prepaid Items

Closing costs are the fees and payments that must be made at closing in order to get a loan. Traditionally, many individual closing costs are paid by the borrower, the seller, or equally divided between them. Other closing costs, such as home inspection, are negotiable.

Closing costs are listed individually on the Closing Disclosure (CD) and divided into a borrower-paid column, a seller-paid column, and a column of expenses paid by others.

A CD might indicate that the borrower pays the following closing costs:

- the lender's loan origination fees
- fees for a credit report
- flood monitoring
- tax monitoring
- pest inspection
- survey fee
- title fees
- government-required recording fees
- prepaid items:
  - homeowner's insurance
  - per diem interest
  - property taxes
- initial money to set up the escrow account
- homeowner association (HOA) fees
- owner's title insurance
- half of the home inspection fee

Closing costs paid by the seller may include the following:

- government-required transfer tax
- commissions to the real estate agents involved
- fee for a home warranty protecting the borrowers from immediate large expenses in case of problems
- half of the home inspection fee
- the rest of the seller's loan on the property
- a seller credit to the borrower that reduces the borrower's closing costs.

The appraisal fee could be paid by others.

Quick Review Questions

11. Who pays closing costs?

12. What are typical prepaid items?

Adjustable-Rate Mortgages ARMs (e.g., fully indexed rates)

The interest rate of an adjustable-rate mortgage (ARM) changes during the length of the mortgage. The rate is typically the interest rate of a financial index whose percentage reflects current interest rates plus a **margin**, or a percentage, added by the lender to make a profit. To calculate an ARM rate, the margin must be added to the interest rate. For example:

- At closing, a lender uses an index with a current rate of 2.5%.
- The lender's margin is 2.25%.
- The initial interest rate is calculated by adding the rate to the margin: $2.5\% + 2.25\% = \textbf{4.75}\%$

Over time, if interest rates increase, the new interest rate might be adjusted to match the new index rate. For example:

- The index rate rises at the time of adjustment to 3.75%.
- To find the new ARM rate, the new index rate must be added to the margin: $3.75\% + 2.25\% = 6\%$.

Interest rates may decrease and adjust the ARM rate down. For example:

- The new index rate might be adjusted to 1.75%.
- To find the new ARM rate, add the new index rate to the margin: $1.75\% + 2.25\% = 4\%$.

The interest rates of most ARMs are limited or **capped** to minimum and maximum percentages. Capping helps borrowers and lenders decide whether the monthly mortgage payments will be manageable:

- A **floor** is the minimum percentage rate of the loan if interest rates go down before the first adjustment.
  - A mortgage with a floor of 3% will never go below that level.
- The **initial adjustment cap** is the maximum amount the interest rate can be raised at the time of first adjustment.
  - Per CFPB, the initial adjustment cap is usually either 2% or 5%.
  - A mortgage with a 4% rate could be raised to 6% or 9%.
- Most ARMs have a **lifetime cap** to provide a maximum interest rate for the length of the loan.
  - According to the CFPB, the cap is usually 5%.
  - Thus, a loan that begins at 3% can never go higher than 8%.
- Some ARMs have a **periodic cap**—the maximum an interest rate can rise at a single adjustment.
  - For instance, if the periodic cap is 1.5%, then a 3% mortgage cannot increase beyond 4.5% at the next adjustment.
  - If the mortgage goes only to 4%, then it cannot increase beyond 5.5% at the next adjustment, and so on.

Some ARMs have a **teaser rate**, where, as a marketing tactic, the interest rate is lower than the typical index plus margin for some period of time. After that time, the rate is adjusted up to the index rate plus margin.

Helpful Hint:
Any caps should be listed in the TILA disclosure.

For example, if index + margin = 6%, a lender might offer a teaser rate of 4% for the first three years. Then, the lender adjusts the rate up to the index + margin rate of 6%, or even higher if the index rate goes up by more than $(6 - 4) = 2\%$ in the first three years of the loan.

Quick Review Question

13. At closing, a lender uses an index with a current rate of 6.25%. The margin is 2.5%. What is the initial interest rate?

14. If the new index rate for the mortgage in Question 15 is adjusted up to 7%, what would the new rate be?

15. If the new index rate for the mortgage in Question 15 decreases to 4.75%, what would the new rate be?

Answer Key

1. The new borrower pays per diem interest for the closing date and the remainder of the days in the month as part of the closing costs; however, the original borrower must pay the per diem interest for the days between (and including) the first day of the month and the closing date.

2. To find the per diem interest for a $500,000 loan with a 6.25% annual interest rate, multiply the loan amount by the annual interest rate:

$$\$500{,}000 \times 0.0625 = \$31{,}250$$

Divide the product by the number of days in the calendar year:

$$\$31{,}250 \div 365 = \$85.62$$

Multiply the quotient by the number of days remaining in the month, including the day of closing:

$$\$85.62 \times 3 = \mathbf{\$256.85}$$

3. The annual cost of private mortgage insurance (PMI) for most mortgages is 80 basis points, or 0.8% of the loan amount.

4. To calculate the total monthly payment, first, calculate the taxes and insurance. To calculate monthly taxes, divide the annual tax rate by twelve:

$$\frac{\$2{,}100}{12} = \mathbf{\$175}$$

To calculate monthly homeowner's insurance, divide the premium by twelve:

$$\frac{\$1{,}200}{12} = \mathbf{\$100}$$

Because the down payment is 20% of the property price, the borrower does not need to pay private mortgage insurance (PMI). Add taxes and insurance to the monthly principal and interest as given in the question:

- monthly principal = $1,375.43
- monthly interest = $2,000
- monthly taxes = $175
- monthly homeowner's insurance = $100
- $1,375.43 + $2,000 + $175 + $100 = $3,650.43

The total monthly payment is **$3,650.43**.

5. To find the down payment and loan amounts for a property with a purchase price of $420,000 and a 10% down payment:

- First, find the value of a 10% down payment for a purchase price of $420,000:
  - $420,000 × 0.10 = **$42,000**
- Then, find the value of the loan (purchase price less down payment):
  - $420,000 − $42,000 = **$378,000**

6. To find the down payment and loan amounts for a property with a purchase price of $550,000 and a 20% down payment:

- First, find the value of a 20% down payment for a purchase price of $550,000:
  - ○ $550,000 × 0.20 = $110,000
- Then, find the value of the loan (purchase price less down payment):
  - ○ $550,000 − $110,000 = **$440,000**

7. To determine the borrower's debt-to-income (DTI) ratio:

- First, determine the borrower's total monthly debt: $300 + $450 + $1,500 = $2,250
- The borrower's monthly income is $4,000. Use that information and the formula to determine the debt-to-income (DTI) ratio: $\frac{\text{debt}}{\text{income}} = \frac{\$2,250}{\$4,000} = 0.562 = \mathbf{56.2\%}$

8. To determine the borrower's debt-to-income (DTI) ratio:

- First determine total monthly debt: $2,200 + $350 = $2,550
- Then, divide that debt by the income: $\frac{\text{debt}}{\text{income}} = \frac{\$2,550}{\$6,000} = 0.425 = \mathbf{42.5\%}$

9. For a $400,000 loan with lender fees of $2,250 + $1\frac{1}{4}$ points, the total fees are calculated as follows:

- $\$2,250 + \left[\left(1\frac{1}{4}\right)(0.01)(400,000)\right]$
- $= 2,250 + 5,000$
- $= \$7,250$

10. To reduce the loan interest rate by 0.25%, the borrower must pay a fee of $\frac{1}{2}$% of $300,000:

- $\frac{1}{2}\% = 0.005$
- $0.005 \times \$300,000$
- $= \$1,500$

With this payment, the lender will reduce the overall interest rate from 4% to 3.75%.

11. Closing costs are paid by the borrower, the seller, or equally divided between them.

12. Typical prepaid items include insurance, per diem interest, and taxes.

13. Calculate the initial interest rate for a lender by using an index with a current rate of 6.25% with a 2.5% margin by adding the index rate to the margin: $6.25\% + 2.5\% = \mathbf{8.75\%}$.

14. If the index rate is 7%, find the new interest rate by adding the new index rate to the margin: $7\% + 2.5\% = \mathbf{9.25\%}$.

15. Determine the new interest rate by adding the new index rate of 4.75% to the margin: $4.75\% + 2.5\% = \mathbf{7.25\%}$

9 Ethics

Ethical Issues

Violations of Law

The **Gramm-Leach-Bliley Act (GLBA)** requires mortgage lenders to create and carry out policies for safeguarding consumers' nonpublic information. **Nonpublic information** includes:

- any financial information that could be connected to the consumer; and

- any lists, descriptions, or other data on consumers gleaned from nonpublic, personally identifiable information.

- A lender with a strong policy of safeguarding nonpublic information has the following:

- an information security program to keep information confidential, protect it from bad actors, and anticipate and guard against new ways to improperly obtain it

- a written risk assessment

- annual testing to ensure that consumer information is being kept secure

- the use of encryption when sending data

- multi-factor authentication (so customers are the only non-lenders who can access their information)

- a written incident response plan to follow if data becomes insecure

> **Did You Know?**
>
> Lenders who do not have policies to safeguard consumers' nonpublic information are violating the law.

A lender must also ensure that companies used for outside services (e.g., appraisers and settlement companies) have their own information security programs. Furthermore, every year lenders must provide a written copy of their privacy policies to each customer. Policy mailings should include information on how consumers can opt out of the lender's marketing outreach and having their personal information shared with nonaffiliated third parties. Loan officers may violate GLBA be doing any of the following:

- letting someone else use their computer while confidential data is being displayed

- taking a coffee break or lunch without closing out confidential data on their computer screen

- providing confidential information about a customer or loan status by any means (e.g., phone, text, email, casual conversation) to a coworker, personal friend or relative, customer's friend or relative, or a company used for outside services

- providing their work-computer password to another person

- using account numbers or other personally identifiable financial information to create a database for future marketing efforts

- sending confidential data electronically without encrypting it first

- keeping confidential data in a non-confidential location

- using a company for outside services that does not have an information security plan

- keeping the names of clients in a marketing database after they have opted out of it

- hiding any of the above from their boss or company executives

Quick Review Questions

1. What law requires mortgage lenders to create and carry out policies for safeguarding consumers' nonpublic information?

2. A settlement company has a data breach because of outdated systems. Is the lender liable?

Prohibited Acts

The Real Estate Settlement Procedures Act (RESPA) prohibits loan officers from certain practices. Some of these prohibited and unethical acts are discussed in this section.

In the 1930s, the FHA refused to insure mortgages for houses within neighborhoods deemed "Black." Red lines were drawn on maps to indicate areas of cities where the federal government would not insure mortgages. This racist practice, known as **redlining**, is now illegal. Lenders may not use such maps to refuse to insure or provide mortgages within minority neighborhoods or to make it harder or more expensive to buy or sell property in a minority neighborhood.

It is also illegal to give or receive anything of value as payment for referring settlement business. The thing of value is often called a **kickback**. Kickbacks are illegal partly because their cost may be passed on to other participants in the transaction without their knowledge. Examples of kickbacks include the following:

- An appraiser charges a seller $500 for a home appraisal but keeps only $400 as the regular fee and "kicks back" the other $100 to pay the loan officer or lender for giving him the job.

- A title company charges $1,000 for title insurance, keeping $750 as their regular fee and kicking back the other $250 to pay the loan officer or lender for using their company.

In both of the examples given, the buyer and/or seller are charged more than they should be, and the difference is given illegally to the loan officer or lender as a kickback, or unearned fee. Anyone convicted of giving or receiving kickbacks will face fines and imprisonment. Under RESPA, it is also illegal for a lender to

- charge money, other than credit report cost, to generate a good faith estimate;

- charge money to prepare any document required by federal law;

- require more money to be put into an escrow account than needed;

- leave known settlement charges out of a good faith estimate; and/or

- hide important information about a loan from a buyer.

As noted in previous chapters, in order to verify a borrower's identity, employment, income, and assets a loan officer needs a certain amount of personal information from a borrower as part of the loan application. After that information is obtained, a loan officer may put that information into a software package and discuss it with the lender's underwriters when deciding whether to approve a loan. But loan officers should not ask for more personal information than absolutely required, and they should never ask for irrelevant details (e.g., the birth dates of a buyer's children).

Quick Review Questions

3. An illegal gift given or received as payment for referring settlement business is called what?

4. May a lender charge any money to generate a good faith estimate?

Fairness in Lending

The Equal Credit Opportunity Act (ECOA) and the Fair Housing Act require lenders to treat all applicants with the same level of fairness. It is illegal to discriminate against applicants on the basis of the following attributes:

- race or color

- national origin

- age

- sex

- marital status

- family status

- religion

- source of income

- disability

- applicants exercising their rights under the Consumer Credit Protection Act

- whether the applicants are buying or renting a property

Many loan officers and lenders develop a network of **referrals**, or people/companies who will recommend the loan officer/lender to prospective borrowers and will receive a fee if the borrower uses those recommendations. Referrals, and their fees, are legal if borrowers gets written notification of referral arrangements between companies they are working with and if they are told in writing that they do not have to use any of the companies in the referral relationship if they prefer someone else.

9. Ethics

121

Coercion is an illegal practice whereby a borrower is forced to use referrals under duress. Coercion could include threatening the borrower with extra fees, paperwork, or other hassles to get the loan, or denying the loan altogether unless referred people/companies are used. Borrowers cannot be forced to use the referrals they receive.

In most cases, property appraisers are unbiased in their assessment of what a property is worth; however, there are times when the appraiser may develop a conflict of interest (e.g., if the appraiser is personal friends with the buyer or seller). Any conflict of interest by an appraiser should be discussed with the buyer, seller, and lender to uphold the fairness of all loan transactions.

Quick Review Questions

5. When are referrals, and their fees, legal?

6. An unscrupulous lender tells borrowers they will be charged an extra fee if they use a home inspector of their choice. What term describes this illegal practice?

Predatory Lending and Steering

Steering is a discriminatory and illegal practice. One type of steering is the discrimination practiced by real estate agents who steer, or encourage, buyers who are White to only buy houses in predominantly White neighborhoods and buyers of color to only buy houses in predominantly non-White neighborhoods. Another illegal steering practice is discriminating against borrowers, especially borrowers of color, by encouraging or forcing them to accept predatory loans. **Predatory loans** are riskier and more expensive than the buyer would typically require

> **Helpful Hint:**
>
> Review Chapter 5 for more on the suitability of products and programs.

because either the house is in a mostly minority neighborhood, or because the lender and loan officer would make more money on such loans.

In recent years, steering has been reduced by fair lending rules; loan officers can no longer make extra money for selling riskier home loans. In addition, the rule that lenders must consider the suitability of a loan for a specific borrower reduces temptations to give borrowers higher-risk loans than they can actually handle.

Loan officers should not focus on a borrower's race or color; rather, they should concentrate only on what a borrower is looking for and what that borrower can afford.

Quick Review Questions

7. A loan officer encourages a borrower who is Latino to take on a risky loan because the loan officer will make a higher commission. What term describes this illegal practice?

8. Loans that are risker and more expensive than a borrower needs to take on are called what?

Fraud Detection

Types of Fraud

Some borrowers may try to commit fraud by lying to a lender about aspects of their current financial situation. The following are types of borrower fraud:

- Asset fraud is claiming more, or more valuable, assets than actually owned—or even borrowing someone else's assets to get the loan and then giving them back afterward.

- Occupancy fraud is claiming a property will be a borrower's primary residence when it is actually an investment property or someone else's primary residence. Trying to reach the income needed to buy an investment property by including the property's anticipated rental income as income the borrower already receives is also fraudulent.

- Income fraud is claiming a higher income than a borrower really has (e.g., to get the mortgage); claiming a lower income than a borrower really has (e.g., to receive incentives for lower-income buyers); or committing identity theft.

- Employment fraud is claiming a job, a higher-level job title, or a longer period of employment than a borrower actually has; claiming a nonexistent side business, hiding an existing side business, or hiding a status as an independent contractor and claiming to be an employee instead (or vice-versa).

- Liability **fraud** is not mentioning existing debts, or applying for multiple mortgages at the same time for the same property.

Quick Review Questions

9. A borrower claims to have an investment account worth $100,000 on her mortgage application, but the account only contains $10,000. What type of fraud might this borrower be committing?

10. A borrower claims to have been a full-time employee for three years at a company, but the company says the borrower is only a part-time employee. What type of fraud might the borrower be committing?

Red Flags and Suspicious Activity

Federal law requires that lenders create a written program they will follow to minimize the chances of their customers' identities being stolen. That program must follow the FTC Red Flags Rule by identifying what the institution considers its **red flags**—suspicious things the institution notices that may indicate identity theft.

Typically, red flags consider ways that identity theft could happen when opening a new account or accessing a current account. Loan officers who notice a red flag must address it as quickly as possible in accordance with their lender's program. This may include contacting the customer or notifying law enforcement. While *evaluating* a borrower's application, examples of red flags include

- suspicious identifying information;

- fake-looking documentation;

- incorrect or fraudulent information provided by a borrower;

- blank spaces on the application that are usually filled in;

- different handwriting in various places, including numbers that look changed; or

- handwritten W-2 forms.

While *verifying* a borrower's application, red flags could include

- information from an employer that does not match the application;

- an employer whose address is only a post office box;

- the same phone numbers for the employer and the borrower;

- assets that seem more expensive than can be afforded on stated income;

- debt not mentioned on the application;

- an immediate or unexpected change of address;

- a fraud alert, or a consumer report that the borrower's credit has been frozen;

- verifications completed and sent on a weekend or national holiday;

- source of earnest money that is undetectable; and/or

- delinquent taxes.

A borrower can create red flags by suddenly having different banking activity, including

- big changes in financial habits, including multiple new accounts;

- an account inactive for a long time that is suddenly being used again;

- the unusual use of a current account; and/or

- a new credit account being used in a way that usually indicates fraud.

A borrower may create red flags by participating in unusual transactions that could trigger a Suspicious Activity Report (SAR) from the lender to the federal government, such as

- bringing in, or asking for, $5,000 or more in cash, especially if the amount is just less than $10,000;

- a transaction with no apparent business purpose; or

9. Ethics

- something the borrower has not done in the past.

- After closing, other red flags might include

- a borrower being unable to answer challenge questions to access the borrower's account,

- a customer not making the first payment or making the first but none after that,

- a customer notifying the lender of unauthorized transactions, and/or

- a customer or law enforcement confirming that the customer's identity has been stolen.

Some red flags do not involve identity theft but may be related to a property's sales contract, especially if the seller seems to be hiding information from the borrower that is commonly disclosed in the mortgage process or that suddenly appears on the contract at or near closing. Loan officers should be particularly suspicious of the following:

- sellers who claim they know nothing of a property's current condition or past history

- "kick-out" clauses that allow a seller to take a higher offer even after final signatures

- appraisal values that are markedly higher or lower than expected

- unusual contingencies in the contract, inserted by either side

- interest rates or extra fees that are different than what the borrower was previously told

- an earnest money check from a buyer that is not written on the buyer's account

Quick Review Questions

11. What does a red flag typically indicate?

12. Why should a borrower avoid opening a new account during the mortgage application process?

Advertising

Misleading Advertising

It is illegal for advertisements to include information that can be considered misleading. All advertising by a lender must undergo **due diligence**—careful review for possible mistaken impressions—before it is published.

One illegal practice, called **bait and switch**, is when an offer that sounds too good to be true is published as "bait" to attract customers. Examples might be a very low interest rate or a mortgage "with no extra fees." But when customers take the bait and apply for a mortgage, they are told that, unfortunately, they do not qualify for the bait offer in some way. All the lender can offer is a deal, "switched" from the bait offer, whose interest rate or fee structure is more expensive than the bait.

> **Helpful Hint:**
>
> Chapter 2 discusses the advertising of mortgage credit products. Much of the information that must be accurate, as listed there, must also be accurate in advertising all other lender products.

Anything considered unfair, deceptive, or abusive in selling mortgages or related products can result in fines to a lender under the Dodd-Frank Act as well as disciplinary measures for both the lender and the mortgage officer involved.

Table 9.1. Understanding Unfair, Deceptive, and Abusive Advertising Tactics		
Description	**Definition**	**Examples**
Unfair	<ul><li>causes substantial injury to a buyer</li><li>is not reasonably avoidable</li><li>is not balanced out by benefits in other parts of the mortgage process</li></ul>	<ul><li>a higher interest rate on the closing disclosure than on the good faith estimate (without telling the borrower)</li><li>language in the mortgage package that charges a late fee in scenarios that the borrower cannot reasonably avoid</li></ul>
Deceptive	<ul><li>misleads or is likely to mislead a borrower</li><li>allows for the borrower to reasonably interpret it in a way that is different from what the lender meant</li><li>because of being misleading, may unnecessarily cost a borrower money</li></ul>	<ul><li>bait-and-switch advertising</li><li>including an important note in small print at the bottom of a page that is different from the large print at the top of the page</li></ul>
Abusive	<ul><li>makes it hard for a borrower to understand the mortgage</li><li>takes unreasonable advantage of a borrower who is not experienced with mortgages</li><li>causes a problem because the borrower trusted a loan officer to look out for him and the loan officer did not</li></ul>	<ul><li>using words in a contract that a borrower whose native language is not English might not fully understand</li><li>a borrower being assessed an extra fee because of an uncorrected mistake by a loan officer</li></ul>

Quick Review Questions

13. What term describes carefully reviewing advertising for possible mistaken impressions before it is published?

14. An advertising tactic that misleads a borrower may be what?

Lawful Advertising

By law, every item of information in a commercial communication must be accurate, even those mentioned only by implication or indirect means. It is a violation to materially misrepresent any term of any mortgage-related product. Loan officers must never hide or misrepresent any aspect of their mortgage process or of the products they sell.

Lenders can—and should—mention "unpleasant" possibilities related to their products; borrowers should know that such things can happen and be able to prepare themselves. For example, borrowers should know that

- interest rates and monthly payments may go up with an adjustable-rate mortgage (ARM);

- any product purchased, even financial counseling, costs money;

- prepaying a mortgage may incur a penalty; and

- late fees are assessed if the mortgage is not paid on time each month.

The federal **Mortgage Acts and Practices-Advertising (MAP) Rule**, or **Regulation N**, governs commercial communication. **Commercial communication** includes

- materials written on paper,

- radio ads,

- television infomercials,

- telemarketing scripts,

- websites,

- posters,

- videos,

- movies,

- billboards,

- slides from presentation software, and

- oral statements.

As long as Regulation N is followed, all of these methods can be used in lawful advertising to the general public, especially the material below on "truth in marketing and advertising."

Helpful Hint:

All materials used in advertising of any type must be kept for two years after they are no longer used.

As discussed in Chapter 2, it is okay to use publicly available information to create a list of names and street addresses for marketing purposes, but the list cannot be created from personally identifiable financial information. Once a year, a lender must provide a written copy of its privacy policy to each customer, including information on how to opt out of the lender's marketing outreach.

Besides marketing to the general public, lenders may send out solicitations, including telemarketing calls, to specific consumers who already have an **established business**

relationship with the lender. Solicitations, including telemarketing, can be used to contact current customers as well as:

- those who owe the lender money

- those whose mortgages have been sold by the lender to someone else;

- those who inquire for information, or who submit a loan application (but only for three months after the date of the application); and

- those who give the lender written permission to contact them.

<table>
<tr><td>

If a consumer requests that a telemarketer not call again, the lender must stop calling. See Chapter 2 for more rules on telemarketing.

</td><td>

Did You Know?

Solicitations may only be sent out for eighteen months after the consumer's last purchase or last payment.

</td></tr>
</table>

Ethical Behavior Related to Loan Origination Activities

All requirements discussed in previous chapters about the paperwork needed for a loan, from both the lender and the borrower, as well as the rules for how a lender treats its borrowers, can be encompassed within the term *compliance*. **Compliance** means following the federal and state laws and regulations of the mortgage industry.

Loan officers who try their best to use common sense in approving loans, keep the paperwork required by federal and state law as organized as possible for each borrower and loan, treat all applicants as cordially as possible without discrimination, and keep all applicants' private information private, will generally be "in compliance" with the law. Nearly all problems with mortgage loans are caused by forgetting one of these four major concepts in some way.

Occasionally, a loan officer discovers material information that should be conveyed to the lender even if the information jeopardizes a loan. In those cases, keeping that information from the lender always causes more problems than it is worth. It is always better to delay or turn down a loan than to approve a loan that should not be approved and then deal with financial issues, headaches and lawsuits later on. In cases where such material information comes from an employer's candid opinion of a borrower, the information should be given to the lender but otherwise kept as private as possible, both for courtesy and for legal reasons.

A lender's loan estimate must provide a good faith estimate of the fees that will be paid by a borrower to get a mortgage, including zero tolerance fees, ten percent tolerance, and good faith tolerances. In some cases, a lender may change the closing costs or fees without referring to the tolerances. See Chapter 5 for details.

As mentioned earlier in this chapter, many loan officers and lenders develop a network of referrals. Referrals and their fees are legal under certain circumstances. A borrower cannot be forced to use the referrals given; however, as also mentioned earlier, referral fees are illegal if given to—or taken from—a settlement company. **Splitting**—dividing fees with a settlement company—is only allowed if payment is made just for the actual services performed.

If money goes missing or is misused after a loan settlement (e.g., when a settlement company steals the money it is given instead of paying off a previous home loan or paying for title insurance as agreed), it can trigger intervention by a state insurance administration, suspension of licenses for everyone involved, the forced closing of a settlement company, and criminal charges.

Quick Review Questions

17. What term describes following the federal and state laws and regulations of the mortgage industry?

18. When is splitting allowed?

Borrower and Consumer Relationships

Loan officers should always acknowledge a customer's complaints and feelings, even if they seem unreasonable. It is best practice to explain how a situation will be addressed and why any steps are taken. The Consumer Financial Protection Bureau (CFPB) has identified three common borrower complaints about mortgage lenders and the steps that loan officers should take:

1. If a borrower falls behind on payments, the loan officer must

    - be as clear as possible about late fees and possible foreclosure,

    - preserve all documentation regarding possible foreclosure, and

    - ensure that a borrower submits related documentation only one time.

2. When a loan is transferred to a new servicer, the loan officer should
    - notify the borrower of the transfer (if possible),

    - know how and where the borrower should make payments after the transfer; and

    - make the transfer process as smooth as possible.

3. In all aspects of the mortgage process, loan officers should err on the side of too much communication with borrowers rather than too little since borrowers have reported poor overall communication concerning the many aspects involved in a mortgage.

Loan officers and lenders are considered to have a fiduciary relationship with consumers. In a **fiduciary relationship**, loan officers and lenders are legally and ethically bound to act in a consumer's best interest at all times, even if a consumer never becomes one of their customers.

> **Helpful Hint:**
>
> Many of the recommendations made in previous chapters relate to the fiduciary relationship; exam questions about this relationship often come down to treating others as you would want to be treated.

The following duties can be part of a fiduciary relationship between lenders and borrowers:

- handling a customer's personal information with great care

- caring about a borrower's situation enough to find out all information needed for a loan

- keeping borrowers' best interests at heart, protecting them from loans they probably cannot afford and encouraging loans they can afford

- avoiding conflicts of interest that could benefit the lender or an affiliate of the lender more than they benefit the borrower

- always acting within the requirements of law

- communicating clearly at all times to prevent misunderstanding and later problems, especially when discussing specific money-related topics like affordability and how much the closing costs and monthly payments will be

Loan officers also have a fiduciary relationship to the lenders employing them and should treat the lenders as fairly as they treat consumers. Loan officers therefore have a duty to protect their lenders from lending money to a borrower who will be unlikely to pay back the loan:

- As mentioned above, whenever loan officers find that borrowers may be hiding the true state of their finances, they are bound to inform the lender and the lender's underwriter of the situation.

- It is always better to delay or turn down a loan application than to approve a loan that should not be approved and then deal with the resulting fallout later.

As discussed in previous chapters, sometimes borrowers try to hide aspects of how much money they have and where that money is coming from. Though a loan officer tries to help borrowers as much as possible, the help cannot extend to hiding a borrower's potential financial issues from a lender. Any questions regarding down payment, job, income, sourcing deposits, multiple mortgage applications from other lenders, or anything else that looks suspicious must be passed on to the loan officer's supervisor.

In some cases, third parties other than the lender and borrower try to get involved in a loan transaction through identity theft or by hacking into a lender's or borrower's email or bank accounts. This is especially true as a loan nears closing and large amounts of money must be wired from a borrower to a lender.

A loan officer should ensure **cybersecurity** during wiring by double-checking closing and wiring instructions from both the actual borrower and actual lender to ensure that money ends up where it should and not with a bad actor. Any questions about this must be resolved before the wiring takes place. Ensuring that the borrower's bank has correct instructions (through direct contact with the bank), and that the borrower's bank is actually the borrower's bank will help prevent trouble.

A **code of ethics** lays out ethical expectations and penalties for subverting them. The **National Association of Mortgage Brokers (NAMB)** has a code of ethics for loan officers that encourages

- honesty and integrity,

- professional conduct,

- honesty in advertising,

- confidentiality,

- compliance with the law, and

- the disclosure of financial interests.

Quick Review Questions

19. Loan officers and lenders must act in a consumer's best interest at all times. What term describes this relationship?

20. Where can a loan officer find ethical guidelines for business practice?

Answer Key

1. The Gramm-Leach-Bliley Act (GLBA) requires mortgage lenders to create and carry out policies for safeguarding consumers' nonpublic information.

2. Since lenders must ensure that companies used for outside services have their own information security programs, the lender might be liable.

3. A kickback is anything of value that is given or received as payment for referring settlement business. Kickbacks are illegal.

4. A lender may only charge the cost of the credit report to generate a good faith estimate.

5. Referrals and their fees are legal if borrowers get written notification of referral arrangements between companies they are working with and if borrowers are told in writing that they do not have to use any of the companies in the referral relationship.

6. The term *coercion* describes the example of telling borrowers that they will be charged an extra fee if they choose to use a home inspector of their choice.

7. The term *steering* describes the example of a loan officer encouraging a borrower who is Latino to take on a risky loan because the loan officer will make a higher commission. Steering is illegal.

8. Predatory loans are unnecessarily risky and more expensive than the borrower needs.

9. This borrower may be committing asset fraud, which involves claiming more or more valuable assets than the borrower actually owns.

10. Employment fraud is when a borrower claims a job, higher-level job title, or longer period of employment than the borrower actually has.

11. Red flags typically indicate identity theft; however, they can also be related to a property's sales contract.

12. When a borrower opens a new account during the application process, it may be interpreted as a red flag.

13. The term *due diligence* describes conducting a careful review of advertisements for possible mistaken impressions before they are published.

14. An advertising tactic that misleads a borrower may be deceptive.

15. All materials used in advertising must be kept for two years after they are no longer used.

16. If a consumer requests that a telemarketer stop calling, the telemarketer working on behalf of the lender must stop calling.

17. The term *compliance* describes following the federal and state laws and regulations of the mortgage industry.

18. Splitting—dividing fees with a settlement company—is only allowed if payment is made just for the actual services performed.

19. The term *fiduciary relationship* describes loan officers and lenders acting in a consumer's best interest at all times.

20. The National Association of Mortgage Brokers (NAMB) offers a code of ethics for mortgage brokers that encourages honesty, compliance, and other ethical behavior.

10 Uniform State Content

SAFE Act and CSBS/AARMR Model State Law

State Mortgage Regulatory Agencies

The Secure and Fair Enforcement for Mortgage Licensing Act of 2008 (**SAFE Act**) created a **Nationwide Multistate Licensing System and Registry (NMLS)** for residential mortgage loan officers. The NMLS and its Registry is maintained by the Conference of State Bank Supervisors (CSBS) and the American Association of Residential Mortgage Regulators (AARMR).

The **Conference of State Bank Supervisors (CSBS)** works with those who regulate banks in each state to make state regulation and supervision of each bank easier to do for both regulators and banks.

The **American Association of Residential Mortgage Regulators (AARMR)** works with those who regulate mortgage companies in each state to make state regulation and supervision of each mortgage company easier for both regulators and mortgage companies.

The SAFE Act requires that MLOs who work for covered financial institutions be federally registered with their own **unique identifier** numbers that stay the same—even if an MLO relocates to another state. MLOs not working for covered financial institutions must have a state license instead, along with their own unique identifier at the state level. **Covered financial institutions** include

- national banks,
- member banks,
- insured state nonmember banks,
- savings associations,
- Farm Credit System institutions, and
- federally insured credit unions.

NMLS keeps all regulation/registration information for both levels of MLOs in the same online location. This is useful for MLOs because NMLS keeps track of what is needed in each state, and one state's licensing requirements are often different than those of neighboring states. NMLS also lets borrowers check that their MLO is licensed and registered in the state where they are buying property; borrowers can also read through their MLO's employment history as a check against possible fraud.

Regulation H was created by the CFPB to implement the SAFE Act and requires each state to create its own **mortgage regulatory agency** to monitor MLOs and their performance. The CSBS and AARMR worked together to create a **model state law** to help state licensing authorities maintain their standards. If a state mortgage regulatory agency does not meet the minimum standards of Regulation H, the CFPB could take over, create its own system for overseeing MLOs, and require the state to use it. As of 2023, all states have their own agencies that meet the minimum requirements.

Because each state governs its own MLOs, it is **critical** that aspiring MLOs check their state's specific requirements online as part of their exam preparation. This information may be discussed during the twenty-hour exam course (mentioned below); however, personally reading through a state's information is the best way to ensure that anything that might come up on the exam will not be missed.

Quick Review Questions

1. What federal act created the NMLS?

2. Who must have a unique identifier number?

Regulatory Authority

The SAFE Act gives each state's licensing agency certain **regulatory powers**, including the power to investigate complaints or violations of the law. A state agency may do the following in an investigation:

- ask for an MLO's (or the employer's) books and other records

- interview any employee of a licensed company

It is illegal for MLOs or their employers to hide or destroy any information related to a state agency's investigation.

Regulation H allows the CFPB to investigate loan originators in detail at the state level in states where the CFPB set up the state's licensing system; however, since all states have their own regulating agencies, the CFPB generally no longer has any reason to do this.

The **CFPB's loan originator rule** requires MLOs to be registered and licensed. It also requires them to put both their own NMLS identification number (NMLS ID) and their employer's NMLS ID on all loan documents. In addition, the Rule prevents MLOs from being paid based purely on the terms of a single transaction, including being paid more than once for the same transaction. MLOs may not "steer" borrowers to use certain companies that might pay the lender or MLO a kickback (see Chapter 9 for more on steering). MLOs may be paid in the following ways:

- hourly wage

- through a fixed fee for each loan made

- by the number and amount of loans created

- by the quality of loans (based on correct paperwork and on their regular repayments made over time)

- by the number of new loan customers brought in

MLOs may also receive bonuses and retirement benefits if they are based on their employer's overall profits.

Quick Review Questions

3. May an MLO hide or destroy information related to a state agency's investigation?

4. What rule requires MLOs to be licensed, registered, and use their NMLS ID number on all documents?

License Law and Regulation

Licensee Qualifications and Application Process

To obtain an MLO license, a candidate must be at least eighteen years of age and must take at least twenty hours of education approved by NMLS:

- three hours on federal law

- three hours on ethics training

- two hours on lending for nontraditional mortgages

- one elective hour

Aspiring MLOs must achieve a score of at least 75 precent on the NMLS exam. Some states have an extra component in their exams that must also be passed. Those who fail the exam may take it again after thirty days. A second fail requires another thirty-day wait before taking the exam a third time. A third fail requires a six-month wait before trying again.

After passing the exam, prospective MLOs use NMLS to apply for their license online and undergo a **background check** to determine their general fitness to practice. This background check includes

- the submission of fingerprints,

- a credit report and criminal record review; and

- the submission of personal and employment histories.

Those who have been convicted or pled guilty to a felony in the last seven years are **denied** a license. Those who have ever been convicted of or pled guilty to a financial felony such as fraud, bribery, forgery, dishonesty, breach of trust or money laundering are **permanently denied** a license. Those who have ever had their MLO license revoked are reevaluated individually.

Quick Review Questions

5. What is the passing score for the NMLS exam?

6. Who must undergo a background check?

License Maintenance

An MLO license expires at the end of each calendar year. MLOs must receive at least eight hours of continuing education annually in order to keep their license and stay current with changes in laws or in practice from year to year. The eight hours of continuing education includes three hours on federal law, two hours on ethics, and one hour on lending for nontraditional mortgages. The eight hours must come from a different course every year.

> **Did You Know?**
>
> MLOs who become teachers of continuing education only have to teach four hours a year to get eight hours of credit.

Anyone who leaves the loan business for at least five years must retake the NMLS exam but is generally not required to take the twenty-hour course again. Rules on this may vary between states. MLOs and underwriters must maintain active licenses, but clerical staff, government employees, and employees of nonprofit organizations generally do not need a license to do their jobs.

Quick Review Questions

7. How many hours of continuing education are required for MLOs to retain their licenses?

8. Why is continuing education required for MLOs?

NMLS Requirements

Because MLOs are regulated at both the state and federal levels, to comply with federal regulations every MLO with a state license must also register with NMLS. Licensing is detailed on the NMLS website. The homepage links to an Individual Form that shows all information that must be submitted to NMLS, including the following:

- proof of identity
- residential history
- employment history
- disclosures of any criminal or legal history
- a background check
- a set of fingerprints
- credit report
- the company sponsor of the application
- an attestation that the information submitted is all correct

All records with NMLS must be kept up to date, reflecting changes in residence, employment, credit status, and so on. The NMLS online account, once established, is the place to enter any new information.

9. An MLO already has a state license. Must the MLO also register with the NMLS?

Compliance

Most states require lenders to keep records of transactions, and of advertising used, for between two and seven years. State rules on record-keeping should always be checked to ensure compliance with state law. State agencies investigating a complaint have the authority to examine licensee books and records as they see fit and interview any employee of a licensed company in the process:

- These records should be submitted to state regulators as quickly as reasonably possible.

- Sometimes consumers submit their own copies of the records in question, which can speed the process of investigation and resolution.

The Model State Law requires that any person originating a residential mortgage loan show their unique identifier clearly on all application forms and advertisements. That extends to business cards, websites, and even email signatures.

> **Did You Know?**
>
> Arkansas and Nevada require lenders to keep mortgage records indefinitely.

MLOs or their employers who fail to follow state rules or break state law may be fined up to $25,000 per incident. They might also have their license suspended, revoked, or renewal denied.

Prohibited acts by MLOs generally include any kind of dishonesty or intent to deceive. Specific examples include

- hiding better loan options from a borrower in order to get paid more,

- stealing money meant for a borrower or lender,

- requiring arbitration to settle disputes (when a consumer could file a lawsuit instead), and

- approving loans that can create negative amortization.

In other words, if an action seems like something an MLO's conscience is telling her not to do, or that looks like it would be bad for a borrower, the MLO should not do it!

Quick Review Questions

10. For how long do most states require lenders to keep records of transactions?

11. If an MLO breaks state law, how much could a potential fine be?

Answer Key

1. The Secure and Fair Enforcement for Mortgage Licensing Act of 2008 (SAFE Act) created the Nationwide Multistate Licensing System and Registry (NMLS).

2. Mortgage Loan Originators (MLOs) who work for covered financial institutions must be federally registered with their own unique identifier numbers.

3. No; it is illegal for a mortgage loan originator (MLO) to hide or destroy information related to a state agency's investigation.

4. The Consumer Financial Protection Bureau's (CFPB) Loan Originator Rule requires Mortgage Loan Originators (MLOs) to be licensed, registered, and use their Nationwide Multistate Licensing System (NMLS) identification number on all documents.

5. Candidates must score at least 75 percent to pass the Nationwide Multistate Licensing System (NMLS) exam.

6. All prospective Mortgage Loan Originators (MLOs) must undergo a background check.

7. Mortgage loan originators (MLOs) must have at least eight hours a year of continuing education to maintain their licenses.

8. Continuing education helps mortgage loan originators (MLOs) stay current with changes in laws or in practice from year to year.

9. Yes; every mortgage loan originator (MLO) with a state license must also register with the Nationwide Multistate Licensing System (NMLS).

10. Most states require lenders to keep records of transactions for between two and seven years.

11. A mortgage loan originator (MLO) who breaks state law may be fined up to $25,000 per incident.

Practice Test #1

1. Which of the following is considered an entitlement when discussing mortgage loans?

   A) a government program that gives money to everyone
   B) a parent's contribution to a borrower's down payment
   C) the borrower's down payment for an FHA loan
   D) the part of a home loan paid by the VA in case of foreclosure

2. John is an MLO who receives $100 from a title company each time he refers a borrower to that title company. What is this illegal practice known as?
   A) coercing
   B) kickbacking
   C) redlining
   D) steering

3. The USA Patriot Act is MOST concerned with which of the following?
   A) identity theft
   B) lending discrimination
   C) private mortgage insurance
   D) written customer identification

4. Which of these tasks can be performed by an unlicensed MLO?
   A) deciding to underwrite a loan
   B) negotiating a loan's interest rate
   C) providing an official loan offer
   D) telling a borrower his loan application is incomplete

5. Which federal law directly governs an MLO's advertising?
   A) Regulation N
   B) the Fair Housing Act
   C) the Gramm-Leach-Bliley Act
   D) the Dodd-Frank Act

6. According to RESPA, as part of an official loan application, a borrower must submit which of the following?
   A) family's full names
   B) current home address
   C) employer's address
   D) Social Security number

7. The index lending rate is currently 4.5%, but a lender's current mortgage rate is 6.5%. The 2% difference in rates is most commonly called the lender's
   A) cost.
   B) escrow.
   C) margin.
   D) profit.

8. As part of a background check before obtaining a license, an MLO must submit which of the following?
   A) a blood test
   B) a mental exam report
   C) a physical health report
   D) a set of fingerprints

9. The new Form 1103 asks whether a borrower has had which of the following?
   A) a marriage
   B) a bankruptcy
   C) gifts donated toward a down payment
   D) homeownership education classes

10. Regulation Z requires that, for a $250,000 loan, the points and fees can add up to NO MORE than how much?
   A) $1,000
   B) $2,500
   C) $7,500
   D) $20,000

11. A borrower says on his application that he owns part of a silver mine in Argentina. An MLO checking this claim discovers that the mine filed for bankruptcy and closed down three years ago. Which type of fraud is the borrower committing?
   A) occupancy
   B) liability
   C) income
   D) asset

12. Which of these has a zero tolerance fee, meaning it cannot increase after disclosure to the borrower?
   A) credit report
   B) home inspection
   C) appraisal
   D) title insurance

13. Kelly and Tiffany, both age 51, are concerned about how to afford a new roof for their house. Which of the following is the MOST helpful suggestion that an MLO could offer?
   A) a home equity line of credit
   B) an interest-only mortgage
   C) a recast
   D) a reverse mortgage

14. A 15% increase in a "10% tolerance" fee must be reported to a borrower within which time frame?
    A)   one day
    B)   three days
    C)   one week
    D)   one month

15. Once a consumer agrees to sign mortgage forms electronically, which of the following can take place?
    A)   He can change to sign them by paper whenever he wants.
    B)   She can orally agree to a form's information without signing anything.
    C)   He must sign them electronically from then on.
    D)   She must keep her computer system up-to-date from then on.

16. A borrower's annual property taxes are $2,000 and his homeowner insurance policy is $1,600 per year; therefore, how much escrow should he include in each of his monthly payments?
    A) $3,600
    B) $1,800
    C) $500
    D) $300

17. The Homeowners Protection Act is MOSTLY designed to protect homeowners from
    A)   racial discrimination
    B)   paying too much for PMI
    C)   identity theft
    D)   hidden fees at closing

18. Mark decides to use his $25,000 bonus from his employer to pay down his mortgage. He can ask his lender to recalculate the monthly payment after his bonus is applied to the loan principal without filing a new loan application. What is this process called?
    A)   reappraising the property
    B)   recasting the loan
    C)   refinancing the loan
    D)   reselling the loan

19. Which of these agencies is part of the Federal Reserve System?
    A)   HUD
    B)   Ginnie Mae
    C)   FHA
    D)   CFPB

20. In the twenty-hour course needed to become an MLO, what percentage of the course specifically covers ethics training?
    A)   10 percent
    B)   15 percent
    C)   25 percent
    D)   50 percent

21. The written mortgage statement sent to borrowers each month must include which of the following?
   A) address of the property
   B) amount of principal still owed
   C) contact information for a housing lawyer
   D) the number of payments remaining

22. A mortgage company's private map divides a city into six areas. The company provides mortgages in four areas, but not in the other two that it considers "high-crime" areas. What is this company illegally doing?
   A) coercing
   B) kick backing
   C) redlining
   D) steering

23. When a borrower receives an adverse action letter that indicates a low credit score, whom should he contact to try to improve the credit score?
   A) the realtor
   B) the developer
   C) the mortgage lender
   D) the credit report company

24. Which of these natural disasters is NOT commonly covered by hazard/homeowner insurance?
   A) earthquake
   B) fire
   C) flood
   D) tornado

25. To receive a qualified mortgage, a borrower with an annual income of $48,000 must NOT have a monthly debt amount greater than which of the following?
   A) $860
   B) $1,720
   C) $2,000
   D) $4,000

26. Which of the following requires a lender to safeguard nonpublic information about consumers?
   A) the Dodd-Frank Act
   B) the Equal Credit Opportunity Act
   C) the Gramm-Leach-Bliley Act
   D) the Secure and Fair Enforcement for Mortgage Licensing (SAFE) Act

27. Markell is buying her first home, with closing costs of $5,000 and a down payment of $10,000. The seller is willing to provide an "interested party contribution" to help Markell. In order to follow Freddie Mac rules, the seller can give Markell NO MORE THAN what amount?
   A) $2,000
   B) $15,000
   C) $10,000
   D) $5,000

28. Which of these costs should be reduced as a goal of RESPA?
    A) a borrower's closing costs
    B) a borrower's down payment
    C) a lender's mortgage processing
    D) a lender's underwriting

29. Which of the following can a lender legally charge a borrower?
    A) $50 to obtain a credit report
    B) $100 to create a Closing Disclosure
    C) $250 to generate a loan estimate
    D) $500 to add unneeded money to an escrow account

30. The "right of rescission" is a three-day period created to allow a borrower to legally do which of the following?
    A) apply for a second mortgage
    B) back out of a mortgage deal
    C) change mortgage lenders
    D) speed up the mortgage process

31. What is a conforming mortgage?
    A) one that allows negative amortization
    B) one that follows Freddie Mac and Fannie Mae rules
    C) one that has no closing costs
    D) one that requires prepayment penalties

32. Judy applies for a mortgage on September 3. The lender has until which day to officially approve or deny the application?
    A) September 6
    B) September 17
    C) October 3
    D) November 3

33. Which piece of information is commonly left off of a borrower's initial loan application?
    A) full name
    B) income level
    C) marital status
    D) Social Security number

34. A borrower of average income with a credit score of 700 who qualifies for an FHA loan only needs a down payment of which percentage?
    A) 3.5%
    B) 5%
    C) 7.5%
    D) 10%

35. What does an Adverse Action Letter explain?
    A)   why the borrower received a bad credit report
    B)   why the borrower doesn't have enough income
    C)   why the lender will not give money to a borrower
    D)   why the lender cannot find needed borrower information

36. How does a lender view an applicant's prior loans that are in repayment?
    A)   as a liability
    B)   as an asset
    C)   as income
    D)   as reserve funds

37. A borrower must prove where he has worked and lived for at LEAST how many years?
    A)   one year
    B)   two years
    C)   five years
    D)   ten years

38. Which of these consumers can legally get an unsolicited telemarketing call from a mortgage lender?
    A)   Diane, who submitted a loan application six months ago but never followed up
    B)   Felicia, who had her mortgage sold by the lender to someone else three years ago
    C)   John, who owes the lender $100,000
    D)   George, who said, "Never call here again!" during the lender's last telemarketing call

39. What is adjustable in an ARM?
    A)   down payment
    B)   interest rate
    C)   mortgage term
    D)   mortgage insurance premium

40. In order to maintain his license every year, an MLO must take how many hours of continuing education?
    A)   4
    B)   8
    C)   16
    D)   20

41. During which times is it ALWAYS legal for a telemarketer to call a customer?
    A)   anytime from 8 a.m. to 9 p.m. in the customer's time zone
    B)   during business hours in the caller's time zone
    C)   before 9 p.m. in the caller's time zone
    D)   at 10 p.m. in the customer's time zone

42. How much would a lender with a loan origination fee of ¾ point would charge for a $500,000 loan?
    A) $5,000
    B) $3,750
    C) $2,500
    D) $750

43. A borrower sues a lender for $20,000 for RESPA violations. If the lender is found to have violated RESPA, what is the MAXIMUM amount it would have to pay the borrower?
- A) $20,000
- B) $60,000
- C) $100,000
- D) $200,000

44. For a borrower buying a $250,000 property with a 10% down payment, the loan amount will be how much?
- A) $2,500,000
- B) $225,000
- C) $125,000
- D) $25,000

45. After a closing, which of these entities is in charge of making sure everyone involved gets their money in a timely fashion?
- A) local HUD office
- B) lender
- C) seller's realtor
- D) title company

46. If Melanie is scheduled to close on her new home on a Friday, her lender must provide her with the closing documents by which day?
- A) Thursday
- B) Wednesday
- C) Tuesday
- D) Monday

47. A Servicing Transfer Statement is sent to a borrower when the lender does which of the following?
- A) sells the mortgage to another lender
- B) pays the borrower's property tax from escrow
- C) provides a good faith estimate of closing costs
- D) accepts the first mortgage payment from the borrower

48. The CFPB loan originator rule requires MLOs to put which information on each loan document?
- A) work telephone
- B) Social Security
- C) NMLS ID
- D) closing cost

49. Which type of agent most commonly schedules the day and time of a closing and provides copies of all important documents to both buyer and seller?
- A) transfer agent
- B) settlement agent
- C) real estate advisor
- D) financial counselor

50. Which of these is MOST likely to be a red flag that a borrower may be having his identity stolen?
    A) The borrower has opened three new credit card accounts in the last sixty days.
    B) The borrower's application is missing one digit of his driver's license number.
    C) The borrower asks a bank teller to cash his $2,000 federal income tax refund check.
    D) The borrower receives $3,000 in his bank account, sourced from relatives helping with a down payment.

51. A 32-year-old woman applying for a mortgage tells her MLO that the job promotion and raise she has been promised will provide enough money to make the mortgage payments. Why might the MLO decide to reject the mortgage application?
    A) The woman has no children.
    B) The house is too small.
    C) The mortgage is unsuitable.
    D) The down payment is not large enough.

52. The Homeownership Counseling Disclosure lists counseling agencies approved by which of the following?
    A) Dodd-Frank Act
    B) Gramm-Leach-Bliley Act
    C) HUD
    D) SEC

53. Annette does not pass her MLO exam when she takes it for the first time on April 1. When is the EARLIEST day she can take the exam again?
    A) April 15
    B) May 1
    C) July 1
    D) October 1

54. Which of the following would be paid by a buyer at closing to reduce his mortgage interest rate from 4.75% to 4.5%?

    A) title insurance
    B) survey fee
    C) origination fee
    D) discount points

55. Which of the following describes the function of a mortgage broker?
    A) someone who works with one lender to benefit the borrower
    B) someone who maximizes lender profits
    C) someone who works with many lenders to benefit the borrower
    D) someone who minimizes lender profits

56. One purpose of closing is to remove which of the following from a property, including paying off the seller's mortgage and satisfying any liens for unpaid property taxes?
    A) easements
    B) encumbrances
    C) promissory notes
    D) reconveyances

57. What is the minimum age for an MLO to be allowed to receive her license?
    A) sixteen
    B) eighteen
    C) twenty-one
    D) twenty-five

58. Which of the following is considered an asset that must be verified by a lender?
    A) a $1,000 credit card balance
    B) a $10,000 savings account
    C) a $50,000 annual salary
    D) a $100,000 second mortgage

59. According to Section 9 of RESPA, a borrower can purchase title insurance from which of the following?
    A) any title company she wants
    B) only a title company recommended by the lender
    C) only a title company recommended by the seller
    D) only a title company in the same town as the property

60. Who is allowed to give Jocelyn a gift of $3,000 toward buying her first home?
    A) her realtor
    B) her new home builder
    C) her MLO
    D) her godmother

61. Which of the following specifies how much of a monthly mortgage payment will be held by the lender to pay property taxes and homeowner insurance?
    A) escrow analysis statement
    B) note disclosure
    C) promissory note
    D) power of attorney

62. A lender can be fined under the Dodd-Frank Act for practices that are considered
    A) abusive.
    B) expensive.
    C) ordinary.
    D) commonplace.

63. A borrower's escrow account is usually set up to allow the lender to submit the borrower's
    A) down payment.
    B) home appraisal cost.
    C) property taxes.
    D) property repair costs.

64. Which of the following is MOST likely a "change in circumstance" that could require a delay in closing on the property?
    A) A home appraisal is $100,000 less than expected.
    B) A lower interest rate is locked in.
    C) The borrower needs an extra week to close.
    D) Part of the down payment will come from another source.

65. If an MLO discovers a discrepancy between a borrower's statement of her income and her supervisor's statement of her income, the borrower may be trying to commit which type of fraud?
    A) occupancy
    B) liability
    C) income
    D) asset

66. As part of a loan application, a borrower may be asked about which of the following?
    A) age
    B) marital status
    C) race
    D) religion

67. Thomas applied for a mortgage on June 2, so the lender must officially approve or deny the application by which date?
    A) June 9
    B) June 16
    C) July 1
    D) August 2

68. Which of the following numbers can legally be used as a basis for deciding how much an MLO is paid in a month?
    A) the number of times the MLO is paid for the same work
    B) the number of transactions the MLO steers to another company
    C) the number of loan applications the MLO rejects
    D) the number of loans the MLO creates

69. Which of these bank deposits would be considered "seasoned"?
    A) a $1,000 paycheck deposited yesterday
    B) a $500 gift deposited two days ago
    C) a $250 credit card refund deposited two weeks ago
    D) a $900 tax refund deposited two months ago

70. Sam is buying a house at a low interest rate and wants his son's family to take over his mortgage at the same interest rate if Sam has not paid the mortgage off by the time of his death. To do this, both Sam and the lender must agree to which of the following?
   A) a promissory note
   B) a deed of reconveyance
   C) an assumption clause
   D) a security instrument

71. Stephanie's statements to her MLO after completing her loan application indicate that she is unlikely to be able to pay back a home mortgage. As part of his fiduciary relationship with his lender, Stephanie's MLO should do which of the following?
   A) approve her loan immediately
   B) keep quiet and assume the lender's underwriter will notice the problems
   C) inform the lender of her statements
   D) deny her loan immediately

72. A borrower requesting a $250,000 loan for a $300,000 property will have an LTV ratio of about how much?
   A) 16.7%
   B) 20.0%
   C) 50.0%
   D) 83.3%

73. Which of the following terms is usually found in a qualified mortgage?
   A) 40-year length
   B) points and fees equal to 10% of the loan
   C) equal monthly payments
   D) balloon payment after 10 years

74. Which important documents do TransUnion and Equifax provide to lenders and consumers?
   A) title insurance
   B) mortgage money
   C) credit reports
   D) property appraisals

75. The URAR form is most often filled out by which of the following?
   A) an appraiser
   B) a borrower
   C) a lender
   D) a realtor

76. John is a first-time homeowner who knows little about the process of obtaining a loan. Which of the lender's responsibilities would require her to explain these concepts to John?
   A) fiduciary
   B) hostile
   C) legal
   D) personal

77. A borrower's income is commonly verified by checking which of the following?
   A)   current mortgage status
   B)   current retirement accounts
   C)   recent stock trades
   D)   recent tax returns

78. Which of the following is considered a "dwelling" under the Home Mortgage Disclosure Act?
   A)   commercial warehouse
   B)   condominium
   C)   mobile home
   D)   motel

79. Steve's monthly debt is $1 500. In order to receive a qualified mortgage his annual income must be AT LEAST which of the following?
   A) $4000
   B) $8000
   C) $42000
   D) $49000

80. The FTC's Red Flags Rule is designed to protect consumers from which of the following?
   A)   fraudulent appraisals
   B)   identity theft
   C)   racial discrimination
   D)   hidden closing costs

81. Which type of insurance is usually purchased by a lender and then charged to a borrower?
   A)   flood
   B)   force-placed
   C)   life
   D)   private mortgage

82. Which person is MOST likely to benefit from a reverse mortgage?
   A)   Barbara, age 57, who wants smaller monthly payments
   B)   Dirk, age 61, who wants to move to a smaller house
   C)   Henry, age 69, who still works 40 hours a week in construction
   D)   Lila, age 81, who has been very sick for several years

83. Which of these people would be denied an MLO license for at least seven years beginning from the date of the incident?

   A)   Xavier, who got a parking ticket last year but paid the fine
   B)   Sarah, who was convicted two years ago of felony drug possession
   C)   Larry, who was found "not guilty" four years ago for impaired driving
   D)   Hope, who pled guilty six years ago to misdemeanor "driving without a license"

84. A borrower who closes her loan on August 19 will have her first monthly payment due on which date?
    A) September 1
    B) September 19
    C) October 1
    D) October 19

85. After a Suspicious Activity Report has been filed regarding a consumer's financial transactions, the consumer
    A) can be asked about it by his bank.
    B) cannot have another report filed about him.
    C) is not told about it.
    D) is warned the report has been filed.

86. How much is the annual PMI cost for a $400 000 mortgage?
    A) $1,600
    B) $2,400
    C) $3,200
    D) $4,000

87. Which of these people would be permanently denied an MLO license?
    A) William, convicted six months ago of speeding
    B) Sophia, convicted three years ago of marijuana possession
    C) Jeremy, who pled guilty five years ago to felony impaired driving
    D) Catherine, who pled guilty ten years ago to felony bribery

88. Which of these closing costs is typically paid entirely by the seller?
    A) pre-paid costs
    B) credit report fee
    C) HOA fees
    D) realtors' commissions

89. After ten years of payments, which of these mortgages will have the HIGHEST interest rate?
    A) an ARM starting at 3%, with a 2% increase after one year
    B) an ARM starting at 4%, with a 3% increase after three years
    C) an ARM starting at 5%, with a 1% increase after five years
    D) a fixed 30-year rate of 6%

90. Most current mortgages in an area are being issued with an APR of 4 – 5% and closing costs of about $6000. Which of the following mortgage terms is MOST likely to be considered "predatory" for a mortgage in this particular area?
    A) APR 4.25%, closing costs $5,500
    B) APR 4.75%, closing costs $7,000
    C) APR 5.25%, closing costs $4,800
    D) APR 6.75%, closing costs $9,600

91. How much would a lender with a loan origination fee of $500 $+ \frac{1}{2}$ point charge for a $300 000 loan?
   A) $3,000
   B) $2,500
   C) $2,000
   D) $1,500

92. What is the cash transaction amount limit that requires lenders to file a Currency Transaction Report with the US Treasury Department?
   A) $5,000
   B) $10,000
   C) $25,000
   D) $50,000

93. According to the Equal Credit Opportunity and Fair Housing Acts, a lender may not discriminate on the basis of a borrower's
   A) past credit history.
   B) current assets.
   C) current monthly income.
   D) current status as a renter.

94. Unless otherwise specified, what is the typical lifetime cap of an ARM that begins at 4.25%?
   A) 9.25%
   B) 7.25%
   C) 6.25%
   D) 5.25%

95. Oscar is selling his home where he has lived for forty years; for most of that time, he has allowed his neighbor to park on the corner of his property. In order for the neighbor to be allowed to continue to do this, the person buying Oscar's home will need to sign which document at closing?
   A) an easement
   B) an encumbrance
   C) a power of attorney
   D) a title

96. Which of the following is the computer system used by MLOs to begin the process of licensing?
   A) AARMR
   B) CSBS
   C) NMLS
   D) SAFE

97. Within three days of receiving an official loan inquiry with all necessary information, a lender must provide the applicant with which of the following?
   A) the Closing Disclosure
   B) the loan estimate
   C) the mortgage insurance quote
   D) a title search

98. Which of these, if approved by an MLO as part of a loan, is considered a "prohibited act"?
    A) negative amortization
    B) an interest rate that is lower than expected
    C) closing costs that are higher than expected
    D) an escrow account

99. Which of the following is commonly verified with an applicant's federal tax returns?
    A) assets
    B) current mortgage
    C) employment
    D) income

100. Which of the following would violate GLBA rules about safeguarding a consumer's nonpublic information?
    A) texting a spouse that a new loan applicant who lives two blocks from the loan office
    B) contacting current account holders who allow marketing communications
    C) emailing a supervisor an encrypted email containing a borrower's Social Security number
    D) allowing a coworker to use your computer without your logging out first

101. What is form 1003 used for?
    A) applying for a loan
    B) reporting a sale to the government
    C) preparing the property for the realtor to list it
    D) submitting an appraisal to the lender

102. According to the Equal Credit Opportunity Act and Fair Housing Act, a lender can legally refuse to make a loan based on a borrower's
    A) annual income.
    B) family status.
    C) national origin.
    D) physical handicap.

103. Which of the following covers the lender's costs of foreclosing on a home whose mortgage payments have not been made?
    A) homeowner insurance
    B) origination fee
    C) recording fee
    D) title insurance

104. Which of the following governs the advertising of mortgage credit products?
    A) Regulation C
    B) Regulation H
    C) Regulation N
    D) Regulation Z

105. A loan application says that a borrower will live in the house, but the borrower privately tells his MLO that his sister will be living in the house. Which type of fraud is this?
   A) occupancy
   B) liability
   C) employment
   D) income

106. Which of the following is considered a "zero tolerance" fee that cannot increase before closing?
   A) homeowner insurance
   B) inspection fee
   C) title insurance
   D) transfer taxes

107. MLOs should always "read the fine print" of their advertisements to ensure that the ads are not
   A) cheap.
   B) expensive.
   C) misleading.
   D) accurate.

108. A 75-year-old man applying for a mortgage tells his MLO that he is using the rest of his retirement savings as the down payment on a house. He is planning to renovate the house while he lives there and then sell the house at a profit three years from now. What is the MOST likely reason for which the MLO might decide to reject the mortgage application?
   A) The man is too old.
   B) The house is too expensive.
   C) The mortgage is unsuitable.
   D) The down payment is not large enough.

109. Which of these is typically found in a Closing Disclosure but NOT in a loan estimate?
   A) interest rate
   B) estimated monthly payment
   C) cash needed to close
   D) costs paid by a seller

110. After his advertising communication has been shared with the public, an MLO must keep a copy of that communication for at least how long?
   A) ninety days
   B) six months
   C) one year
   D) two years

111. A borrower's $210,000 loan at 5% interest closes on February 8 in a non-leap year. How much will the borrower owe in per diem interest at closing?
   A) $218.75
   B) $437.50
   C) $656.25
   D) $875.00

112. If a borrower receives referrals from her mortgage lender for mortgage-related services, what should she do?
    A) use those companies because they are used to working with her lender
    B) consider them but ultimately choose whichever company will work best for her finances
    C) work with one of those companies, since doing so is a legal obligation
    D) avoid those companies no matter what

113. Which appraisal method is MOST often used for existing owner-occupied homes?
    A) cost approach
    B) income approach
    C) sales approach
    D) future value approach

114. Naomi is buying a $300 000 house and will need private mortgage insurance unless her down payment is at least how much?
    A) $10,500
    B) $20,000
    C) $30,000
    D) $60,000

115. A mortgage's "loan origination fee" is typically the commission paid to which of the following?
    A) the lender
    B) the title company
    C) the realtor
    D) the MLO

116. A state regulatory agency has asked a lender to let them see an MLO's loan records for the last six months. When the MLO hears of this, what should he do FIRST?
    A) gather all of his recent records for the lender to see
    B) hide his records for a questionable loan he approved
    C) prepare for an oral interview with agency representatives
    D) schedule his annual vacation for the days when the state agency will visit

117. How much is Martin's first monthly payment on his new loan under the following conditions?

Conditions for a Loan	Costs
Monthly principal	$395. 46
Monthly interest	$1,300. 47
Annual taxes	$1,440. 00
Annual homeowner's insurance	$1,500. 00

    A) $4,635.93
    B) $3,315.93
    C) $3,260.93
    D) $1,940.93

118. Which of the following requires each US state to create its own mortgage regulatory agency?
   A) AARMR
   B) CSBS
   C) Regulation H
   D) Dodd-Frank Act

119. According to the Real Estate Settlement Procedures Act (RESPA), which document must be reviewed and signed by the borrower at least three business days prior to closing?
   A) the loan estimate
   B) the intent to proceed
   C) the deed of trust
   D) the Closing Disclosure

120. Based on a 365-day calendar, what is the per diem interest on a $250,000 loan with a 7.5% interest rate?
   A) $49
   B) $51
   C) $53
   D) $55

Answer Key

1. D: An entitlement is the part of a home loan paid by the VA in case of foreclosure.

2. B: John is receiving kickbacks from the title company, where a kickback is anything paid for a referral of settlement business.

3. D: Written customer identification is part of the USA Patriot Act's emphasis on preventing terrorism and money laundering.

4. A: Unlicensed MLOs may not offer or negotiate loans, nor directly contact a borrower; however, they may decide to underwrite the loan since this does not involve contacting the borrower directly.

5. A: Regulation N directly governs "commercial communication," which includes advertising.

6. D: A borrower's Social Security number is on the Real Estate Settlement Procedure Act's (RESPA's) list of the six pieces of information needed to submit an official loan application; the other options are not.

7. C: A lender's margin is the difference between its current mortgage rate and the current index lending rate.

8. D: Fingerprints are required as part of a background check and must be submitted by most financial professionals before becoming licensed.

9. D: Asking whether a borrower has had homeownership education classes is a question on Form 1103—Supplemental Consumer Information.

10. C: For loans of $100,000 or more, points and fees can be no more than 3 percent of the loan, so $250,000 × 0.03 = $7,500.

11. D: Borrowers commit asset fraud by claiming they own valuable things that actually have no value—in this case, a closed-down silver mine.

12. A: The credit report fee cannot increase, but the other options might in certain circumstances.

13. A: A home equity line of credit (HELOC) loans money from the equity in a home. It is commonly used for major home renovation projects.

14. B: A borrower has three days to decide whether to continue the loan process in case his finances can't support a 15% increase.

15. A: A consumer can always change back to signing documents by paper, though he must be told if doing so will cost him money.

16. D: The monthly escrow amount is (2,000 + 1,600) ÷ 12 = $300.

17. B: The Homeowners Protection Act provides guidelines for when private mortgage insurance (PMI) must be canceled.

18. B: Recasting the loan allows the new monthly payment on a loan to be determined after a large amount of principal is suddenly paid back. A new loan application is not needed.

19. D: The Consumer Finance Protection Bureau is part of the Federal Reserve System.

20. B: Three hours of the twenty-hour course discuss ethics, which comprises 15 percent of the entire course.

21. B: The amount of principal still owed must be updated on the written mortgage statement each month.

22. C: Redlining is the discriminatory practice of refusing to allow certain borrowers to obtain mortgages in some areas but not in others.

23. D: Credit score problems should be discussed with the credit report company, as it is the only entity that can correct a credit report.

24. C: Flood insurance is not part of most homeowner insurance policies; when needed or desired, it must be purchased separately by a borrower in addition to homeowner insurance.

25. B: The maximum monthly debt-to-income (DTI) ratio for qualified mortgages is 43 percent. Since the borrower makes $\frac{\$48,000}{12} = \$4,000$ per month, his maximum DTI must be $4,000 \times 0.43 = \$1,720$.

26. C: The Gramm-Leach-Bliley Act safeguards nonpublic information.

27. D: Seller contributions can only pay for closing costs, in this case up to $5,000.

28. A: The *S* in RESPA is for *settlement*. The Real Estate Settlement Procedures Act (RESPA) was created to reduce a borrower's settlement costs at closing.

29. A: Lenders may charge clients for obtaining a credit report; the other options are illegal according to the Real Estate Settlement Procedures Act (RESPA).

30. B: The right of rescission allows a borrower three days to change her mind at no cost before making a large purchase.

31. B: Conforming or conventional mortgages follow (or "conform to") Freddie Mac and Fannie Mae rules.

32. C: A lender has thirty days to approve or deny an application.

33. C: Marital status is not one of the six pieces of information needed to create an initial loan application; the others options listed are required.

34. A: Federal Housing Administration (FHA) borrowers with a credit score above 580 only need a 3.5% down payment.

35. C: The Adverse Action Letter explains why a borrower's mortgage application was denied.

36. A: Any debt that must be repaid is considered a "liability" by a lender.

37. B: Borrowers must show employment and address histories for at least the past two years.

38. C: Consumers who owe money to lenders can receive unsolicited telemarketing calls. Note that loan applicants can be contacted for only three months after submitting their applications.

39. B: As economic conditions change, adjustable-rate mortgages (ARMs) may have their interest rates changed during the term of the mortgage.

40. B: Eight hours of continuing education is required each year to keep an MLO license current.

41. A: Calls can be made between 8 a.m. and 9 p.m. in the customer's time zone.

42. B: A point is 1% of the loan amount, so $\frac{3}{4}$ point would be $\frac{3}{4} \times 0.01 \times 500,000 = \$3,750$.

43. B: The Real Estate Settlement Procedures Act (RESPA) allows treble damages in some cases, which in this scenario might be as much as $\$20,000 \times 3 = \$60,000$.

44. B: The loan amount will be 90% of the $250,000 price, or $225,000.

45. D: The title company takes care of the money and sends it to all parties involved as required.

46. C: Closing documents must be given to the buyer at least three days before closing, so Melanie would need these by Tuesday if she is closing on Friday.

47. A: The Servicing Transfer Statement tells a borrower about the new lender "servicing" his loan after the old lender has "transferred" the loan to them.

48. C: MLOs must put both their own and their employer's Nationwide Multistate Licensing System and Registry (NMLS) ID number on each loan document.

49. B: Closing arrangements are usually made by a settlement agent.

50. A: Multiple new credit card accounts in a short time is a common red flag for identify theft.

51. C: Planning to make payments on only the promise of a raise is so risky that an MLO would be likely to reject the application on the grounds of unsuitability.

52. C: The Department of Housing and Urban Development (HUD) approves homeowner counseling agencies.

53. B: At least thirty days must pass before Annette can take the exam again.

54. D: Discount points are a form of prepaid interest, paid by the buyer to reduce a mortgage interest rate.

55. C: Mortgage brokers have access to multiple lenders, which they search to find the best mortgage possible for a borrower.

56. B: An encumbrance is any issue preventing a buyer from owning a property free and clear, including a current mortgage or unpaid tax.

57. B: MLOs must be at least eighteen years old to receive their license.

58. B: A savings account is considered an asset that can be used or sold to pay a mortgage if needed.

59. A: The Real Estate Settlement Procedure Act (RESPA) prohibits the seller from requiring that a particular title company be used, so the borrower is free to use any company she wants.

60. D: A godmother is considered a "non-relative" who can provide gift money toward buying a home. The other options cannot give gifts because of their involvement in the transaction.

61. A: Taxes and insurance go into an escrow account, whose contents are described in an escrow analysis statement.

62. A: The Dodd-Frank Act prohibits practices considered "unfair, deceptive or abusive."

63. C: To ensure the taxes are paid on time, a lender usually submits the borrower's property taxes with money from the escrow account.

64. A: Borrowers would need at least two more weeks for the lender to reconsider the loan because of a "change in circumstance" due to the house's new lower appraisal rate.

65. C: Income fraud is claiming a higher or lower salary than what a person is actually paid.

66. B: A lender may ask if a borrower is currently married but may not ask about age, race, or religion.

67. C: A lender has thirty days to approve or deny an application.

68. D: It is permissible to pay an MLO based on the number of loans she creates in a month.

69. D: The word *seasoned* describes any cash that is in an account for more than sixty days; therefore, any deposits from two months ago would be considered "seasoned."

70. C: An assumption clause would allow Sam's son's family to "assume," or take over, the loan at the same interest rate Sam had.

71. C: Negative information should be passed on to the lender so that it can be included in their final decision. An MLO should not approve or deny the loan immediately (in case the lender would make a different decision) and should never hide such information from the lender.

72. D: The loan-to-value (LTV) ratio is $\frac{250,000}{300,000} = 0.833$, or 83.3%.

73. C: Qualified mortgages typically require equal monthly payments for the term of the mortgage.

74. C: TransUnion and Equifax both provide the credit reports that lenders use to estimate whether a borrower will be able to repay her loan.

75. A: The Uniform Residential Appraisal Report (URAR) is filled out by an appraiser.

76. A: Their fiduciary relationship obliges John's MLO to explain basic finance as needed during the loan process.

77. D: Tax returns are used to verify past income, as misstatements on tax forms are a crime.

78. B: A condominium is considered a "dwelling," which is defined as a "residential structure"; the other options are not considered dwellings.

79. C: For qualified mortgages, the monthly debt-to-income ratio can be no larger than 43%; therefore, Steve's annual income must be at least $\left(\frac{\$1,500}{0.43}\right) \times 12 = \$41,860$.

80. B: The Federal Trade Commission's (FTC's) Red Flags Rule covers unusual "red flag" situations that may indicate that identity theft is occurring.

81. B: Force-placed insurance is usually purchased by a lender to cover a home where the borrower has let his homeowner insurance expire. The lender then charges the borrower for the insurance.

82. D: Reverse mortgages work best for people over age 62 who can no longer work and thus might not be able to make monthly mortgage payments. From the options given, Lila would therefore be the most likely person to benefit from a reverse mortgage.

83. B: Felony convictions unrelated to money require that an MLO license be denied for seven years after conviction.

84. C: The first payment is due at the beginning of the second month after closing, which is October 1.

85. C: Consumers are never told when a report has been filed about them.

86. C: Annual private mortgage insurance (PMI) cost is 0.8% of the loan amount, or $400,000 \times \left(\frac{0.8}{100}\right) =$ $3,200.

87. D: Permanent license denials are for those convicted of—or who plead guilty to—finance-related crimes.

88. D: The seller typically pays both realtors' commissions: the buyer's realtor for bringing him a buyer, and the seller's realtor for doing the work to get the house sold.

89. B: After ten years, option A's rate will be 5%, option B's rate will be 7%, option C's rate will be 6%, and option D's rate will be 6%; therefore, option B will have the highest interest rate.

90. D: An illegal predatory loan usually has a much higher annual percentage rate (APR) and much higher closing costs than normal for an area. Only option D has both an APR and closing costs that are much higher than normal for the area.

91. B: A point is 1% of the loan amount, so $500 $+\frac{1}{2}$ point would be $500 $+\frac{1}{2}$ $(0.01 \times 300,000) =$ $500 + 1,500 = $2,000.

92. B: Cash transaction amount limits of $10,000 require a Currency Transaction Report, whereas $5,000 requires a Suspicious Activity Report.

93. D: It is illegal to discriminate based on whether a borrower is renting a home instead of buying it.

94. A: The Consumer Financial Protection Bureau (CFPB) says that adjustable-rate mortgages (ARMs) typically have a cap of 5%, so $4.25 + 5 = 9.25\%$.

95. A: Easements must be granted by buyers in order for neighbors to legally use any part of the buyer's property.

96. C: The Nationwide Multistate Licensing System and Registry (NMLS)is used by MLOs to begin the licensing process.

97. B: The loan estimate spells out the main terms of a loan so that a borrower can decide whether or not to accept them.

98. A: Negative amortization, where the amount to pay back increases even when monthly payments are made on time, is considered a "prohibited act."

99. D: It is assumed that federal tax returns accurately show income; otherwise, a borrower could be guilty of tax evasion.

100. D: According to the Gramm-Leach-Bliley Act (GLBA), it is forbidden to allow a coworker to use your computer before you have logged out; coworkers should use their own accounts to access computer systems.

101. A: Form 1003 is a borrower's loan application, so it is used to collect all of the financial and identification information that the lender needs to consider the loan.

102. A: Annual income can be a cause for refusing a loan because a borrower may not have enough income to afford the monthly payments.

103. D: Title insurance, usually purchased by the buyer, covers foreclosure costs if they are required.

104. C: Regulation N governs the advertising of mortgage credit products.

105. A: Lying about who will live in a property is occupancy fraud.

106. D: Because the amount of transfer taxes can be exactly known beforehand, it is considered a "zero tolerance fee" that cannot increase before closing.

107. C: MLO advertisements must not mislead consumers about loan terms or fees.

108. C: In the situation described, the man's idea is so risky, and uses so much of his resources, that an MLO would be likely to reject the application on the grounds of unsuitability.

109. D: The loan estimate has no need to list costs paid by a seller since it concentrates only on the terms of the borrower's loan.

110. D: The minimum time for keeping old advertising communications is two years.

111. C: The per diem interest covers the last twenty-one days in February, including the day of closing. Thus, per diem interest is $(\$210,000 \times 0.05) \div 12 \times \left(\frac{21}{28}\right) = \$656.25$.

112. B: According to the law, a borrower cannot be forced to use a mortgage lender's referrals, but she may do so if she wants to.

113. C: Appraisals on existing owner-occupied homes are usually made by a sales approach, which focuses on the values of recent sales in the area.

114. D: Private mortgage insurance (PMI) is required for mortgages with less than a 20% down payment, so Naomi would need a down payment of $\$300,000 \times 0.2 = \$60,000$ to avoid PMI.

115. D: The loan origination fee, although given to the lender as part of closing costs, is usually the commission paid to the MLO.

116. A: An MLO must fully cooperate with any records request from a state agency.

117. D: Both the taxes and homeowner's insurance amounts must be divided by 12 to find the amount payable each month; therefore, the payment is $\$395.46 + \$1,300.47 + (\$1,440 \div 12) + (\$1,500 \div 12) = \$1,940.93$.

118. C: Regulation H, which implements the Secure and Fair Enforcement for Mortgage Licensing (SAFE) Act requires that each US state create its own mortgage regulatory agency.

119. **D:** Per the Real Estate Settlement Procedures Act (RESPA), the borrower must review and sign the Closing Disclosure (CD) at least three business days prior to closing.

120. B: The per diem interest would be $51: $250,000 $\times \frac{7.5\%}{365}$ = $51.37.

Practice Test #2

1. In order to attract many potential borrowers, a mortgage lender advertises reduced fees and a mortgage with an interest rate that is significantly below market average; however, upon applying, borrowers are told they do not qualify for the advertised mortgage and instead are offered a different mortgage with an average interest rate and average fees. What is this practice called?

A) marketing
B) steering
C) due diligence
D) bait and switch

2. Which of the following is typically a prepaid item for which several months' worth are paid into an escrow account at closing?
A) appraisal fee
B) pest inspection fee
C) PMI
D) realtor commission

3. Which of the following is an easement?
A) a lien placed by a roofer who has not been paid for repairing storm damage
B) a document indicating that a mortgage has been fully paid off
C) an amount of seller's money used to pay a buyer's closing costs
D) permission granting a neighbor to cross the owner's lawn in order to get to a park

4. By law, which of the following must Acme Credit Union keep track of for each MLO it employs?
A) NMLS ID number
B) family status
C) salary
D) race

5. What is the general relationship between a mortgage's APR and its stated interest rate?
A) The interest rate is higher.
B) The APR is higher.
C) Both are equal.
D) The two are unrelated.

6. What is the GMI of a salaried borrower who is paid a gross income of $3 200 per week?

    A) $12 800.00
    B) $12 866.66
    C) $13 800.00
    D) $13 866.66

7. Which of these groups provides a specific code of ethics for loan officers?
    A)   National Association of Mortgage Brokers (NAMB)
    B)   Housing and Urban Development (HUD)
    C)   Conference of State Bank Supervisors (CSBS)
    D)   Consumer Financial Protection Bureau (CFPB)

8. Carl comes to his closing on Wednesday and is given his final Closing Disclosure with an interest rate that is higher than expected. He is told that the interest rate on his loan estimate was actually a clerical error by the lender. Carl has until which day to decide whether to close the loan or not?
    A)   Thursday
    B)   Friday
    C)   Monday
    D)   the following Wednesday

9. In the twenty-hour course needed to become an MLO, how many hours discuss non-traditional mortgage lending?
    A)   eight
    B)   three
    C)   two
    D)   ten

10. What is the term for the illegal practice where lenders refuse (or make it more difficult) for borrowers to receive mortgages within specific, minority neighborhoods?
    A)   redlining
    B)   bait and switch
    C)   red flag
    D)   coercion

11. Under the Homeowners Protection Act, if a borrower's original mortgage amount is $200 000, how much principal must be paid before PMI is automatically canceled by the lender?
    A) $20,000
    B) $22,000
    C) $40,000
    D) $44,000

12. Which of these people would be permanently denied an MLO license?
    A)   Marjorie, found not guilty of arson ten years ago
    B)   Lamont, who paid a $100 fine for littering six months ago
    C)   Kyle, convicted three years ago on felony charges of check forgery
    D)   Naomi, convicted five years ago of assaulting a police officer

13. Margaret is purchasing a $75 000 mobile home with a 5% down payment. According to Regulation Z, the closing costs for her mortgage can be no more than which of the following?
   A) $1,000
   B) $2,250
   C) $3,000
   D) $3,750

14. Which of the following is a mortgage in which the interest rate remains unchanged for the entire term of the loan?
   A) adjustable-rate mortgage
   B) locked interest rate Mortgage
   C) fixed-rate mortgage
   D) 10/1 ARM

15. A borrower's loan application says that he is a vice president of a construction company, but an MLO checking this statement finds that the borrower was fired as vice president two weeks before submitting the application. Which type of fraud is this?
   A) asset
   B) employment
   C) income
   D) liability

16. How many rows are in the amortization table of a 30-year mortgage?
   A) 360
   B) 180
   C) 60
   D) 30

17. Which of these people would be denied an MLO license for at least seven years beginning from the date of the incident?
   A) Phyllis, who pled guilty to misdemeanor driving without a license
   B) Quenton, who was arrested for misdemeanor marijuana possession
   C) Roger, who was found not guilty of felony bank robbery
   D) Scarlet, who pled guilty to felony drunk driving

18. The Home Mortgage Disclosure Act (HMDA) requirement for lenders to obtain information on (or to estimate) a borrower's ethnicity is MOST intended to prevent which of the following?
   A) financial fraud
   B) identity theft
   C) mortgage foreclosure
   D) racial discrimination

19. At closing, the borrower signs which document, agreeing to repay the lender?
   A) credit report
   B) loan estimate
   C) promissory note
   D) title search

20. While applying for a mortgage, a borrower claims to make less than what he actually earns in order to receive an incentive that is only given to low-income borrowers. Which type of fraud is the borrower committing?
   A)   money fraud
   B)   income fraud
   C)   employment fraud
   D)   asset fraud

21. Rafael has a credit score of 700 and Makendra has a credit score of 500. The idea of "risk-based pricing" says that
   A)   Rafael's mortgage will be more expensive.
   B)   Makendra's mortgage will be more expensive.
   C)   Both mortgages will cost the same.
   D)   The two mortgage costs are totally unrelated.

22. Elena's monthly income is $4,000. Her monthly debt, including her new mortgage, will be $1,400. Which of the following will be her DTI ratio?
   A)   10%
   B)   35%
   C)   74%
   D)   286%

23. A mortgage lender installs an electronic billboard in front of its building. Whenever an MLO is featured on the billboard, the billboard must show the MLO's name and which number?
   A)   personal cellphone
   B)   work telephone
   C)   NMLS ID
   D)   Social Security

24. Which of the following is governed by Regulation N?
   A)   a mortgage lender's television ad
   B)   a case of racial discrimination
   C)   a case of identity theft
   D)   a request for information on a borrower

25. Ziggy wants to buy a $400,000 house with a $380,000 mortgage. What is the LTV ratio of the house?
   A)   95%
   B)   80%
   C)   20%
   D)   5%

26. What is the procedure to ensure a borrower is not a terrorist?
   A)   Call the applicant's personal references.
   B)   Check the applicant's credit report and credit accounts.
   C)   Check the list of terrorists for the applicant's name.
   D)   Ask the realtor if the applicant said anything suspicious.

27. Which of these consumers can legally get an unsolicited telemarketing call from a mortgage lender?
    A) Gustav, who has opted in to receive communications from his lender
    B) Sally, who told her lender's telemarketer a month ago to put her on the "do not call" list
    C) Olga, whose mortgage from the lender was sold two months ago to another servicer
    D) LaBron, who paid off his debts to the lender six months ago

28. Which of the following is true about monthly payments on a 15-year loan and monthly payments on a 30-year loan?
    A) The 15-year loan payments are typically higher.
    B) The 30-year loan payments are typically higher.
    C) Both loan payments are about equal.
    D) The two payments are totally unrelated.

29. To ensure compliance with fair lending practices, which federal law requires mortgage lenders to collect and regularly report data to the government about loan applications received for the purchase of a dwelling?
    A) the Dodd-Frank Act
    B) the Fair Credit Reporting Act (FCRA)
    C) the Home Mortgage Disclosure Act (HMDA)
    D) the Gramm-Leach-Bliley Act (GLBA)

30. Which of the following must be submitted by an applicant for MLO licensing?
    A) marriage license
    B) high school diploma
    C) college transcript
    D) credit report

31. Which process is MOST helped by the Freddie Mac software called "Loan Program Advisor"?
    A) underwriting
    B) counseling
    C) closing
    D) appraising

32. What is the annual PMI cost for a $240 000 mortgage?
    A) $1,920
    B) $2,400
    C) $3,000
    D) $4,800

33. A borrower receiving a FACTA disclosure from a lender gets information about his own
    A) tax situation.
    B) mortgage interest rate.
    C) credit score.
    D) employment history.

34. Which type of loan is used exclusively for rural properties?
    A) VA loan
    B) FHA loan
    C) SBA loan
    D) USDA Section 502 loan

35. Which of the following, if unexpected, is MOST likely to be a sign that a borrower has had her identity stolen?
    A) a $3,000 withdrawal from his checking account
    B) a $2,000 payment toward his credit card bill
    C) a $1,000 deposit of his most recent paycheck
    D) a $500 refund from a retail store

36. Which of the following terms BEST describes mortgages of more than a million dollars?
    A) assumable
    B) conventional
    C) jumbo
    D) qualified

37. Under Regulation B of the ECOA, if a borrower's mortgage loan application is denied, how many days does the lender have to provide the reason for denial in writing?
    A) three business days
    B) five business days
    C) three days
    D) thirty days

38. If a lender is "in compliance," it means the lender is generally
    A) hiring more employees over time.
    B) obeying federal and state laws regarding mortgages.
    C) practicing racial discrimination.
    D) profitable each year.

39. Ursula's $200,000 mortgage with a single $40,000 payment due at the very end of the term is which kind of mortgage?
    A) qualified
    B) balloon
    C) conforming
    D) jumbo

40. Which of the following does NOT factor into a borrower's back-end DTI ratio?
    A) utilities
    B) child support
    C) car payment
    D) alimony

41. Under Regulation B of the ECOA, which of the following factors can be cause for denying a loan application?
    A) marital status
    B) sex
    C) income
    D) religion

42. Which part of a monthly payment goes to paying back the original loan amount?
    A) principal
    B) interest
    C) taxes
    D) insurance

43. When calculating a borrower's back-end DTI, which of the following should be excluded?
    A) credit cards
    B) car lease payments
    C) child support
    D) utility payments

44. Nestor completes his loan application on Tuesday. The lender has until when to mail Nestor the loan disclosures?
    A) Wednesday
    B) Friday
    C) Monday
    D) Tuesday

45. A 5/1 ARM means that the mortgage rate
    A) stays the same for five years and then adjusts once each year after that.
    B) begins at a 5% interest rate and then adjusts upward 1% each year.
    C) begins at a 1% interest rate and then adjusts upward each year until it reaches 6%.
    D) stays the same for one year, and then adjusts once every five years after that.

46. A borrower's annual property taxes are $1,500, his PMI is $75 per month, and his homeowner insurance is $100 per month. Each of his monthly payments should therefore include an escrow amount of how much?
    A) $3,600
    B) $1,800
    C) $600
    D) $300

47. Which documents have nearly the same information on them?
    A) the loan estimate and the Closing Disclosure
    B) the loan application and the deed of sale
    C) the property title and the HUD disclosures
    D) the credit report and the property listing

48. As part of explaining "unpleasant" possibilities, an MLO should explain which of the following about ARM to a borrower?
    A) that a higher interest rate means a higher monthly payment
    B) that a higher interest rate means more frequent payments
    C) that a lower interest rate means a higher monthly payment
    D) that a lower interest rate means more frequent payments.

49. Which party is responsible for recording the title and deed of a property with the local government after closing?
    A) the mortgage lender
    B) the borrower
    C) the settlement agent
    D) the real estate agent

50. With a reverse mortgage, who receives money?
    A) the lender
    B) the state
    C) the current owner
    D) the escrow account

51. A suspicious activity report should be filed with the US Treasury Department for any transaction greater than which of the following?
    A) $5,000
    B) $10,000
    C) $25,000
    D) $50,000

52. Which of the following ensures that the seller of a property is its rightful owner?
    A) the appraisal
    B) the title search
    C) the survey
    D) the inspection

53. How often must a lender send written copies of its privacy policies to its borrowers?

    A) once a month
    B) once a quarter
    C) once a year
    D) once at the start of a mortgage

54. A real estate agent is showing homes to a preapproved Latino couple who are shopping for their first home. Because the couple is Latino, the real estate agent is purposely omitting homes in White neighborhoods and only showing the couple homes in predominantly minority neighborhoods. What is this called?

A) steering
B) redlining
C) splitting
D) kickback

55. Stella's $370,000 loan at 4.5% interest closes on April 16. How much will she owe in per diem interest at closing?

A) $46.25
B) $671.37
C) $693.75
D) $1,387.50

56. Under Section 10 of RESPA, which of the following are lenders prohibited from doing to borrower's escrow accounts?

A) submitting payments for taxes more than two weeks early
B) collecting too much money from borrowers and holding escrows that are larger than necessary
C) requiring borrowers to pay monthly into their escrow accounts
D) raising the borrower's monthly mortgage payment due to an escrow shortage

57. Robert owns 100,000 shares of Acme Company stock that he could sell if needed to pay his mortgage. An MLO will ensure that Robert owns the stock and that the stock is worth what Robert claims by completing which form?

A) credit report
B) deed of trust
C) proof of assets
D) proof of income

58. Section 8 of RESPA prohibits which of the following from occurring?

A) originating adjustable-rate mortgages (ARMs)
B) denying an applicant because of the neighborhood in which the property is located
C) giving or accepting a fee or kickback for business referrals
D) requiring the borrower to provide certain personal information (e.g., number of children)

59. What is an optional cost the borrower can pay to the lender in order to receive a reduced interest rate on a loan?

A) an origination fee
B) per diem interest
C) discount points
D) prepaid interest

60. In order to qualify for a larger loan, a borrower does not disclose the court ordered alimony payments he makes to his former wife. Is this mortgage fraud? If so, which type of fraud is the borrower committing?
    A) Yes, this is income fraud.
    B) No, since alimony is not on the credit report, it is not required to be disclosed.
    C) Yes, this is liability fraud.
    D) No, alimony should only be included if it is garnished from the borrower's wages.

61. Which of the following mortgage types allows the borrower to NOT make monthly principal or interest payments to the lender and instead receive payment(s) from the lender?
    A) balloon mortgage
    B) reverse mortgage
    C) interest-only mortgage
    D) subordinate mortgage

62. If a borrower earns $1050 a week and nets $775 a week after taxes and deductions, what is the borrower's gross monthly income?
    A) $3,100
    B) $3,358
    C) $4,200
    D) $4,550

63. Which entity currently has authority to enforce compliance and supervise the regulations set forth in the ECOA?
    A) The Federal Reserve
    B) The Consumer Financial Protection Bureau (CFPB)
    C) The Federal Housing Administration (FHA)
    D) The US Department of Housing and Urban Development (HUD)

64. Private mortgage insurance on a $200 000 loan can be automatically removed as soon as the borrower has how much equity?
    A) $160,000
    B) $156,000
    C) $44,000
    D) $40,000

65. Kyle gets a new interest only mortgage with a $100,000 principal. After making payments every month for three years, how much does Kyle owe?
    A) $120,000
    B) $100,000
    C) $80,000
    D) $60,000

66. Which of the following do annuities most commonly provide for a borrower?
    A) assets
    B) gift funds
    C) liabilities
    D) reserve funds

67. Which of the following is MOST often used as an index when calculating a mortgage's interest rate?
    A) the Dow Jones industrial average
    B) the Federal Reserve discount rate
    C) the NASDAQ composite average
    D) the US Treasury Bond rate

68. John received $10,000 in capital gains last year and has received $30,000 in capital gains this year. An MLO now verifying John's income should use which number as John's average annual capital gains income?
    A) $30,000
    B) $20,000
    C) $10,000
    D) $0

69. Stan sits down at his desk to make some nighttime telemarketing calls to potential customers in a different time zone. At which time in the customer's time zone must he stop calling for the night?
    A) 6 p.m.
    B) 7 p.m.
    C) 8 p.m.
    D) 9 p.m.

70. Which of the following people officially estimates the value of a property?
    A) seller
    B) realtor
    C) lender
    D) appraiser

71. A borrower wants to purchase an income property but does not have enough money for the down payment. The borrower knows that the down payment requirement for a primary residence is significantly lower, so she tells the mortgage loan officer that this property will be her primary residence. Which type of fraud is the borrower committing?
    A) liability fraud
    B) borrower fraud
    C) occupancy fraud
    D) asset fraud

72. Because James has just made the last payment on his 30-year mortgage, he will soon receive which document that transfers the property's title to him?
    A) an encumbrance
    B) a deed of reconveyance
    C) a note of disclosure
    D) a title search

73. According to RESPA, the Mortgage Servicing Disclosure Statement must be provided to the borrower within three business days of which of the following?
   A)   the closing of the loan
   B)   the loan application
   C)   the loan being sold to another lender
   D)   the first payment date

74. Which of the following natural disasters can often be covered by a separate federal hazard insurance policy?
   A)   earthquake
   B)   flood
   C)   fire
   D)   tornado

75. An MLO is allowed to be paid by which of the following?
   A)   commission only
   B)   salary only
   C)   both commission and salary
   D)   neither commission nor salary

76. To buy a $600 000 home without paying for monthly PMI, a borrower must have a down payment of AT LEAST how much?
   A) $30,000
   B) $60,000
   C) $120,000
   D) $150,000

77. A lender with a loan origination fee of ($300 + ¼ point) would charge how much for a $300,000 loan?
   A) $3,300
   B) $1,050
   C) $750
   D) $300

78. The term splitting describes a legal division of fees between a lender and which of the following?
   A)   a buyer
   B)   a construction company
   C)   a realtor
   D)   a settlement company

79. Under the following conditions, how much will Victor's first monthly payment on his new mortgage be?

Conditions for a Loan	Costs
Monthly principal	$288.63
Monthly interest	$1,100.11
Annual taxes	$1,800.00
Annual homeowner's insurance	$1,200.00
Annual PMI	$1,500.00

A) $5,888.74
B) $3,638.74
C) $1,763.74
D) $1,388.74

80. Which of the following documents can be legally signed by electronic means?
A) a mortgage foreclosure notice
B) a Closing Disclosure
C) a mortgage default notice
D) an eviction notice

81. The interest rate for Francisco's ARM has a floor of 4%, a current index of 5.25%, and a margin of 2.5%. What is Francisco's interest rate right now?
A) 6.5%
B) 7.75%
C) 9.25%
D) 11.75%

82. Which of the following is legal under the Dodd-Frank Act?
A) bait-and-switch advertisement
B) clear language in a mortgage document
C) an interest rate increase on Closing Document
D) an unexpected fee at closing

83. A conventional home mortgage is most likely to be issued by which of the following?
A) the federal government
B) a state government
C) a private bank
D) the Veteran's Administration

84. Which of the following occupancy types would a mortgage lender consider as owner-occupied?
A) a vacation home
B) an investment property
C) a primary residence
D) a second home

85. Which disclosure is provided to borrowers and informs them whether or not a lender will service their loan or sell their loan to another lender or investor?
    A) the Servicing Transfer Statement
    B) the Affiliated Business Arrangement Disclosure
    C) the good faith estimate
    D) the Mortgage Servicing Disclosure Statement

86. Which of the following equations would successfully calculate the LTV ratio?
    A) loan amount − appraised value
    B) down payment ÷ loan amount
    C) loan amount ÷ appraised value
    D) purchase price − down payment

87. Which of the following is a reason why kickbacks are illegal?
    A) The loan officer makes undocumented income.
    B) They are not listed on the Closing Disclosure.
    C) The mortgage lender that the loan officer works for does not get a cut of the kickback.
    D) The cost of the kickback is most likely passed on to the borrower unknowingly.

88. Connie is up to date on her current $200 000 mortgage that has an APR of 7%. When she applies for refinancing, which of these new mortgages would allow her MLO to skip income verification?
    A) $200,000 mortgage, APR 6%, $5,000 fees
    B) $195,000 mortgage, APR 8%, $3,000 fees
    C) $205,000 mortgage, APR 5%, $4,000 fees
    D) $200,000 mortgage, APR 7%, $7,000 fees

89. How much is one discount point?
    A) $1,000
    B) 1% of the purchase price
    C) $500
    D) 1% of the loan amount

90. Jonathan left the mortgage loan business eight years ago to try a new career. If he decides to go back to the business of mortgage loans, he must FIRST do which of the following?
    A) clear his criminal record
    B) pass the MLO exam again
    C) pass a new MLO licensing course
    D) surrender his driver's license to his state

91. Which agency is led by a secretary who is appointed by the US president and confirmed by the US Senate?
    A) the Consumer Financial Protection Bureau (CFPB)
    B) the Federal Trade Commission (FTC)
    C) the Government National Mortgage Association (GNMA)
    D) the Department of Housing and Urban Development (HUD)

92. Who serves the intermediary between the mortgage lender and the appraiser?
    A) the title company
    B) the settlement agent
    C) the appraisal management company
    D) the attorney

93. A mortgage loan officer refuses to accept an application because the borrower is looking to refinance the property in a specific minority neighborhood. This is an example of which illegal practice?

    A) redlining
    B) steering
    C) a kickback
    D) bait and switch

94. Jamie's first mortgage for $300,000 is with Alpha Mortgage Company. Three years later, Jamie gets a second mortgage for $100,000 with Beta Mortgage Company. Two years after that, Jamie's house goes into foreclosure and is sold for $350,000. What happens to the proceeds of the sale?
    A) Jamie gets all of the profit and can pay the lenders off if she wants to.
    B) Alpha gets fully paid back, and Beta gets what is left.
    C) Alpha and Beta each get partly paid back.
    D) Beta gets fully paid back, and Alpha gets what is left.

95. Which of these tasks must be performed by a licensed loan originator?
    A) emailing a loan offer to a prospective borrower
    B) showing a house to a prospective borrower
    C) putting a printed loan application into a filing cabinet
    D) emailing a completed loan application to a lender

96. Which agency created the term red flag to describe something that may indicate identity theft to a lender?
    A) the Consumer Financial Protection Bureau (CFPB)
    B) the Department of Housing and Urban Development (HUD)
    C) the Federal Trade Commission (FTC)
    D) the Securities and Exchange Commission (SEC)

97. Which of the following is considered a liability by lenders?
    A) a $1,000 certificate of deposit
    B) a $2,000 tax refund
    C) a $5,000 credit card balance
    D) a $10,000 life insurance policy

98. Michelle passes her MLO exam and becomes licensed with NMLS on November 4 2023. When does her new MLO license expire?
    A) December 31, 2023
    B) February 4, 2024
    C) November 4, 2024
    D) December 31, 2024

99. Which term describes a mortgage where the buyer can take over payments on the same terms and conditions as the seller had?
- A) assumable
- B) conforming
- C) conventional
- D) qualified

100. When qualifying a borrower for a mortgage, which credit score from the three credit bureaus on the credit report is used?
- A) the lowest score
- B) the average score
- C) the middle score
- D) the highest score

101. An MLO's duty to practice cybersecurity includes ensuring that
- A) numbers match each other on the good faith estimate and Closing Document.
- B) money is wired successfully from borrower to lender.
- C) anti-discrimination laws are properly followed.
- D) borrower applications contain all necessary information.

102. Lamont cannot attend the closing on his house, so he must give his realtor which document beforehand so that the realtor can legally sign on his behalf?
- A) power of attorney
- B) security instrument
- C) settlement statement
- D) title search

103. Which document is a legally binding agreement between the lender and borrower which states that the borrower will repay the loan in accordance with the terms and conditions outlined within the document?
- A) a promissory note
- B) a Closing Disclosure
- C) a mortgage
- D) a deed of trust

104. Mark works for a credit union and has never been registered with NMLS as an MLO. The SAFE Act allows Mark to process mortgage loans without NMLS registration as long as he
- A) works at the credit union and not at a bank.
- B) processes fewer than six mortgage loans per year.
- C) processes mortgage loans less than $100,000.
- D) does all of his work as a volunteer without pay.

105. Which type of appraisal uses the land as value and takes into consideration the cost of construction/improvements as well as the depreciation of any structures currently on the land?
   A) market data approach
   B) sales comparison appraisal
   C) income approach appraisal
   D) cost approach appraisal

106. A lender may charge a prepayment penalty on a qualified mortgage for up to how many years?
   A) five
   B) one
   C) three
   D) ten

107. The 2013 HOEPA rule requires borrowers to be given a list of which of the following?
   A) local mortgage lenders
   B) local real estate agents
   C) local title insurance companies
   D) local homeowner counselors

108. An immigrant who does not speak English very well applies for a mortgage to buy a home. Because of the language barrier, the loan officer thinks he can make a higher commission by giving the borrower a mortgage that is more expensive than what the borrower requires. Which term below BEST describes this?
   A) a steering loan
   B) a predatory loan
   C) a split loan
   D) a bait-and-switch loan

109. When calculating a borrower's front-end DTI ratio, which of the following should be excluded?
   A) car lease payment
   B) PMI (if applicable)
   C) property taxes
   D) hazard insurance

110. Which of the following includes the phrase "to ensure the ability of state mortgage regulators to provide effective mortgage supervision" as part of its mission statement?
   A) the American Association of Residential Mortgage Regulators (AARMR)
   B) the Conference of State Bank Supervisors (CSBS)
   C) then National Mortgage Licensing System (NMLS)
   D) the SAFE Act

111. In which instance can mortgage loan officers receive a fee for referring borrowers to a company?
   A) if the price of the service to the borrower is still within market average
   B) if the referral fee is listed on the Closing Disclosure as a kickback
   C) if borrowers are told in writing of the referral arrangement and that they are not required to use the referred company
   D) if the price of the service to the borrower is within 10% of what was quoted in the loan estimate

112. Which of the following people typically schedules a closing?
    A)   the buyer
    B)   the realtor
    C)   the seller
    D)   the settlement agent

113. Which of the following mortgage transactions is protected under RESPA?
    A)   new home purchases
    B)   vacant land purchases
    C)   commercial property purchases
    D)   agriculture structure purchases

114. A borrower is MOST likely to access the NMLS database to find information on which of the following?
    A)   the terms of his loan
    B)   the status of his loan application
    C)   the employment history of his MLO
    D)   the firm employing his realtor

115. Section 9 of RESPA prohibits the seller of a property from doing which of the following?
    A)   requiring the buyer to purchase title insurance through a specific title company
    B)   speaking with the buyer's mortgage loan originator
    C)   requiring the buyer to have a property inspection
    D)   requiring the buyer to provide a copy of his credit report

116. If a borrower states she is purchasing a home on the beach that she plans to vacation at as well as rent out when not in use, which occupancy type would this be considered?
    A)   vacation home
    B)   investment property
    C)   second home
    D)   primary residence

117. Brock took the MLO exam for the third time on May 17 and still did not pass. What is the EARLIEST day he can take the exam again?
    A)   May 24
    B)   June 17
    C)   August 17
    D)   November 17

118. Regulation N must be followed in a lender's
    A)   underwriting process.
    B)   good faith estimates.
    C)   credit practices.
    D)   advertising.

119. Which of the following mortgage loans requires a Closing Disclosure?
    A)   a first-time-buyer loan
    B)   a houseboat loan
    C)   a home equity loan
    D)   a reverse mortgage

120. Corey has budgeted to pay his first mortgage payment on May 1; therefore, what is the LATEST day he should close on his house?
    A)   March 31
    B)   April 1
    C)   April 15
    D)   April 30

Answer Key

1. D: Bait and switch is the illegal practice of baiting potential borrowers with an enticing but unattainable offer and then switching to a less desirable offer once the borrowers apply.

2. C: Private mortgage insurance (PMI) is paid monthly; therefore, several months of PMI are typically prepaid into an escrow account at closing.

3. D: An owner grants an easement by legally allowing someone else access to her property.

4. A: Acme must ensure that each MLO is registered with his own NMLS ID number.

5. B: The annual percentage rate (APR) is calculated to include not only the mortgage's stated interest rate, but also the mortgage's fees and insurance costs; therefore, the APR is typically higher than the mortgage's stated interest rate.

6. D: To calculate the gross monthly income (GMI) of a salaried borrower who is paid weekly, the gross weekly pay would be multiplied by 52 (weeks in a year) and then divided by 12 (months in a year). (E.g., $\$3,200 \times 52 = \frac{\$166,400}{12} = \$13,866.66$.)

7. A: The National Association of Mortgage Brokers provides a specific code of ethics for loan officers.

8. A: Clerical errors allow one extra day for a borrower to decide whether to accept the loan terms.

9. C: Nontraditional mortgage lending is discussed for two of the twenty hours.

10. A: The term *redlining* defines the practice used by mortgage lenders to refuse (or make it more difficult) for borrowers to receive mortgages in specific, minority neighborhoods.

11. D: Per the Homeowners Protection Act, the lender must automatically cancel private mortgage insurance (PMI) after 22% of the original mortgage amount has been repaid; in this case, $\$200,000 \times 0.22 = \$44,000$.

12. C: Permanent denial of MLO licensing comes from a conviction for any financial felony, such as forging checks.

13. C: Regulation Z specifies that for all loans between $60,000 and $100,000, closing costs can be no more than $3,000.

14. C: The interest rate remains unchanged in a fixed-rate mortgage.

15. B: By claiming to have a job that he does not have, this borrower is committing employment fraud.

16. A: A mortgage's amortization table contains one row for each month of the mortgage's length, detailing how much principal and interest are being paid with each payment, as well as how much total principal is left to pay. Thus, a 30-year mortgage's table has 360 rows.

17. D: MLO licensure is denied for at least seven years for people who have been convicted of—or have pleaded guilty to—a felony.

18. D: Data on borrower ethnicity is collected to ensure that lenders do not discriminate against borrowers on the basis of race.

19. C: The promissory note is the official list of terms and conditions of the loan.

20. B: When borrowers claim that their income is higher or lower than what it actually is, it is a form of income fraud.

21. B:"Risk-based pricing" means that higher credit scores allow for lower mortgage costs and lower credit scores result in higher mortgage costs.

22. B: The debt-to-income (DTI) ratio is $\frac{1,400}{4,000} = 35\%$.

23. C: The model state law requires that an MLO's NMLS ID number appear on all advertising, which includes electronic billboards.

24. A: Regulation N governs a lender's advertising, including TV ads.

25. A: The loan-to-value (LTV) ratio is $\frac{380,000}{400,000} = 0.95$ or 95%.

26. C: The USA Patriot Act requires lenders to check borrowers' names against a list of known terrorists.

27. A: People who opt in to receive communications from their lender can get unsolicited telemarketing calls.

28. A: Because a 15-year loan is paid off in half the time of a 30-year loan, the monthly payments for a 15-year loan are typically higher.

29. C: To ensure that lenders are adhering to fair lending practices, the Home Mortgage Disclosure Act (HMDA) requires lenders to collect or generate forty-eight pieces of data for each dwelling loan application it receives and to report all of this data to the federal government.

30. D: A credit report is required to give evidence of an MLO's responsibility with his personal finances.

31. A: Freddie Mac's "Loan Program Advisor" software helps evaluate whether a lender should underwrite a new mortgage.

32. A: Annual PMI cost is 0.8% of the loan amount, or $240,000 \times \left(\frac{0.8}{100}\right) = \$1,920$.

33. C: A Fair and Accurate Credit Transactions Act (FACTA) disclosure provides borrowers with their credit reports and credit scores.

34. D: US Department of Agriculture (USDA) loans are for properties in rural areas.

35. A: Unexpected withdrawals of money are most likely to indicate identity theft. Unexpected additions to a bank account are generally less likely to indicate identity theft.

36. C: Jumbo mortgages are for properties valued over the million-dollar limit on government-backed mortgages.

37. D: The Equal Credit Opportunity Act (ECOA) Regulation B states that the lender must provide the reason(s) for denying a borrower's mortgage loan application within thirty days.

38. B: Compliance is the concept of "complying with," or obeying, federal and state laws.

39. B: Balloon mortgages have unusually large payments—much larger than typical monthly payments—that are due at the end of the term.

40. A: The monthly payments for utilities should be excluded from a borrower' back-end debt-to-income (DTI) ratio.

41. C: In accordance with the Equal Credit Opportunity Act's (ECOA's) Regulation B, income can be cause for denying a loan application.

42. A: The principal is the original loan amount.

43. D: Utility payments are not liabilities that are used when calculating a borrower's back-end debt-to-income ratio (DTI).

44. B: Not including the day on which the application was submitted, the lender has three business days to mail loan disclosures.

45. A: The first number in an adjustable-rate mortgage (ARM) is the number of years when the mortgage rate stays the same; the second number is how many years after the first adjustment the mortgage can be adjusted.

46. D: The monthly escrow amount is $\left(\frac{1,500}{12}\right) + 75 + 100 = \$300$.

47. A: Though a Closing Disclosure often contains slightly different information than a loan estimate, the main information on both documents is generally the same.

48. A: Higher interest rates require higher mortgage payments.

49. C: One of the responsibilities of the settlement agent is to work with the county clerk and county recorder to record the title and deed of a property after closing.

50. C: In a reverse mortgage, a lender sends money to the current owner each month.

51. A: A $5,000 transaction requires a suspicious activity report, and a transaction of $10,000 requires a currency transaction report.

52. B: Title insurance covers any problems arising from a title search indicating that the seller may not be the rightful owner.

53. C: Privacy policies are sent to borrowers annually.

54. A: Real estate agents who encourage their buyers to purchase in a neighborhood that is predominantly the same race or ethnicity as them is a form of steering.

55. C: The per diem interest covers the last fifteen days in April, including the day of closing; therefore, per diem interest is $(\$370,000 \times 0.045) \div 12 \times \left(\frac{15}{30}\right) = \$693.75$.

56. B: Borrowers are protected under Section 10 of RESPA from having lenders collect too much money and holding large escrows. Depending on the time of year, there is a limit to how much money lenders can collect up front to be held in escrow.

57. C: An asset is something valuable (e.g., stock in a company) that can be sold for cash to pay off a debt if needed.

58. C: Under Section 8 of the Real Estate Settlement Procedures Act (RESPA), giving or accepting a fee, kickback, or anything of monetary value in exchange for referrals is prohibited.

59. C: Discount points are optional and can be paid by the borrower to the lender to reduce the loan's interest rate.

60. C: Failure to disclose *any* existing debts or payments, such as child support or alimony, is classified as liability fraud.

61. B: A reverse mortgage allows borrowers to borrow against the equity in their home without having to make principal or interest payments to their lender.

62. D: The borrower's gross monthly income would be $4,550:

$$\$1,050 \times 52 = \frac{\$54,600}{12} = \$4,550$$

63. B: Since the Dodd-Frank Act was enacted in 2010, supervisory and compliance enforcement authority for the Equal Credit Opportunity Act (ECOA) was transferred from the Federal Reserve to the Consumer Financial Protection Bureau (CFPB).

64. C: Private mortgage insurance (PMI) is automatically removed when equity reaches 22% of the loan, which is $200,000 \times 0.22 = \$44,000$.

65. B: Interest-rate mortgages pay off no principal, so the borrower owes just as much as in the beginning.

66. D: Annuities are most commonly kept as reserve funds to be used only in case of an emergency lack of income.

67. D: The US Treasury Bond rate has a certain percentage of margin added to create a mortgage's actual interest rate.

68. B: The capital gains amounts for the last two years should be averaged: ($10,000 + $30,000)/2 = $20,000.

69. D: Calls can be made between 8 a.m. and 9 p.m. in the customer's time zone.

70. D: An appraiser writes a report—an appraisal—that estimates the value of a property.

71. C: When a borrower lies about the intended occupancy of a property, it is a form of occupancy fraud.

72. B: The deed "reconveys," or returns, the property's title to its owner.

73. B: The Real Estate Settlement Procedures Act (RESPA) requires the Mortgage Servicing Disclosure to be provided to the borrower within three business days of the loan application.

74. B: Flood insurance is not part of most private homeowner insurance policies, but it can be purchased through the Federal Emergency Management Agency (FEMA).

75. C: An MLO may receive both a commission and a salary from a lender but may not be paid by both the borrower and lender for the same loan.

76. C: In order to avoid private mortgage insurance (PMI), a buyer must put down at least 20%, or in this case, over $120,000.

77. B: A point is 1% of the loan amount, so $\frac{1}{4}$ point is $\frac{1}{4} \times 0.01 \times 300,000 = \$750$. The total fee would therefore be $\$300 + \$750 = \$1,050$.

78. D: Splitting divides fees between a lender and a settlement company.

79. C: The taxes, homeowner's insurance, and private mortgage insurance (PMI) must be divided by 12 to find the amount payable each month; therefore, the monthly payment is:

$$\$288.63 + \$1,100.11 + \left(\frac{\$1,800}{12}\right) + \left(\frac{\$1,200}{12}\right) + \left(\frac{\$1,500}{12}\right) = \$1,763.74$$

80. B: The Electronic Signatures in Global and National Commerce (E-Sign) Act allows Closing Disclosures to be signed electronically.

81. B: The interest rate right now is the current index plus the margin, or $5.25 + 2.5 = 7.75\%$.

82. B: Clear language in a mortgage document is expected and legal; the other options would be considered "unfair, deceptive, or abusive."

83. C: In mortgage terms, a conventional loan is one which is not backed by the government.

84. C: A primary residence is the only occupancy type that a mortgage lender considers to be owner-occupied.

85. D: The Mortgage Servicing Disclosure Statement is provided to borrowers within three business days of the loan application and states whether or not their loan will be serviced by the originating lender or sold to a different lender or investor on the secondary market.

86. C: The loan-to-value (LTV) ratio is calculated by dividing the loan amount by the appraised value of the property. (E.g., $80,000 loan amount ÷ $100,000 appraised value = 0.80 or 80%).

87. D: Borrowers may unknowingly pay for the kickback when they pay for the service that is giving the kickback to the referring party. For example, if a house inspection typically costs $500, the inspector could charge the borrower $700 for the inspection and give $200 to the referring party as a kickback while keeping the $500 to complete the inspection.

88. A: Income verification can be skipped for refinances that do not increase the amount owed, have a lower interest rate, and have fees less than 3% of the refinanced amount. Option A is the only one that meets all three of these conditions.

89. D: A discount point is 1% of the loan amount.

90. B: Leaving the mortgage profession for more than five years requires a retake of the MLO exam. In most states, the licensing course is not required a second time.

91. D: The Department of Housing and Urban Development (HUD) is a cabinet-level agency, led by a secretary appointed by the US president and confirmed by the US Senate.

92. C: An appraisal management company acts as an intermediary between the mortgage lender and the appraiser in order to prevent any collusion.

93. A: Refusing to accept an application because the subject property is within a minority neighborhood is an example of redlining.

94. B: A first mortgage gets paid back before a second mortgage, so Alpha would get fully paid back and Beta would get what is left.

95. A: Only licensed loan originators are allowed to negotiate with borrowers; this includes sending an email of an offer to a borrower.

96. C: The Federal Trade Commission's (FTC's) Red Flags Rule concerns issues that may indicate identity theft.

97. C: A liability is money owed to someone else; therefore, a balance owed to a credit card company is considered a liability.

98. A: MLO licensing expires at the end of each calendar year, so even though Michelle has not been licensed for very long, her license will still expire on December 31, 2023.

99. A: An assumable mortgage is one that allows the buyer to "assume" the loan's payments, terms, and conditions.

100. C: A borrower's middle credit score is used when qualifying for a mortgage. For example, if a borrower has the following credit scores on her credit report—Transunion (696); Equifax (667); Experian (686)—the borrower would qualify with the 686 (Experian) credit score.

101. B: An MLO should perform each task listed in the options, but cybersecurity is computer security, especially when money is being wired between parties.

102. A: A power of attorney granted by a buyer or seller allows another person (e.g., a realtor) to legally sign documents for that buyer or seller at closing when that buyer or seller is unavailable in person.

103. A: The promissory note is a legally binding document that is an agreement between the lender and the borrower which states that the borrower agrees to repay the loan per the terms and conditions contained within the document.

104. B: A de minimis exception of the Secure and Fair Enforcement for Mortgage Licensing (SAFE) Act allows a never-before-registered person to process mortgage loans as long as he does five or fewer within a twelve-month period.

105. D: The cost approach appraisal uses the land value plus the cost of construction and/or improvements to a structure on the property and then subtracts any depreciation to determine the value.

106. C: After three years, no prepayment penalty is allowed.

107. D: The 2013 HOEPA rule requires that borrowers be given a list of homeowner counselors near or within the borrower's zip code.

108. B: Predatory loans are more expensive than necessary and benefit the loan officer and/or lender. Encouraging or even forcing borrowers to accept these loans is an illegal practice.

109. A: The front-end debt-to-income (DTI) ratio is used to determine the percentage of a borrower's gross monthly income that will be dedicated to housing expenses, such as principal, interest, taxes and insurance (hazard and PMI, if applicable).

110. A: The American Association of Residential Mortgage Regulators (AARMR) helps mortgage regulators in each state properly supervise their mortgage lenders and the lenders' employees.

111. C: Referrals and referral fees are legal when written notification disclosing the referral arrangements is given to borrowers and when they are told in writing that they can use another company and are not required to use the referred company.

112. D: A settlement agent (or closing agent) typically schedules a closing.

113. A: The Real Estate Settlement Procedures Act (RESPA) is designed to benefit and protect consumers during mortgage transactions on residential properties, such as new home purchases.

114. C: One reason for the NMLS database's existence is to allow a borrower to search the employment history of his MLO to ensure that person is properly licensed and works for the company she claims to work for.

115. A: Under Section 9 of the Real Estate Settlement Procedures Act (RESPA), the seller may not insist or require that a buyer purchase title insurance through a particular title company.

116. B: Since the borrower's intentions include generating rental income with this property, the mortgage loan officer must consider this an investment property.

117. D: After failing the exam three times, a candidate must wait six months before taking the exam again.

118. D: Regulation N covers truth in lender advertising.

119. A: All first-time homebuyers must receive a copy of the TILA-RESPA Integrated Disclosures (TRID).

120. A: The first payment is due at the beginning of the second month after closing, so Corey would need to close on or before March 31 to have the first payment due on May 1.

Practice Test #3

1. Which of the following is the term for suspicious things an institution may notice that could indicate identity theft?

   A)   red flag
   B)   steering
   C)   fraud flag
   D)   redlining

2. According to the GLBA, how often are mortgage lenders required to provide all customers with written copies of their privacy policies?

   A)   every month
   B)   every quarter
   C)   every year
   D)   every other year

3. When qualifying for a mortgage, the extra money that a borrower may be required to have that is intended to cover the mortgage payments in the event the borrower faces financial difficulty is called what?

   A)   safe harbor funds
   B)   residual income
   C)   gift funds
   D)   reserve funds

4. On an ARM, which of the following changes during the term of the loan?

   A)   the margin
   B)   the amortization schedule
   C)   the payment date
   D)   the fully indexed rate

5. A loan officer refers her borrower to a title company that pays the loan officer $100 for every referral. The loan officer provides a written statement to the borrower that discloses the referral arrangement and states that the borrower is not required to use this title company. When the loan officer makes the referral and gives the borrower the written statement, she also informs the borrower that if he does not use the

referred title company the loan will not close in time, the borrower will be responsible for extension fees, and the seller may back out if the closing date is missed. Why is this considered illegal?

  A) The loan officer should not have waited so close to the closing date.

  B) The loan officer is receiving a kickback.

  C) The loan officer is using coercion to force a referral.

  D) This is not illegal since the loan officer provided the written disclosure to the borrower.

6. When may a borrower use cash as an asset when applying for a mortgage?

  A) immediately after being deposited

  B) thirty days after being deposited

  C) forty-five days after being deposited

  D) sixty days after being deposited

7. On which type of loan is mortgage insurance always required?

  A) VA

  B) FHA

  C) USDA

  D) Conventional

8. Which entity works with regulators in each state to create and facilitate the regulation and supervision of mortgage companies?

  A) the Consumer Financial Protection Bureau (CFPB)

  B) the American Association of Residential Mortgage Regulators (AARMR)

  C) the Conference of State Bank Supervisors (CSBS)

  D) the Nationwide Multistate Licensing System and Registry (NMLS)

9. Which of the following laws regulates the advertising of mortgage products?

  A) the Homeowner Protection Act

  B) Regulation N

  C) the Real Estate Settlement Procedures Act (RESPA)

  D) the Fair and Accurate Credit Transactions Act (FACTA)

10. What would the LTV ratio be if a borrower purchases a home for $277,000 and puts down $39,000?

  A) 14%

  B) 71%

  C) 72%

  D) 86%

11. Which of the following was the Gramm-Leach-Bliley Act (GLBA) designed to safeguard for consumers?

  A) nonpublic information

  B) telephone numbers

  C) criminal records

  D) home sales price

12. What happens if the borrower does NOT sign the Closing Disclosure three business days prior to closing?

    A)   The lender is charged a fee.

    B)   The closing date must be pushed back.

    C)   The loan must be re-originated.

    D)   The borrower is charged a fee.

13. In 2012, a borrower used a 7/1 ARM to purchase a home; the loan has a 5% interest rate. If the lender's margin is 2%, and in 2021 their current interest rate is 9%, what would the current index rate be?

    A)   5%

    B)   3%

    C)   11%

    D)   7%

14. What is the term for a fee imposed on borrowers who pay their loans off earlier than specified in their contracts?

    A)   early termination penalty

    B)   sudden repayment fee

    C)   prepayment penalty

    D)   early repayment penalty

15. In accordance with the Homeowners Protection Act, if a borrower's mortgage payments are current, at what loan-to-value (LTV) ratio must their private mortgage insurance be automatically canceled?

    A)   78%

    B)   80%

    C)   88%

    D)   90%

16. Prior to qualifying for a mortgage, a borrower transfers assets from his mother to ensure he will qualify and then intends to transfer these assets back to his mother once the loan closes. Is this considered fraud? If so which type of fraud would this be?

    A)   No, as long as the assets are transferred sixty days prior to applying for the mortgage, it is legal.

    B)   No, since the assets belong to the mother and will most likely be inherited by the borrower, this is legal.

    C)   Yes, this is income fraud.

    D)   Yes, this is asset fraud.

17. Which of the following is part of the background check required by the NMLS to obtain an MLO license?

    A)   a review of twenty-four months of bank statements

    B)   a review of high school or college transcripts

    C)   a review of family history of financial crimes

    D)   a review of credit reports and criminal records

18. Which law requires financial institutions to file an SAR with the US Treasury Department on transactions over $10,000?
    A) Gramm-Leach-Bliley Act (GLBA)
    B) USA PATRIOT Act
    C) Bank Secrecy Act (BSA)
    D) Fair and Accurate Credit Transactions Act (FACTA)

19. Under the CFPB's loan originator rule, in which of the following ways is a mortgage loan originator PROHIBITED from being compensated?
    A) hourly pay
    B) based on the total amount of loans originated
    C) on a fixed rate for each loan originated
    D) based on the terms of loans originated

20. Which law was enacted to protect the privacy of consumers by requiring financial institutions to create and implement policies for safeguarding their nonpublic information?
    A) the Truth In Lending Act (TILA)
    B) the Dodd-Frank Act
    C) the Homeowners Protection Act
    D) the Gramm-Leach-Bliley Act (GLBA)

21. What is the total monthly mortgage payment if a borrower's principal and interest payments are $2 250; homeowner's insurance premium is $4800 per year; and taxes are $3600 annually?
    A) $2,400
    B) $2,850
    C) $2,950
    D) $3,600

22. How many times can the NMLS exam be failed until a six-month waiting period is required before the next retake?
    A) once
    B) twice
    C) three times
    D) five times

23. Which of the following could classify as income fraud when applying for a mortgage?
    A) overstating a bank account balance
    B) lying about length of employment
    C) understating salary for low-income benefits
    D) omitting child support payments from debts

24. A mortgage lender who inaccurately advertises mortgage credit products to consumers is in violation of which law?
    A) Regulation Z
    B) the Fair Housing Act
    C) Regulation N
    D) the Homeowners Protection Act

25. Which of the following is used to calculate per diem interest using a 365-day calendar?

A) $\frac{\text{loan amount}}{\text{interestrate}} \times 365$

B) loan amount $\times \frac{\text{interest rate}}{360}$

C) loan amount ÷ interest rate ÷ 365

D) loan amount $\times \frac{\text{interest rate}}{365}$

26. Which of the following loan types is considered nonconforming?

A) conventional
B) USDA
C) FHA
D) jumbo

27. Under TRID, which of the following disclosures replaces the good faith estimate, TIL, and HUD-1?

A) the deed of trust and the promissory note
B) the loan estimate and the Closing Disclosure
C) Form 1003 and the Closing Disclosure
D) the loan estimate and the promissory note

28. A borrower has a 30-year mortgage where the interest rate is fixed at 6% for the first seven years; however, in the eighth year and every year after, the interest rate will be updated. Which type of mortgage does this borrower MOST likely have?

A) a 30-year fixed-rate mortgage
B) a 10/1 adjustable-rate mortgage
C) a balloon mortgage
D) a 7/1 adjustable-rate mortgage

29. What is the back-end DTI ratio for a borrower with an $80,000 gross annual salary, a $3,300 estimated monthly mortgage payment, a $400 monthly car payment, and a $150 monthly car insurance payment?

A) 49.5%
B) 51.8%
C) 55.5%
D) 57.8%

30. Which of the following laws protects borrowers by preventing unreasonable mortgage terms and governing mortgage loan origination fees?

A) the Real Estate Settlement Procedures Act (RESPA)
B) the Homeowners Protection Act
C) the Home Mortgage Disclosure Act (HMDA)
D) the Dodd-Frank Act

31. Which type of loan matures and is required to be paid in full prior to the completion of its amortization schedule?

A) an adjustable-rate mortgage
B) a subordinate mortgage
C) a balloon mortgage
D) a reverse mortgage

32. Which of the following would be a reason for automatic denial when applying for a mortgage loan originator's license?
    A) a person convicted of a felony in the last nine years
    B) a person who previously had her MLO license revoked
    C) a person who is 18 years old but only has his GED
    D) a person who was convicted of a financial felony thirty years ago

33. Which RESPA form must be provided to borrowers if a business relationship exists between the settlement provider and the referring party?
    A) Form 1003
    B) Affiliated Business Arrangement Disclosure
    C) Adverse Action Notice
    D) Uniform Settlement Statement (HUD-1)

34. For a reverse mortgage, which of the following factors will a mortgage loan originator use to qualify a potential borrower?
    A) the borrower's race
    B) the purchase price of the property
    C) the borrower's age
    D) the length of ownership of the property

35. Which of the following loan programs would be the BEST fit for a borrower who wants to purchase a home in the city, can afford a small down payment, has a credit score below 680, and earns a lower-than-average income?
    A) conventional
    B) FHA
    C) jumbo
    D) USDA

36. Which of the following loan types is protected under HOEPA?
    A) reverse mortgage
    B) USDA loan
    C) construction loan
    D) FHA loan

37. Which of the following loan types usually takes a second lien position and is considered a subordinate loan?
    A) a balloon mortgage
    B) a reverse mortgage
    C) a home equity line of credit
    D) an adjustable-rate mortgage

38. Who does title insurance protect?
    A) the lender
    B) the title company
    C) the seller
    D) the homebuyer

39. How many hours of ethics training is required to obtain an MLO license?
   A)   one hour
   B)   three hours
   C)   four hours
   D)   six hours

40. Which of the following does the Bank Secrecy Act/Anti-Money Laundering (BSA/AML) require all financial institutions to do?
   A)   maintain all advertisement materials for two years
   B)   provide customers with their privacy policy annually
   C)   verify customers' identities
   D)   provide denied borrowers with an adverse action notice

41. Which of the following do mortgage lenders use to determine the value of a property?
   A)   assessed value
   B)   appraised value
   C)   purchase price
   D)   real estate agent opinion

42. Which of the following loan types are considered to be the LEAST risky to lenders?
   A)   fixed-rate mortgages
   B)   interest-only mortgages
   C)   home equity lines of credit
   D)   adjustable-rate mortgages

43. If a lender has a maximum LTV of 85% on second homes, what is the minimum down payment on a $195000 property being purchased as a second home?
   A) $22,940
   B) $29,250
   C) $31,120
   D) $43,580

44. Defined by the GLBA, which of the following would be considered nonpublic information?
   A)   first and last name
   B)   home address
   C)   bank account number
   D)   phone number

45. Which two mortgage types will Freddie Mac and Fannie Mae purchase because they are originated and underwritten to the rules and limits they have set forth?
   A)   qualified mortgages and non-qualified mortgages
   B)   conforming and conventional mortgages
   C)   qualified mortgages and jumbo mortgages
   D)   conforming mortgages and jumbo mortgages

46. A borrower calls about refinancing her mortgage: the value of the home is $330,000 and she still owes $191,400. What is the borrower's LTV ratio?

A) 42%

B) 58%

C) 61%

D) 86%

47. Which of the following was established by the Secure and Fair Enforcement for Mortgage Licensing (SAFE) Act?

A) the National Association of Mortgage Brokers

B) the Nationwide Multistate Licensing System and Registry

C) the Consumer Financial Protection Bureau

D) the Mortgage Loan Officer Code of Ethics

48. Which of the following loan types is a government-backed loan?

A) FHA

B) Conventional

C) Jumbo

D) HELOC

49. Under(HMDA, which of the following pieces of information do borrowers have the right to refuse to provide?

A) age

B) income

C) sex

D) marital status

50. A mortgage lender approves a loan with excellent terms for a borrower to buy his first home. At closing, the mortgage lender tells the borrower that he no longer qualifies for that loan but that he is approved for a different loan at less favorable terms. The borrower will lose the house if he does not accept the new loan. This scenario is an example of which practice?

A) steering

B) bait and switch

C) redlining

D) splitting

51. Which type of insurance is required on ALL conventional mortgages?

A) private mortgage insurance

B) flood insurance

C) hazard insurance

D) up-front mortgage insurance premiums

52. Per HOEPA, which of the following total lender points and fees would classify a $70 000 mortgage loan as high cost?
    A) $3,600
    B) $1,200
    C) $3,000
    D) $2,400

53. What is the total gross monthly income if the borrower makes an annual salary of $84,000 and the co borrower makes a biweekly salary of $2,200?
    A) $9,266
    B) $11,400
    C) $11,766
    D) $11,900

54. Under the Bank Secrecy Act (BSA), how long must a financial institution keep an SAR after it has been filed?
    A) 180 days
    B) one year
    C) three years
    D) five years

55. How many points can a borrower buy for $4,500 if he purchases a $170,000 home and puts $20,000 down?
    A) one point
    B) two points
    C) three points
    D) four points

56. On a $150 000 mortgage, what is the maximum amount of points and fees that can be charged while allowing the loan to remain classified as a qualified mortgage (QM)?
    A) $2,500
    B) $3,000
    C) 4,500
    D) $5,500

57. What is the benefit given to a mortgage loan originator who becomes a teacher of continuing education to other mortgage loan originators?
    A) They do not have to complete their own continuing education requirements.
    B) Their license will not expire as long as they are teaching.
    C) They are only required to complete four hours of continuing education annually.
    D) They receive a letter from the NMLS thanking them for their expertise.

58. Which of the following entities established the guidelines for loans to be considered conforming?
    A) the Federal Housing Administration (FHA)
    B) the US Department of Veterans Affairs (VA)
    C) the Federal National Mortgage Association (FNMA)
    D) the Consumer Financial Protection Bureau (CFPB)

59. When purchasing a home, the buyer and seller agreed on a purchase price of $300,000. The buyer negotiated 2% of the purchase price from the seller to be used towards the buyer's closing costs. The buyer is putting 10% down and has $5,000 in closing costs. How much of the seller's credit can be used for the down payment?

A) $0
B) $1,000
C) $3,000
D) $6,000

60. Under the HMDA, also known as Regulation C, which of the following should the MLO do if the borrower declines to provide information pertaining to his race, sex, or ethnicity?

A) indicate on the application that the borrower refused to provide this information and guess the information based on visual observation
B) tell the borrower that this information is optional and can be left blank
C) deny the loan application on the grounds that the borrower refused to provide required information
D) inform the borrower that the lender's HMDA data is nonpublic information and will be safeguarded

61. A mortgage lender advertises an unattainably low interest rate on the radio in the hopes of increasing inbound call volume for mortgage applications. Which law is the mortgage lender in violation of?

A) Regulation N
B) Home Mortgage Disclosure Act
C) Regulation B
D) Homeowners Protection Act

62. Which of the following is a legal document that can be executed by the borrower to appoint another person of authority to sign for them at closing?

A) the deed of trust
B) the Supplemental Consumer Information Form (SCIF)
C) the power of attorney (POA)
D) the Borrower's Signature Authorization

63. What is the PRIMARY purpose of PMI?

A) to protect the borrower
B) to protect the property
C) to protect the lender
D) to protect the seller

64. Which of the following is a standardized mortgage application created by Fannie Mae and called the "Uniform Residential Loan Application"?

A) Form 1003
B) 1099 Form
C) Form 1004
D) Form 1073

65. Before it can be published, what must happen to a mortgage lender's advertising?
   A) It must be reviewed and approved by the CFPB.
   B) It must undergo due diligence for possible mistaken impressions.
   C) It must be reviewed and approved by an industry peer.
   D) It must undergo a focus group test to see how consumers react.

66. What is another name for the Homeowners Protection Act?
   A) the PMI Cancellation Act
   B) the Home Mortgage Disclosure Act (HMDA)
   C) the Truth In Lending Act (TILA)
   D) the Home Ownership and Equity Protection Act (HOEPA)

67. Which appraisal type is MOST commonly used on home purchases?
   A) cost approach appraisal
   B) sales comparison appraisal
   C) income approach appraisal
   D) homebuyer approach appraisal

68. A mortgage loan officer advises his client that if she works with the loan officer's real estate agent connection when buying a house, she will not be charged an out of network agent fee on her loan. Is this illegal?
   A) Yes, this is a form of steering.
   B) No, the client is not being forced.
   C) Yes, this is a form of coercion.
   D) No, the loan officer is saving the borrower money.

69. Which loan type requires a one-time UFMIP?
   A) FHA
   B) conventional
   C) jumbo
   D) VA

70. According to the (ECOA), within how many days must the lender provide the borrower with an adverse action notice if his application is denied?
   A) fifteen days
   B) thirty days
   C) forty-five days
   D) sixty days

71. What is the type of relationship that lenders and mortgage loan officers have with their borrowers where they are ethically and legally required to act in the best interests of the borrowers?

   A) business relationship
   B) fiduciary relationship
   C) confidential relationship
   D) good faith relationship

72. A mortgage loan officer takes advantage of an older adult customer who has difficulty hearing by giving him a more expensive mortgage than he qualifies for because the loan officer will make more money. This is known as which type of loan?
   A)   prime mortgage
   B)   predatory loan
   C)   reverse mortgage
   D)   negative amortization

73. What is the front-end DTI ratio for a borrower with a gross monthly income of $5,000; a monthly principal and interest payment of $1,900; $2,200 in annual taxes; $1,800 in annual insurance premiums; and a $325 per month car loan?
   A)   36%
   B)   41%
   C)   45%
   D)   51%

74. According to HOEPA, a mortgage loan is considered high cost when the total lender fees exceed which amount?
   A) $5,000
   B)   5% of loan amount
   C) $10,000
   D)   10% of loan amount

75. How much is the one-time, up-front mortgage insurance premium (UFMIP) for FHA loans?
   A) $1,750
   B)   1.75% of loan amount
   C) $2,750
   D)   2.75% of loan amount

76. What is the term for the maximum amount the interest rate can go up at the time of the first adjustment on an ARM?

   A)   periodic cap
   B)   initial adjustment cap
   C)   lifetime cap
   D)   interest adjustment cap

77. According to the Electronic Signatures in Global and National Commerce (E-Sign) Act, who must provide agreement to use electronic signatures in a transaction?
   A)   the settlement company
   B)   just the lender
   C)   just the borrower
   D)   both the lender and borrower

78. Which of the following loans are government-backed and specifically designed for properties in rural areas?
   A)   Farmer Housing Authority Loan
   B)   United States Department of Agriculture Loan
   C)   Federal Housing Administration Loan
   D)   Subprime Mortgage Loan

79. Which of the following items on the loan estimate is considered a zero tolerance fee?
   A)   government recording fees
   B)   origination fees
   C)   prepaid interest
   D)   title insurance fees

80. Under the Homeowners Protection Act, which of the following is a requirement in order to cancel private mortgage insurance (PMI) at 80% loan-to-value (LTV)?
   A)   An inspection to determine current condition.
   B)   A new credit report to ensure credit worthiness.
   C)   A written request from the borrower to cancel PMI.
   D)   The mortgage is no more than 60 days past due.

81. A real estate agent with a client who is considered a minority is only showing the client homes in minority neighborhoods and refuses to show homes elsewhere. Which illegal practice is this?
   A)   redlining
   B)   bait and switch
   C)   steering
   D)   splitting

82. What is the front-end DTI ratio for a borrower who makes $108,000 a year and has been preapproved for a $300,000 mortgage with a monthly principal and interest payment of $2,100; annual property taxes of $3,600; annual homeowners insurance of $2,400; monthly utilities of $300; and a $400 a month car lease with nine months of payments remaining?
   A)   22%
   B)   29%
   C)   32%
   D)   37%

83. When does a mortgage loan originator license expire?
   A)   on the applicants birthday
   B)   January 31st of every year
   C)   on the anniversary of when the license was issued
   D)   December 31st of every year

84. A borrower tells his mortgage loan officer that he is purchasing a vacation home on the beach. In order to receive more favorable loan terms he does not disclose that he intends to rent out the beach house while he is not using it. Is this legal?
    A) Yes, it is legal as long as the borrower still intends to vacation at the property.
    B) No, this is a form of liability fraud.
    C) Yes, this is not an investment property.
    D) No, this is a form of occupancy fraud.

85. Which of the following items on the loan estimate is considered a zero tolerance fee?
    A) the lender's title policy
    B) the prepaid interest
    C) the origination fee
    D) the assignment recording fee

86. A $225,000 loan with a 7% interest rate is closing on June 22nd. Including the closing day and using a 365-day calendar, how much per diem interest will the borrower have to pay?

    A) $345.20
    B) $388.36
    C) $393.75
    D) $431.50

87. Which of the following may be required if a borrower is perceived as a higher risk to the lender?
    A) a longer mortgage term
    B) a larger down payment
    C) a lower margin on an adjustable-rate mortgage
    D) hazard insurance

88. What is the gross monthly income for a borrower who makes $1,950 bi weekly and a coborrower who makes $2,100 semi monthly?
    A) $7,325
    B) $8,100
    C) $8,425
    D) $8,775

89. Which entity has a code of ethics within which loan officers are encouraged to work?
    A) the National Association of Mortgage Brokers (NAMB)
    B) Freddie Mac
    C) the Consumer Financial Protection Bureau (CFPB)
    D) Fannie Mae

90. Under the BSA/AML, an SAR should be filed with the Treasury Department by a financial institution on any transactions exceeding which amount?
    A) $100,000
    B) $25,000
    C) $50,000
    D) $10,000

91. How much of a down payment would a borrower need on a $275 000 house if the borrower is preapproved for a loan at 85% LTV?
    A) $33,750
    B) $41,250
    C) $233,750
    D) $241,250

92. What is the front-end DTI ratio for a borrower with a gross annual income of $120,000; an expected monthly principal, interest, tax, and insurance payment of $2,300; and a $500 monthly car payment?
    A) 28%
    B) 2.3%
    C) 23%
    D) 1.9%

93. What is Regulation N also known as?
    A) the Mortgage Acts and Practices-Advertising (MAP) Rule
    B) the Fair and Accurate Credit Transactions Act (FACTA)
    C) the Gramm-Leach-Bliley Act (GLBA)
    D) the Secure and Fair Enforcement for Mortgage Licensing Act (SAFE)

94. If a mortgage lender requires a borrower to put at least $15,000 down on the purchase of a $300,000 home, what would the LTV be?
    A) 85%
    B) 90%
    C) 92.5%
    D) 95%

95. Which of the following fees will the borrower have to pay when applying for a mortgage loan?
    A) the loan officer's time
    B) the cost of the credit report
    C) the pre-approval letter
    D) none

96. In 2017, a borrower receives a 5/1 ARM with a 1.5% margin. In 2022, if the index rate rises from 3% to 4.5%, what is the fully indexed rate of the borrower's loan after the change date?
    A) 4.5%
    B) 3%
    C) 6%
    D) 7.5%

97. If a borrower uses an FHA loan to purchase a $200,000 house, puts down 3.5%, and rolls in the 1.75% FHA upfront mortgage insurance premium, how much will the loan amount be?
    A) $198,500.00
    B) $198,412.50
    C) $196,377.50
    D) $196,500.00

98. A borrower applies for a mortgage that requires her to have two years at her current job. Unfortunately, the borrower has only been at the job for one year but states on the loan application that she has been there for three years. Which type of mortgage fraud is this?
    A) employment fraud
    B) income fraud
    C) occupancy fraud
    D) asset fraud

99. What is the GMI of a salaried borrower who is paid $2,600 gross biweekly?
    A) $5,200.00
    B) $5,233.33
    C) $5,600.00
    D) $5,633.33

100. Which scenario involving a mortgage requires that there be a clear advantage or tangible net benefit to the borrower?
    A) purchase of primary residence
    B) refinancing a mortgage
    C) purchase of investment property
    D) when receiving an ARM

101. Under Section 32 of HOEPA, a mortgage is classified as high cost if the APR exceeds the APOR by how much?
    A) 2.5%
    B) 4.5%
    C) 5.5%
    D) 6.5%

102. Which law was created by the CFPB to implement the SAFE Act?
    A) Regulation H
    B) the Bank Secrecy Act/Anti-Money Laundering (BSA/AML)
    C) Regulation N
    D) the Real Estate Settlement Procedures Act (RESPA)

103. Which of the following would be considered a red flag and may indicate identity theft?
    A) a borrower applying for a mortgage on a property that is in a state outside of where he resides
    B) a borrower providing handwritten W-2 forms and/or pay stubs
    C) a borrower with a cosigner who is not a relative
    D) a borrower who has been at her current job for less than two years

104. What are the two factors that determine the interest rate for an adjustable-rate mortgage after the change date has occurred?
    A) index rate and credit score
    B) credit score and margin
    C) index rate and margin
    D) down payment and index rate

105. Denying a mortgage loan application because of the borrower's disability is a violation of what?
    A)   the Equal Credit Opportunity Act
    B)   the Real Estate Settlement Procedure Act
    C)   the Home Ownership and Equity Protection Act
    D)   the Home Mortgage Disclosure Act

106. When qualifying a borrower, what is the term for the outstanding financial obligations that the borrower owes as a debt to others that is used to calculate their DTI ratio?
    A)   assets
    B)   expenses
    C)   bills
    D)   liabilities

107. Which federal law requires major credit reporting agencies to give consumers easy access to their credit reports and help prevent identity theft?
    A)   the Truth In Lending Act
    B)   the Fair and Accurate Credit Transactions Act
    C)   the USA Patriot Act
    D)   the Dodd-Frank Act

108. What is the minimum score needed to pass the NMLS exam?
    A)   65%
    B)   70%
    C)   75%
    D)   80%

109. A borrower qualifying for a $240 000 mortgage loan would like to purchase 2 points in order to lower the interest rate from 7% to 6.5%. How much would this cost the borrower?
    A) $1,400
    B) $2,400
    C) $2,800
    D) $4,800

110. If an aspiring MLO does not pass the NMLS exam on the second try, how long must she wait until she can retake the exam?
    A)   There is no time requirement to retake the exam.
    B)   thirty days
    C)   sixty days
    D)   six months

111. If a borrower uses a purchase money second mortgage structured as 80/10/10 to buy a home and receives a first mortgage for $240,000, what would be the amount of the purchase money second mortgage?
    A) $24,000
    B) $30,000
    C) $48,000
    D) $60,000

112. A real estate agent has a consultation with a potential seller to be the listing agent of his property. The seller agrees to give the listing to the agent with the condition that the agent does not sell the property to a specific race. Is this illegal?
    A) No, as long as it is not documented in the listing contract.
    B) Yes, this is a form of redlining.
    C) No, this is a personal preference that the agent must respect.
    D) Yes, this is a form of steering.

113. According to the FTC's Red Flag Rule, what triggers a red flag?
    A) a borrower's income not being sufficient for the requested loan amount
    B) an outstanding tax lien on a borrower's credit report
    C) any suspicious activity that indicates identity theft
    D) a property that is located within a flood zone

114. If a lender has a maximum frontend DTI ratio of 36% and a borrower has an annual salary of $130,000, what would the borrower's MAXIMUM housing payment be?
    A) $3,400
    B) $3,611
    C) $3,900
    D) $3,911

115. A state license is required for mortgage loan officers working at which of the following?
    A) federally insured credit unions
    B) member banks
    C) mortgage companies
    D) national banks

116. If a 5/1 ARM has a fully indexed rate of 5%, a margin of 3%, and a periodic cap of 1.5%, what is the MAXIMUM interest rate at the next adjustment?
    A) 4.5%
    B) 6.5%
    C) 8%
    D) 9.5%

117. Which of the following is required when completing continuing education to renew a mortgage loan originator license?
    A) three hours of ethics education
    B) one hour of traditional mortgages education
    C) two hours of compliance education
    D) three hours of federal law education

118. When applying for a mortgage to buy a home, the borrower claims that her 401(k) account has a balance of $250 000; however she only has $50 000 in the account. Since she does not plan on using these funds for the purchase of the home, is this legal?
    A) Yes, the funds are not being used for the purchase of the home.
    B) No, this may be seen as a false compensating factor and considered asset fraud.
    C) Yes, the future value of the 401(k) account could be $250,000.
    D) No, since the borrower's employer contributes to her 401(k), this is income fraud.

119. To remain compliant with the TRID, the lender must provide and have the borrower sign the Closing Disclosure how many days prior to closing?
    A) three business days
    B) three days
    C) five business days
    D) five days

120. What would the loan amount be if a borrower bought a $315 000 home put $30 000 down and received $9000 in credit from the seller?
    A) $275,000
    B) $276,000
    C) $285,000
    D) $286,000

Answer Key

1. A: A red flag is the term for suspicious things that may be noticed by an institution which may indicate possible identity theft.

2. C: Per the requirements set forth by the Gramm-Leach-Bliley Act (GLBA), financial institutions must provide their customers with written copies of their privacy policies once a year.

3. D: Reserve Funds may be required for a borrower to reduce risk and ensure that the borrower has money to continue making mortgage payments in the event of financial difficulties.

4. D: On an adjustable-rate mortgage (ARM), the fully indexed rate, which is the effective interest rate of the loan after the margin and index rate are combined, can be expected to change over the life of the loan.

5. C: Coercion is the illegal practice of forcing a borrower to use a referred party by threatening additional fees, amongst other things.

6. D: Cash may be used as an asset once the borrower has deposited the money into a bank account and the money has been in the account for sixty days or more.

7. B: Federal Housing Administration (FHA) loans require mortgage insurance for the entirety of the loan and may not be waived or removed.

8. B: The American Association of Residential Mortgage Regulators (AARMR) assists state regulators with the supervision and regulation of mortgage companies.

9. B: Regulation N outlines and regulates how mortgage credit products can be advertised.

10. D: The loan-to-value (LTV) ratio would be 86%: $277,000 - \$39,000 = \frac{\$238,000}{\$277,000} = 86\%$.

11. A: The Gramm-Leach-Bliley Act (GLBA) was designed to protect and safeguard consumers' nonpublic information by setting requirements for mortgage lenders to follow.

12. B: If the Closing Disclosure is not signed by the borrower three business days prior to closing, the closing date will be pushed back until three business days have passed.

13. D: Since the margin never changes and is added to the index rate to calculate the interest rate on an adjustable-rate mortgage (ARM), we can determine the current index rate by finding the difference between the interest rate and the margin: 9% (interest rate) − 2% (margin) = 7% (index rate).

14. C: Although they are not common for personal residential mortgages, prepayment penalties may be outlined in a borrower's mortgage terms; in such cases, a fee would be imposed on the borrower if the mortgage is paid off earlier than specified.

15. A: When a borrower is up to date on their mortgage payments, their private mortgage insurance must be automatically canceled when 22% of their original mortgage balance is paid off (78% LTV).

16. D: Claiming more assets—and even borrowing some else's assets—to qualify for a mortgage is considered asset fraud.

17. D: A review of an aspiring MLO's credit report and criminal record is part of the required background check required by the NMLS to obtain an MLO license.

18. C: The Bank Secrecy Act (BSA) requires financial institutions to file a suspicious activity report (SAR) with the US Treasury Department on transactions over $10,000.

19. D: Mortgage loan officers can be compensated in a variety of ways; however, the Consumer Financial Protection Bureau's (CFPB's) loan originator rule prohibits them from being compensated purely based on the terms of the loans they originate. For example, a loan officer cannot be paid more for loans originated at higher interest rates or with higher points.

20. D: The Gramm-Leach-Bliley Act (GLBA) was passed to protect consumers' privacy by establishing requirements for financial institutions pertaining to the safeguarding of nonpublic information.

21. C: The total monthly mortgage payment for the borrower would be $2,950. Taxes and insurance should be divided by 12 and added to the principal and interest payments: $\frac{\$4,800}{12} = \$400$ per month insurance, $+\frac{\$3,600}{12} = \$300$ per month taxes $= \$700$ per month, $+ \$2,250$ per month principal and interest $= \$2,950$ per month.

22. C: A six-month waiting period is required before the NMLS exam can be retaken after someone fails it three times.

23. C: Falsifying information relating to income, such as salary, in an effort to benefit financially could be classified as a form of income fraud.

24. C: Inaccurately advertising a mortgage is a violation of Regulation N, which regulates how mortgage credit products can be advertised.

25. D: Per diem interest is calculated using a 365-day calendar by multiplying the interest rate by the loan amount and dividing by 365: loan amount $\times \frac{\text{interest rate}}{365}$.

26. D: Jumbo loans, which are loans that exceed the limits set by the Federal Home Loan Mortgage Corporation (Freddie Mac) and the Federal National Mortgage Association (Fannie Mae), are nonconforming loans while conventional, FHA, and USDA loans are all conforming.

27. B: The loan estimate (LE) and Closing Disclosure (CD) replace the good faith estimate, Truth in Lending Act (TIL), and HUD-1 under TILA-RESPA Integrated Disclosures (TRID).

28. D: The borrower has a 7/1 adjustable-rate mortgage (ARM) where the loan is amortized over a period of thirty years, but the interest rate is only fixed for the first seven years and adjusts every year thereafter.

29. C: A gross monthly income (GMI) of $6,666.66 $\left(\frac{\$80,000}{12} = \$6,666.66\right)$ and a total monthly debt obligation of $3,700 (car insurance is not a debt obligation) equates to a 55.5% back-end debt-to-income (DTI) ratio $\left(\frac{\$3,700}{\$6,666.66} = 55.5\%\right)$.

30. D: The Dodd-Frank Act protects borrowers in a multitude of ways, including preventing unreasonable mortgage terms and governing mortgage loan origination fees.

31. C: A balloon mortgage is a loan that has a maturity date sooner than the timeframe for which the loan is amortized, which requires the remaining balance to be paid in full upon reaching the maturity date.

32. D: Anyone who has ever been convicted of—or plead guilty to—a financial felony will be permanently banned from receiving an MLO license.

33. B: Under the Real Estate Settlement Procedures Act (RESPA), an Affiliated Business Arrangement Disclosure must be provided to the borrower in her initial loan disclosure package if a business relationship exists between the settlement provider and the referring party. The lender must also disclose whether or not there is a direct financial interest in the business being referred.

34. C: When qualifying a borrower for a reverse mortgage, the mortgage loan officer will verify the borrower's age to confirm the person is at least sixty-two years old.

35. B: An Federal Housing Administration (FHA) loan would most likely be the best fit for this borrower since the home is not in a rural area and the borrower has a small down payment and low credit score.

36. D: The Home Ownership and Equity Protection Act (HOEPA) does not cover reverse mortgages, USDA loans, or construction loans.

37. C: A home equity line of credit (HELOC) is an open-ended mortgage that will take second lien position if a primary mortgage already exists on the property.

38. D: Title insurance protects the homebuyer from any title defects that may negatively impact the homebuyer's legal ownership rights to the property.

39. B: In order to qualify for an MLO license, candidates must have three hours of ethics training approved by the Nationwide Multistate Licensing System and Registry (NMLS, or NMLS).

40. C: The Bank Secrecy Act/Anti-Money Laundering (BSA/AML) requires financial institutions to verify the identities of their customers.

41. B: Mortgage lenders use the appraised value generated during an appraisal to determine a property's value.

42. A: Fixed-rate mortgages are considered to be the least risky mortgages for lenders since the borrower qualifies for the mortgage with a fixed principal and interest payment that will remain the same for the entirety of the loan's term.

43. B: The minimum down payment to meet the 85% LTV requirement is $29,250: $195,000 $\times$ 0.15 = $29,250.

44. C: The Gramm-Leach-Bliley Act (GLBA) defines nonpublic information as any personally identifiable financial information, such as a bank account number. Information such as names, street addresses, and phone numbers are considered public information.

45. B: Both the Federal Home Loan Mortgage Corporation (Freddie Mac) and the Federal National Mortgage Association (Fannie Mae) have rules and limits on the types of mortgages they will buy. These loans are originated and underwritten to those rules and limits and are known as conforming and conventional mortgages.

46. B: The loan-to-value (LTV) ratio of the borrower's current mortgage is 58%: $\frac{191,400}{330,000} = 58\%$.

47. B: The Nationwide Multistate Licensing System and Registry (NMLS, or NMLS) was established by the Secure and Fair Enforcement for Mortgage Licensing (SAFE) Act.

48. A: Federal Housing Administration loans are backed by the government.

49. C: Per the Home Mortgage Disclosure Act (HMDA), borrowers have the right to refuse to provide information regarding their sex.

50. B: "Baiting" a borrower with loan terms that sound too good to be true which are then "switched" to a less desirable loan is an example of a bait-and-switch tactic.

51. C: Hazard insurance is required on all conventional mortgages to provide coverage to the property being financed.

52. A: When the total amount of lender points and fees exceed 5% of the loan amount, the loan is considered high cost per the Home Ownership and Equity Protection Act (HOEPA); in this case $70,000 × .05 = $3,500.

53. C: The gross monthly income of these borrowers combined is $11,766: $2,200 × 26 pay periods = $57,200 per year + $84,000 per year $= \frac{\$141,200}{12} = \$11,766$.

54. D: Once a suspicious activity report (SAR) has been filed, the Bank Secrecy Act (BSA) requires the financial institution to keep the report for five years.

55. C: The borrower could buy three points for $4,500: a point is 1% of the loan amount; in this case, $170,000 − $20,000 = $150,000 × 1% = $1,500 per point.

56. C: In order for a mortgage to be classified as a qualified mortgage (QM), the maximum amount of points and fees cannot exceed 3% of loans over $100,000; in this case: $150,000 × 0.03 = $4,500.

57. C: Only four hours of annual continuing education are required for mortgage loan originators who become teachers of continuing education.

58. C: One of the entities that set the guidelines for loans to be considered conforming is the Federal National Mortgage Association (FNMA), also called Fannie Mae.

59. A: Money received by the borrower from the seller during the purchase of a property cannot be used toward the borrower's down payment. If any credit is left over after all closing costs are paid, the buyer can use the excess funds to purchase discount points and reduce the interest rate on the loan.

60. A: If a borrower declines to provide the Home Mortgage Disclosure Act (HMDA) information on a loan application, the loan officer should guess the information based on visual observation and indicate on the application that the borrower declined to provide the information directly.

61. A: Regulation N governs how mortgages can be advertised to consumers

62. C: A power of attorney (POA) is a legal document that the borrower can execute to authorize another person to act on behalf of the borrower; this includes signing on the borrower's behalf at closing.

63. C: The primary purpose of private mortgage insurance (PMI) is to protect the lender in the event that a borrower fails to repay the loan.

64. A: The Uniform Residential Loan Application, or Form 1003, is Fannie Mae's standardized loan application.

65. B: All mortgage lender advertising must undergo due diligence before it is published.

66. A: The Homeowners Protection Act is also referred to as the PMI Cancellation Act as it streamlines the process of canceling borrower-paid private mortgage insurance (PMI) and unifies the process across the entire country.

67. B: The sales comparison appraisal, also referred to as the market data approach, is the most commonly used appraisal for home purchases.

68. C: Forcing a client to work with a referral under the threat of extra paperwork, hassle, or fees is coercion; it is illegal.

69. A: In addition to monthly mortgage insurance premiums, Federal Housing Administration (FHA) loans also require a one-time mortgage insurance premium to be paid at the time of closing—an up-front mortgage insurance premium (UFMIP). Fortunately for borrowers, this amount is able to be financed with their mortgage.

70. B: The Equal Credit Opportunity Act (ECOA) requires that lenders provide borrowers with adverse action notices within thirty days if their loan applications are denied.

71. B: A "fiduciary relationship" is when lenders or mortgage loan officers act with the borrowers' best interests in mind.

72. B: A predatory loan is when officers give borrowers loans that are more expensive than they require in order for the loan officer to achieve financial gain.

73. C: The front-end debt-to-income (DTI) ratio of this borrower is 45%: $2,200 + $1,800 $= \frac{\$4,000}{12} =$ $333.33 + $1,900 $= \frac{\$2,233.33}{\$5,000} = 0.45$.

74. B: A mortgage loan in which the total lender fees exceed 5% of the loan amount is considered a high-cost mortgage under the Home Ownership and Equity Protection Act (HOEPA).

75. B: The one-time, up-front mortgage insurance premium (UFMIP) required on all Federal Housing Administration FHA loans is 1.75% of the loan amount.

76. B: The initial adjustment cap is the maximum amount the interest rate can go up at the time of the first adjustment on an adjustable-rate mortgage (ARM).

77. D: In order to use electronic signing capabilities in a transaction, both the lender and the borrower must agree to do so under the E-Sign Act.

78. B: The United States Department of Agriculture (USDA) loan is a government-backed loan exclusively offered to borrowers in rural areas.

79. B: Origination Fees are considered zero tolerance fees and must remain unchanged from the first loan estimate provided to the borrower.

80. C: In order to cancel PMI once 20% of the original mortgage amount is paid off (80% LTV), one requirement is a written request from the borrower to cancel PMI.

81. C: Only showing minorities homes in minority neighborhoods and not allowing them to view homes in other neighborhoods is a form of steering.

82. B: With a gross monthly income of $9,000 $\left(\frac{\$108,000}{12} = \$9,000\right)$, the borrower has a 29% front-end debt-to-income (DTI) ratio:

$$\$2,100 + \frac{\$3,600}{12} + \frac{\$2,400}{12} = \frac{\$2,600}{\$9,000} = 28.8$$

83. D: A mortgage loan originator license expires on December 31st of every year.

84. D: Not disclosing—or falsely disclosing—the intended occupancy of a property when applying for a mortgage is not legal and is a form of occupancy fraud.

85. C: An origination fee is a zero tolerance fee and is not allowed to change from what is quoted on the initial loan estimate.

86. B: The borrower would have to pay $388.36 in per diem interest:

$$\$225,000 \times 0.07 = \frac{\$15,750}{365} = \$43.15 \times 9 \text{ days} = \$388.36$$

87. B: The lender may require the borrower to make a larger down payment if the borrower presents a higher overall risk profile. The larger down payment reduces the mortgage amount needed and lowers the chance of default since the borrower is more financially vested in the property.

88. C: The borrowers together have a gross monthly income of $8,425:

$$\$1,950 \times 26 \text{ pay periods} = \frac{\$50,700}{12} = \$4,225 \text{ per month} + \$2,100 \times 2 \text{ pay periods}$$

$$\$4,200 \text{ per month} = \mathbf{\$8,425}$$

89. A: The National Association of Mortgage Brokers (NAMB) has a code of ethics by which loan officers need to abide.

90. D: Under the Bank Secrecy Act/Anti-Money Laundering (BSA/AML), financial Institutions should file a suspicious activity report (SAR) on any transactions over $10,000.

91. B: An 85% loan-to-value (LTV) ratio would make the borrower responsible for a 15% down payment, which is $41,250: $275,000 \times 15\% = \$41,250$.

92. C: Divide the gross annual income by 12 to calculate the borrower's gross monthly income $\left(\frac{\$120,000}{12} = \$10,000\right)$. Since this is a front-end debt-to-income (DTI) ratio, we do not need to include the $500 monthly car payment. Divide the expected monthly principal, interest, taxes, and insurance (PITI) payment by the gross monthly income to find the borrower's front-end DTI $\left(\frac{\$2,300}{\$10,000} = 23\%\right)$.

93. A: Regulation N is also known as the Mortgage Acts and Practices-Advertising (MAP) Rule, which governs commercial communication.

94. D: The LTV would be 95% since the borrower would be putting 5% down: $300,000 - $15,000 = \frac{$285,000}{$300,000} = 0.95$.

95. B: The cost of the credit report is the only fee a mortgage lender can charge the borrower for applying.

96. C: The fully indexed rate would be 6%: index 4.5% + margin 1.5% = fully indexed rate 6%.

97. C: The borrower's loan amount after the down payment and rolling in the FHA UFMIP is $196,377.50: $200,000 × 96.5% = $193,000 × 1.0175 = $196,377.50.

98. A: Claiming a longer period of employment than what one actually has is a form of employment fraud.

99. D: To calculate the gross monthly income (GMI) for a bi-weekly salaried borrower, the bi-weekly gross would be multiplied by 26 (which is the amount of pay periods annual for bi-weekly pay) and then divided by 12 (months in a year). In this case, $2,600 × 26 = \frac{$67,600}{12} = $5,633.33$.

100. B: When refinancing a mortgage, there must be a tangible net benefit or advantage for the borrower.

101. D: In section 32 of the Home Ownership and Equity Protection Act (HOEPA), which outlines high-cost mortgage loans, a mortgage loan is considered high cost when the annual percentage rate (APR) exceeds the average prime offer rate (APOR) by 6.5%.

102. A: To require that each state create its own mortgage regulatory agency, the Consumer Financial Protection Bureau (CFPB) created Regulation H to implement the SAFE Act.

103. B: Suspicious and/or fake-looking documentation, such as handwritten W-2 forms or paystubs, would be considered a red flag and should be addressed as soon as possible.

104. C: On an adjustable-rate mortgage, once the change date has occurred and the fixed-rate period is over, the index rate and margin are used to calculate the new effective interest rate.

105. A: Discriminating based on a borrower's disability is a violation of the Equal Credit Opportunity Act (ECOA).

106. D: Liabilities are outstanding financial obligations that are owed as a debt which is used to calculate the debt-to-income (DTI) ratio when qualifying a borrower.

107. B: The Fair and Accurate Credit Transaction Act (FACTA) is an amendment to the Fair Credit Reporting Act (FCRA) that requires major credit reporting agencies to give consumers access to their credit reports and help prevent identity theft.

108. C: Anyone who takes the NMLS exam must earn a final score of 75% or higher in order to pass.

109. D: Buying 2 points on a $240,000 loan would cost the borrower $4,800: $240,000 × 1% = $2,400 × 2 = $4,800.

110. B: There is a thirty-day waiting period for the second and third attempts on the NMLS exam.

111. B: Knowing that an 80/10/10 purchase-money second mortgage is an 80% first mortgage, 10% second mortgage and 10% down payment, 10% of the purchase price needs to be found. Knowing that $240,000 is 80% of the purchase price, the full purchase price is $\frac{\$240,000}{.80} = \$300,000$. From there, the amount of the 10% purchase-money second mortgage must be calculated: $\$300,000 \times .10 = \$30,000$.

112. D: Encouraging or discouraging the sale of a property to a buyer based on race is a form of steering and is illegal.

113. C: A red flag under the Federal Trade Commission's (FTC's) Red Flags Rule is any suspicious activity that indicates identity theft is occurring or has occurred.

114. C: The maximum housing payment for this borrower would be $3,900 a month: $\frac{\$130,000}{12} = \$10,833.33$ gross monthly income $\times 0.36 = \$3,900$.

115. C: Mortgage companies are not considered covered financial institutions; therefore, they require mortgage loan officers to have a state license.

116. B: With a periodic cap of 1.5%, the interest rate cannot go above 6.5% at the next rate adjustment: 5% rate $+$ 1.5% cap $=$ 6.5%.

117. D: When completing continuing education, three hours of federal law education is required.

118. B: This is not legal; lying about the true value of an asset is considered asset fraud.

119. A: Per the TILA-RESPA Integrated Disclosures (TRID), the lender must deliver and have the borrower sign (or electronically sign) the Closing Disclosure three business days before closing.

120. C: The loan amount would be $285,000 since the credit from the seller cannot be used as a down payment or to reduce the loan amount: $\$315,000 - \$30,000 = \$285,000$.

Online Resources

T rivium includes online resources with the purchase of this study guide to help you fully prepare for the exam.

Practice Tests

In addition to the practice tests included in this book, we also offer an online exam. Since many exams today are computer based, practicing your test-taking skills on the computer is a great way to prepare.

From Stress to Success

Watch "From Stress to Success," a brief but insightful YouTube video that offers the tips, tricks, and secrets experts use to score higher on the exam.

Reviews

Leave a review, send us helpful feedback, or sign up for Cirrus promotions—including free books!

Access these materials at: www.triviumtestprep.com/nmls-online-resources

Made in the USA
Las Vegas, NV
21 February 2024

86027692R00129